Introducing Management
A Development Guide

Kate Williams and Bob Johnson

Second edition

ELSEVIER
BUTTERWORTH
HEINEMANN

AMSTERDAM BOSTON HEIDELBERG LONDON NEW YORK OXFORD
PARIS SAN DIEGO SAN FRANCISCO SINGAPORE SYDNEY TOKYO

Elsevier Butterworth-Heinemann
Linacre House, Jordan Hill, Oxford OX2 8DP
200 Wheeler Road, Burlington, MA 01803

First published 1999
Reprinted 2001 (twice)
Second edition 2004

Permissions may be sought directly from Elsevier's Science and Technology
Rights Department in Oxford, UK: phone: (+44) (0) 1865 843830; fax: (+44)
(0) 1865 853333; e-mail: permissions@elsevier.co.uk. You may also complete
your request on-line via the Elsevier homepage (http://www.elsevier.com),
by selecting 'Customer Support' and then 'Obtaining Permissions'

British Library Cataloguing in Publication Data
A catalogue record for this book is available from the British Library

Library of Congress Cataloguing in Publication Data
A catalogue record for this book is available from the Library of Congress

ISBN 0 7506 5920 3

For more information on all Butterworth-Heinemann
publications please visit our website at www.bh.com

Printed and bound in Great Britain

PLANT A TREE
British Trust for Conservation Volunteers
FOR EVERY TITLE THAT WE PUBLISH, BUTTERWORTH-HEINEMANN
WILL PAY FOR BTCV TO PLANT AND CARE FOR A TREE.

Introducing Ma

Contents

305309

CONTENTS

CONTENTS

Preface

The business environment is increasingly one of turbulence and uncertainty and a number of organizations are under pressure to increase profitability and reduce costs. Many organizations, both private and public sector, are identifying and developing ways that will ensure their continued survival in this environment. Organizations need a skilled, flexible and responsive workforce in which managers play an integral part. The role of a manager is both challenging and complex.

This book aims to be a development guide for both new and existing managers to assist them in their role. It provides under-pinning knowledge, based on management concepts and theories and explores the key responsibilities of a manager: people, activities, information and resources.

This book is an essential resource when studying for a recognised management qualification through, for example, the ILM, CMI or an N/SVQ. You will find this book beneficial to your learning and development as it is closely linked to the knowledge requirements for all Level 3 qualifications in management.

Management is essentially a practical skill and this book reflects this. It contains short case studies, insights and practical examples taken from different sectors that enable you to apply the concepts and principles to your own work situation.

This second edition has been fully revised and contains updated and new material, including website addresses. We have been careful to retain the same approach, features and user friendliness of the first edition.

The role of a manager has never been more challenging. We hope you find this book helpful in assisting you to make sense of the complexities within your role and that it encourages you to study further so that you can effectively and successfully meet those challenges.

Kate Williams

Learning Structure

Introducing Management: a development guide has a thorough, easy-to-follow learning structure to guide readers through their introduction to the management role.

The book is divided into five sections, which comprehensively cover the key areas of management.

The sections are as follows:

Section 1: Managing in Context – this section sets out to give a brief explanation of the work managers can expect to do and the results for which they are responsible. It also describes the way in which changes in the wider world can affect organizations and impact on the job of a manager. Finally, it explains some different shapes or structure that an organization can take and the influence of culture (the way we do things around here) on decision-making and methods of working. As its title suggests, the purpose of this section is to set the manager's job into the context of the whole organization, and beyond. For many managers, particularly at a more junior level, it is easy to get caught up in the day-to-day, hour-by-hour activities, and overlook what the organization expects them to achieve in the longer term and the influence of external factors. Section 1 is intended to put that right and encourages the reader to consider the bigger picture.

Each of the remaining four sections deals with one of a manager's key responsibilities. These are generally considered to be:

- Managing People
- Managing Activities
- Managing Information
- Managing Resources

The starting point for **Section 2: Managing People** – is the recognition that people are a manager's most important and valuable resource; they need the right knowledge, skills and attitude to enable them to contribute in achieving both team and organizational goals. The manager needs to demonstrate clear direction and effective leadership. Section 2 starts by examining motivation – how to get people to do what you as a manager want them to do. It goes on to explore a range of ideas about leadership – how the people issues of management fit within the context of the job of management and some techniques for effective delegation. Teams deliver results and the next part looks at the manager's role in building a successful team. Finally Section 2 examines ways to improve individual performance and how to successfully involve people in the change process.

Section 3: Managing Activities – has three main themes: quality, customers and productivity. It stresses the importance of identifying your customers, both internal and external, and what they expect from you. It defines quality as 'meeting and exceeding customer expectations' and points out that adding value should be the highest priority for managers and their teams. It then looks at ways of increasing efficiency and making more productive use of resources all in the context of health, safety and the environment.

Section 4: Managing Information – starts from the position that accurate, timely and relevant information is an essential basis for quality management decisions. It offers a range of problem solving and decision making techniques and examines the importance of recording and processing information. Finally it points out that information is not an end in itself – we pass on information to achieve results. Section 4, therefore, finishes with a description of the communication process and looks at ways of improving your communication skills both in writing and face-to-face.

Section 5: Managing Resources – focuses on the use and interpretation of financial statements. It provides an overview of company financial information, including budgeting and stock control and how manager's actions in this area will affect the team. For example, it explains how financial information, if presented wrongly, has adverse affects on the morale of your team and how this information affects strategic decisions. It looks at budgets and the controls and decisions that have to be made to effectively manage them. Finally, it offers advice on effective ways of managing and controlling resources, information and time.

Introducing Management includes the following features to guide your learning:

Chapter Objectives

Bullet points at the beginning of each chapter serve as a guide to the content and the learning that will be covered.

Insights

Short anecdotes about different situations a manager may find themselves in followed by questions to provoke discussion.

Case Studies

These are used to bring a real-life aspect to the information and as with the Insights are intended to contextualize the reading for the learner. They are also followed by discussion questions, which require more thinking and time.

Example

Examples are highlighted throughout the text to illustrate the information to help understanding.

Discussion

Questions for discussion are placed at regular intervals so that readers can take time out from the text to discuss the information and relate it to their own experience.

Review

Each chapter ends with some review questions. These reinforce and check the knowledge and understanding from the chapter that has just been read.

Workplace Activity

These activities relate the knowledge gained back to the workplace of the reader. This helps to contextualize the learning and encourages the reader to reflect and improve on their own management style and skills.

Website addresses

Relevant website addresses are included at the end of each section. These are intended as an additional resource and as a source of reference to assist the reader in their role.

Glossary

A list of all key vocabulary and terms that have been used throughout the text, are collected at the back of the book.

Section 1   Managing in Context

- *What is management?*
- *What do managers do?*
- *What resources do managers have?*
- *Where do resources come from?*
- *Who are our customers?*
- *What do they buy?*
- *How does culture affect an organization's performance?*
- *What affects an organization's success — or failure?*

europee
-first management book - Henry Ford

1 Achieving results

You may not have 'manager' in your job title. In fact many organizations avoid the term, particularly for jobs which have a management element at a junior level. For example, the Civil Service typically uses the titles 'Administrative Officer' and 'Executive Officer' for such positions. Many companies call their junior managers 'supervisors' or 'team leaders'. On the other hand in some small firms, the Directors are also responsible for day-to-day management.

That's all very well but not very helpful without some understanding of what the management role involves. There are many differing views amongst writers on management, which help towards our understanding.

Many of the early writers on management have significantly influenced the way we view the management role. For example, in the first European book on management Henri Fayol said that management involved: ⁵ elements.

- Forecasting and planning
- Organization
- Command
- Control
- Co-ordination.

MANAGING IN CONTEXT

3

E. F. L. Brech described management as:

'A social process entailing responsibility for the effective and economical planning and regulation of the operations of an enterprise, in fulfilment of a given purpose or task'.

Harold Koontz on the other hand, in his book *Towards a Unified Theory of Management,* argued that management was:

'. . . the art of getting things done through and with people in formally organized groups'.

More recent definitions include:

'Management is . . . the organ of society specifically charged with making resources productive'
(Peter Drucker)

'Deciding what should be done and then getting other people to do it'
(Rosemary Stewart)

'Management is fundamental to the effective operation of work organizations'
(Laurie Mullins)

There is a common thread that links these views:

- Management involves making plans and decisions about the future needs of the business
- Management is about making cost-effective use of resources through efficient organization and control
- Management is about getting the best out of people to achieve objectives.

In some organizations people have 'manager' in their title, make plans and decisions, manage physical resources but are not responsible for staff.

Consider this situation:

Insight

Albert is the Despatch Manager of a small stationery wholesaling company. Each day he analyses the orders scheduled for delivery that day, removes the stock from the warehouse and assembles it for collection by drivers employed by a local haulage contractor.

Is Albert really a manager?

In our view the short answer is 'No'. His plans and decisions are dictated for him by the orders he receives — which probably are prepared elsewhere in the organization. He may have access to resources — a ladder perhaps or even a forklift truck, but that is no more than you would expect of any warehouse operative. And finally the drivers do not report to him — they are managed and controlled by the haulage company which employs them.

Of course you may have reached a different conclusion based on different assumptions.

If Albert schedules his own work AND

If he is responsible for the layout and organization of the warehouse AND

If he is entitled to give instructions to the drivers

THEN his title is justifiably that of manager.

Your role as a manager

It is the *content* of your job which makes you a manager *not your job title*. Regardless of the title, a genuine management job involves:

- Forecasting the future nature of the business and of your operation and the challenges (environmental factors) affecting it;
- Planning the targets and objectives your operation will deliver either in the short-term (day-to-day) or in the long-term, or both;
- Ensuring you have the resources (people, equipment, budget, materials) to meet your objectives;
- Making cost-effective use of those resources;
- Giving clear and relevant instructions to your staff;
- Gaining and maintaining staff commitment to the organization and to their work.

5

These activities reflect the content of a manager's job whatever the level. However, the balance of activities varies according to whether we are considering a junior, middle or senior manager. Research in America quoted by Rosemary Stewart shows that junior managers are much more involved in short-term relatively simple day-to-day decisions. At higher levels, decisions take longer to make and put into practice.

Decisions at the lower levels are often more clear cut. They usually have to be done quickly and there is less uncertainty about the result than at higher levels. Recent trends are to reduce the number of management levels and put decision-making responsibility and leadership roles further down the organization. Nevertheless it is still the case that:

- First-line managers are mainly responsible for day-by-day and hour-by-hour decisions;
- Their decisions tend to be followed by immediate action which allows an early chance to see if they have worked;
- First-line management decisions usually deal with fairly straightforward issues where the results and effects of the decision are obvious.

At the same time, not all decisions at a junior level are of this short-term, straightforward nature. Increasingly, managers at this level are being expected to make or suggest improvements to working practices, the use of resources and the quality of their output and to take responsibility for longer-term issues like staff recruitment and customer satisfaction.

However, not all the work a manager does is truly management work. Consider this situation:

Insight

Ranjit Khan is the manager of a small neighbourhood supermarket. Each morning he comes in early to open the shop and serves at the checkout until his staff arrive. He then gives them their duties for the day. During the day, he meets sales representatives and places orders for next week. When the shop is busy, he refills the shelves. In quiet moments he prepares wage packets, checks stock levels and pays bills.

Which of Ranjit's jobs are management jobs?

The following are the management elements we see in Ranjit's job:

- **Managing Resources**
  This involves opening the shop, checking stock levels and placing orders.

- **Managing People**
  This involves giving his staff their duties and presumably supervising them during the day.

- **Managing Activities**
  Ranjit's presence in the shop enables him to assess the extent to which it is providing customer satisfaction and to make improvements.

- **Managing Information**
  The jobs of preparing wage packets and paying bills are not management jobs. However, they may encourage him to seek more effective ways of managing the payroll or keeping accounts.

In a small operation like this it would be unrealistic to expect that the manager will manage all the time. Ranjit is not managing when he serves at the checkout or refills the shelves. But those activities do keep him close to customers and aware of the issues and problems facing his staff when they do the same jobs. This is one of the main considerations which have led to the delegation of decision making – decisions should be taken by the people affected by them and who will understand the consequences.

For many junior managers the jobs they do are an uncomfortable mix of managerial and 'hands-on' work. It is important to be aware of the difference. Managerial work involves the activities of forecasting, planning, managing resources and managing people we have already described. 'Hands-on' work involves the basic tasks which keep the operation running.

Review

Now check your understanding of this chapter by completing the following tasks:

1 Henri Fayol listed five elements of management. What words did he use to describe the following activities:

(a) Looking to the future and deciding what to do about it

P _ _ _

(b) getting together the necessary resources and procedures to deliver objectives

O _ _ _ _ _ _ _

(c) Giving instructions and granting authority

C _ _ _ _ _ _ _

(d) Checking results and taking corrective action

C _ _ _ _ _ _

(e) Keeping everything and everybody working towards defined goals

C _ _ _ _ _ _ _ _ _

2 List the four types of resources which managers manage.

_____   _____

_____   _____

3 What does the word '**delegation**' mean to you?

_____

Workplace Activity

If you are currently doing a management job relate this chapter to your own experience by answering the following questions:

1 Identify the main activities you undertake at work. Decide roughly what percentage of the working week you spend on each. What percentage of the week do you spend on managerial activity?

2 What do you know about the aims of your organization?

3 What aspects of your role enable you to contribute to the achievement of these aims?

4 How far can you influence the resources you manage?

5 What are your responsibilities to and for the people you manage?

6 To what extent can you change/influence the quality of the output from your operation?

References

1 Fayol, H. (1916) *General + Industrial Management*, Pitman: London.
2 Brech, E. F. L. (1953) *Principles and Practice of Management*, Longman: London.
3 Koontz, H. (1914) *Towards a Unified Theory of Management*, McGraw-Hill: New York.
4 Drucker, P. F. (1954) *The Practice of Management*, Butterworth-Heinemann: Oxford.

5 Stewart, R. (1999) The Reality of Management, Butterworth-Heinemann: Oxford.
6 Mullins, L. (2002) *Management and Organization Behaviour*, FT Prentice Hall: Harlow.

2 Managing resources

- *What resources do managers have?*
- *Where do resources come from?*

Increasingly in today's competitive markets there is a need for managers to **add value** through the work that they do. In fact this does not only apply to managers. The main idea is that the only way people can justify their employment is by producing something which is more valuable or desirable than the raw materials they started with. Here are some examples:

- An assembly line worker adds value by (for example) turning lengths of wood into table legs.

- An accounts clerk turns orders and delivery notes into invoices (which are of greater value to the organization because they ultimately result in income).

- A haulage driver adds value by moving goods from their starting point to where they are wanted.

- A good waiter adds value by providing a superior level of service whilst projecting a sparky personality.

The manager's contribution to this process of adding value is to ensure that through the process of '**transformation**' the final result is worth more than the combined cost of the raw materials and the resources used.

This process of **transformation** involves:

- Getting hold of the necessary raw materials;

- Making sure the tools, machinery or equipment are in place to change them into something more valuable;

- Managing the people involved;

- Continually checking that the final result meets the expectation of customers and their willingness to pay.

To achieve all that means the manager is competent in:

- **Managing activities** (with an emphasis on customer requirements);
- **Managing resources** (with an emphasis on arranging for necessary equipment to be available now and for the future);
- **Managing people** (with an emphasis on ensuring staff know what to do and have the skills and motivation to do it);
- **Managing information** (with an emphasis on gathering and monitoring cost and performance information).

Therefore, you will find ideas and thoughts which illustrate the process of transformation and adding value throughout this book.

For the moment though we want to concentrate on the resources on which managers depend, where they come from and how difficult they are to get hold of. This will then lead us into looking at how the organization and the environment have an effect in the final two chapters of this section.

In the previous chapter we explained that managers depend on the resources of:

- people
- equipment
- budget
- materials.

These four are all **'inputs'**. They form the resources which are then **transformed** into the products and services needed by customers. Inputs or resources can be split into two categories:

Consumable resources

As the name implies these are used up as the process of transformation takes place. Some examples of consumable resources are:

- Raw materials
- Energy in the form of heat and light
- Time
- Budget (which pays for energy and time).

11

Renewable resources

These are resources necessary for the transformation process but which can be used repeatedly over time. Examples are:

- Equipment or machinery
- Staff experience and expertise
- Premises, space
- Furniture, computers, calculators and the like.

Picture the staff canteen in a corporate headquarters office block. The canteen is subsidized and serves morning coffee, afternoon tea, snacks and lunches.

What inputs does the canteen need?

Which are consumable and which are renewable?

What differences would it make if the canteen were expected to make a profit?

We thought that:

The canteen's *consumable resources* would consist of:

- Raw materials like instant coffee, teabags, water, milk, sugar, meat, vegetables, salad and so on
- Energy (gas or electricity to heat drinks and cook the food)
- Pre-packed snacks like biscuits, cakes or sandwiches (assuming the canteen staff do not make sandwiches themselves)
- The canteen staff's time
- Money (a budget to subsidize the canteen).

Renewable resources would be made up of:

- Teapots and coffee urns
- Cups, saucers, plates, cutlery (unless the canteen uses disposable versions which would be thrown away after use and therefore consumable resources)
- Cookers
- Refrigerators and freezers

INTRODUCING MANAGEMENT

- Canteen furniture (dining tables and chairs)
- Sinks for washing-up
- The cooks' expertise in preparing and cooking food
- Serving staff's ability to, for example, operate the tills, serve the food and clear the tables.

If the canteen were not subsidized two main differences would come into play. Firstly the prices in the canteen would increase as the canteen would have to make a profit in order to fund itself. The office staff would therefore become customers who could choose to use the canteen or go elsewhere. Which raises our second difference. We said just now that part of the manager's role in managing resources was to make sure that products or services satisfied customers. If the canteen received no subsidy it would be even more important that the quality and value offered by the canteen met customer expectations and compared successfully with competitors outside. We shall return to this theme both briefly in the next chapter and at greater length in Section 3.

Obtaining resources

Managers often complain that they have insufficient resources to meet their particular needs of the business. Lack of necessary resources is an understandable source of frustration. However it is important for managers to recognize the wider context in which their operations take place.

The amounts an organization can afford to spend on resources are partly the result of past income and expenditure and partly the result of external constraints. In an ideal world senior managers would predict their likely resource needs in future years and set money aside to pay for them. However such an ideal situation often does not apply.

Example	A commercial business may not achieve the sales turnover and resulting profit it expected. In years of really poor sales performance it may even trade at a loss. As a result money which should have been set aside for future resources will either not be there or will be used to keep the business running.

Government funded bodies such as the health or defence services are generally not allowed to put money aside to spend in future years. Any surplus budget at the end of a financial year is lost. Consequently the amount of money a Civil Service department has available to spend on new or extra resources depend on the generosity or otherwise of government at the time that year's budget is prepared. In other words the obtaining of resources depends on the 'political' environment, i.e. the agendas and 'rules' within that company — a factor we shall return to in the final chapter of this section.

Publicly funded operations often find that the demand for their services is greater than they have forecasted. There are several possible reasons for this. In the health service progress in diagnosis and treatment has meant that doctors can now treat diseases which were previously incurable. The treatment will be available but at a greater cost than that forecast because the treatment did not exist when the forecasts were made.

For road maintenance programmes, severe weather may demand greater road maintenance than anticipated. As their processes become more sophisticated employers may need greater numbers of staff with degrees. As a result society expects more people to attend university. Any of these causes of **higher-than-forecast demand** will mean that past money set aside for resources will be inadequate.

Consider this situation:

Case Study

> The Copy Shop is an independent business offering a printing and photocopying service in the small town of Swinford. It was set up five years ago with two leased photocopiers and a second-hand printing press. Last year was a profitable one. So the owner set some of his profits aside to buy a new printing press because the current second-hand machine needs expensive maintenance and is no longer able to produce the quality customers expect. Unfortunately a national chain has set up a printing and photocopying branch in the town. The Copy Shop has lost two major customers, turnover has dropped by 20% and it is currently trading at a loss.
>
> The owner calculates that he can afford to continue paying his staff for another four months without touching the reserves he has put aside for the new printing press.

What choices are open to the owner?

What would you advise him to do?

It seems to us that the owner can choose between the following decisions:

- Buy the new printing press, keep his staff and mount a marketing campaign to restore the lost business. A high risk decision but commercial decisions are risky by definition!

- Forget the new press and use the money to pay his staff for longer than four months. But he may find it difficult to maintain and increase his business if the quality produced by the old press is not competitive.

- Find ways of reducing the cost of resources. For example could the new press be leased rather than bought? (More expensive in the long term but cheaper in the short term.) Will staff accept a drop in wages? (Or can they find better-paid jobs elsewhere?) Can new materials such as paper and ink be bought more cheaply? (Or will the quality suffer?)

- Cut back on the scale of his business. Ending the lease on one of his photocopiers, making staff redundant or even moving to smaller premises would all reduce overheads (although the photocopier lease almost certainly contains a penalty clause for early termination, staff will be entitled to redundancy payments and there will be costs involved in moving premises).

Faced with these alternatives what advice would you give? There is no 'right' answer to this question. However any action to reduce costs without attempting to rebuild the business is likely to lead to a further decline in The Copy Shop's turnover and profit. But at the same time the owner cannot afford to upgrade his resources, keep all his staff and pay the costs of an advertising campaign. The only approach to this crisis which is likely to have any chance of success will need to combine cost savings, the development of a more competitive service and major marketing activity.

External factors

That last case study shows that historical success in building up reserves to increase or upgrade resources can often be hindered by

15

external factors outside an organization's control. So far in this chapter we have mentioned the impact of:

- Customer choice
- Political decisions
- Technological improvements
- Competitor activity
- Social change
- The weather.

All of these affect an organization's operations by affecting the cost and availability of resources.

Example	A coffee manufacturer will find raw materials (coffee beans) scarce and expensive if bad weather leads to a crop failure.
	New, improved operating methods and technology may require staff with different experience and qualifications. If the country's education and training system has not caught up with the changes, staff with relevant backgrounds will also be hard to find and costly.
	Both of these problems (raw materials and staffing) will be aggravated if competitors are seeking the same resources.

Many governments have now limited or banned the exploitation of natural resources like hardwoods. Organizations with processes which depend on them need to find alternative sources or to re-design their processes.

Discoveries, e.g. the risks to health of asbestos as an insulating material, may make certain resources illegal and force future changes to processes.

Resources and you

This chapter has presented a 'big-picture' view of resources emphasizing an organization's need to be aware of external influences when planning resource needs or seeking to obtain them.

You may be wondering what these strategic considerations have to do with you. There are two answers to this question. The first is that **managers do not work in isolation.** To be effective, managers need to have an interest in and understanding of the wider world they are in, so they can effectively plan resource needs. Such an understanding is essential if managers are to make sense of decisions taken elsewhere in the organization (and be able to explain them to their staff). As far as managing resources is concerned, these decisions may involve:

- Changes to products or new materials
- Changes to processes
- Changes to budgets
- Why necessary resources can or cannot be made available.

These references to change lead on to our second answer. **Management is an ever-changing, dynamic process.** Much of a manager's work should involve looking for, making or recommending improvements. In order for improvements to be relevant and desirable, they need to take account of the organization's past performance, future plans and the environment in which it operates.

Review

Now check your understanding of this chapter by completing the following activities:

Pg331

1   Managers are responsible for a _ _ _ _ _ v _ _ _ _
    (complete the words)

2   Resources are also known as i _ _ _ _ _
    (fill in the gap)

3   What are the two categories of resources?
    c _ _ _ _ _ able
    r _ _ _ _ able

4   List four external factors which might affect resource availability

    _____   _____

    _____   _____

5   Give two reasons why managers need to understand the context in which their organizations operate

    _____   _____

    _____   _____

If you are currently doing a management job relate this chapter to your own experience by answering the following questions:

1 What resources do you manage?

2 What changes are you responsible for?

3 How does your organization fund extra or upgraded resources?

4 What improvements would you like to see to the resources you manage?

5 How practical are those improvements in view of the context in which your organization operates?

6 What are the foreseeable changes for your organization which may affect availability of resources?

3 Focusing on customers

| Chapter Objectives | • *Who are our customers?*
• *What do they buy?* |

Many managers have little or no contact with their organization's external customers. In fact, for many organizations like government departments and hospitals the idea that the people they serve are customers at all is a comparatively recent one.

However, in the past few years, management thinking and management literature have placed considerable emphasis on the need for '**customer orientation**', i.e. basing the majority of actions and decisions on the needs and wants of the customer. Here are some quotations which make the point:

'There have always been strategic advantages in staying close to customers. Good customer relationships reverberate not only in current sales but also in future effectiveness and growth. Satisfied customers are the single best source of new business. Timely knowledge of changing customer requirements makes it possible to guide production more efficiently, reducing waste, inventory costs and returns.'
(Rosabeth Moss Kanter)

'If we are to define quality in a way which is useful in its management then we must recognize the need to include in the assessment of quality the time requirement of the customer'.
(John S. Oakland)

'To say that 'the customer is king' is an understatement of many of our successful companies. For them good customer relations and a deep knowledge of the market in which they operate are

MANAGING IN CONTEXT

19

essential, routine and unquestioned parts of their day-to-day method of doing business.'
(Walter Goldsmith and David Clutterbuck)

There are two themes that are important to this emphasis on customers. The first is the theme of **change.** Of the authors we have quoted, Rosabeth Moss Kanter stresses that all organizations now operate in environments where change is massively unpredictable and taking place at a bewildering speed. Many other management writers make the same point. Their response to change is that organizations, in order to keep their operations relevant, must check constantly on their customers' expectations and requirements because customer satisfaction should be their primary goal.

The second theme is that of **Total Quality Management** or continuous quality improvement as it is sometimes called. The TQM philosophy is also based on the principle that customer satisfaction is the main objective of any organization. But it goes further. Total Quality Management starts from the position that everybody in an organization is somebody else's internal customer. A closer look at some of these internal customer—supplier relationships reveals some unexpected links. As John Oakland points out:

'How many executives really bother to find out what their customers' – their secretaries' – requirements are? Can their handwriting be read; do they have clear instructions; do the secretaries always know where the boss is? Equally, do the secretaries establish what their bosses need – error-free typing, clear messages, a tidy office?'

The TQM theme is related to the theme of change because it is founded on the idea that internal relationships make up a **supply chain** which ultimately leads to the external customer.

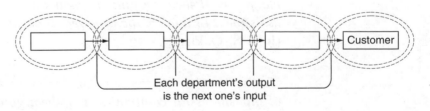

Figure 3.1

20

If that supply chain is working properly to identify customer needs at each stage, the whole organization will be able to adapt to the changing needs of external customers. We shall return to the topics of customer satisfaction and the internal supply chain in Section 3.

Therefore, an organization is full of customers. Your colleagues are your customers and you are their customer. They can fulfil your needs and requirements by carrying out their role efficiently and vice versa. For example:

Insight

Katie works in the internal communications department in the Head Office of a large retail company. She must edit and collate all the information from the relevant departments in order for it to be clear, understandable information that can be sent out to all departments. In this scenario, the members of staff working in the other departments are Katie's customers. She serves their needs and requirements in order for them to carry out their jobs efficiently. However, Katie is also a customer. She is a customer of the IT department. They must keep her computer and printer in good working condition so that she can input all the information she has received into her computer, before it can be distributed to the departments. If the IT department do not keep her computer working, they have failed to serve her needs and requirements and she becomes an unhappy customer.

Because they all work for the same company everyone here is an 'internal' customer.

Who are your *'internal' customers?*

We are all the 'external' customers of shops for example. If a shop does not serve our needs or requirements satisfactorily, we will cease to visit it. It won't get any customers and eventually will make so little money that it will be forced to shut down.

Just as Katie relied on the IT department to keep her computer functioning in order for her to distribute information, the shop relies on us in order to make enough money to sustain itself. For

21

the moment though we shall explore the needs of external customers and how these are affected by their environment.

Customers and quality

The TQM literature takes as its starting point the idea that:

customers buy quality

It is important to understand what quality means in this context. It does not mean the same as 'high quality', 'top quality' or even 'good quality'. Instead TQM emphasizes that quality should be 'satisfactory' — in other words it should meet the needs of customers. Quotations from two of the early Total Quality gurus clarify this point.

Joseph Juran defined quality as 'fitness for purpose or use'. *Philip Crosby used the phrase* 'conformance to specification'.

From the customer's viewpoint therefore, quality describes *the extent to which a product or service meets their needs or satisfies their expectations.*

Insight

Two friends have gone to the High Street to buy cutlery — sets of table knives, forks and spoons. The first wants them for a holiday caravan the family has just bought, which they plan to use for their annual holidays and occasional weekends. The second wants them to give to her nephew as a wedding present.

Based on this limited information what do you think would constitute 'quality' in each case?

Without being able to ask the customers we have to make some assumptions. It seems reasonable to assume that cutlery for the holiday caravan should ideally be robust and relatively inexpensive without needing to look particularly special. The cutlery for the wedding present on the other hand will itself need to be impressive — with a well-known maker's name, possibly silver-plated and with the weight and design to give a positive message about the good wishes and generosity of the givers.

External influences

Of course making assumptions like these are subjective and unreliable. That is why in Section 3 we shall go into greater detail about the need to carry out proper and frequent research into customer requirements. But it is also essential to recognize that customer needs are in part a reflection of the external factors affecting customers. Here are some basic examples:

<table>
<tr><td>

Example

</td><td>

- More rigorous drink-driving laws in the UK have increased pub sales of soft drinks.

- Greater public awareness of environmental issues has led to an increase in supermarket sales of recyclable products and organically farmed foods.

- Both travel and airline companies worldwide were affected by a dramatic reduction in customers who were reluctant to travel in the aftermath of the terrorist attack on the US in September 2001.

</td></tr>
</table>

In each of these cases something in the wider world has changed. Customers, manufacturers and suppliers will have had little or no influence on that change. However the change has either increased or reduced the amount of a product or service that customers were willing to buy. In other words, external factors brought about a change in customer expectations or requirements.

In a similar way external factors can influence what customers see as 'satisfactory quality'. For senior executives a company car delivers satisfaction in a number of ways:

- As a means of transport for getting from A to B
- As a source of comfort on journeys
- As a status symbol.

Any car will meet the first requirement. The second is to do with a range of considerations like seat design, whether the car has air-conditioning, the smoothness of the ride. The third requirement has historically been met by a combination of size and brand.

Today's senior executive still requires a car to deliver transport, comfort and status. But a change in external considerations has added an extra requirement and brought different expectations about the way the original three are delivered. These days big cars are being criticized as:

- 'Gas guzzlers'
- Wasteful of national resources
- Environmentally unfriendly.

Big company cars are consequently seen as reflecting badly on the environmental sensitivity of both their drivers and the employing organizations.

Discussion	What response to this change would you expect from: • customers? • car manufacturers?

The typical customer response was to move to smaller cars which offered the same standard of comfort they had been used to in their previously preferred larger cars. However manufacturers like Jaguar and BMW did not make smaller cars. As a result their sales declined. In response they broke with tradition by developing their own compact models – the X400 in the case of Jaguar and the Compact in the case of BMW. Once again a change in the external environment had forced suppliers to change their product range in order to remain responsive to customer requirements. Alternatively and more charitably you would argue that prestige car manufacturers had predicted and planned for changes in customer requirement but slightly mis-timed their response.

Comparable changes in the external environment have resulted in other changes in customer definitions of 'satisfactory quality'.

Example	• Removal of the price-fixing Net Book Agreement in the UK led customers to expect to be able to buy popular book titles at a discount.

- Competition from Far Eastern car manufacturers led customers to expect higher levels of equipment from base level European made cars.

- A move from state-run to privatized public transport has led to higher customer expectations of service, convenience and price.

Your contribution to customer satisfaction

As we mentioned at the start of this chapter, many managers have little or no contact with external customers. And if your organization has not moved down the Total Quality route you may have no formal way of identifying the requirements and expectations of your external customers. Nevertheless this does not remove your need to be aware of what your organization's customers expect from your products or services.

So what can you do?

Follow the three steps . . .

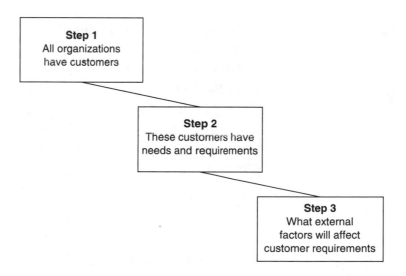

The **first step** is to recognize that all organizations have customers:

- Patients are the customers of hospitals and doctors' surgeries.
- Taxpayers are the customers of the tax offices.

- Road users are the customers of local government road maintenance departments.
- Churchgoers are the customers of their local vicars.

We have deliberately chosen examples from non-profit making sectors in order to demonstrate the fact that all organizations have an obligation to identify and satisfy their customers' expectations and requirements.

The **second step** is to make yourself aware of what those customers' expectations and requirements are. Building on our earlier examples:

- Patients expect prompt and courteous attention, successful and relatively painless treatment.
- Taxpayers expect accurate advice delivered in a supportive and understanding way.
- Road users expect safe, smooth roads maintained with the minimum of inconvenience.
- Churchgoers expect stimulating sermons, lively hymns and comfortable pews.

Discussion	• **Who are your organization's customers?** • **What do they expect?** • **How do you and your team contribute to meeting their expectations?**

The **third step** is to find out the external factors which are likely to influence those customers' expectations and requirements. Of course that is not always easy. All well-run organizations monitor their own and their customers' external environment in order to identify:

- What the future demand for their products and services will be.
- How easily they will be able to acquire the resources to meet that demand.
- How much they will have to pay for those resources.
- The satisfaction their customers expect from their products or services.

- What competition they will face.
- Any external factors which will influence their customers' expectations.
- How those expectations will change as a result.

They do all this as part of the strategic planning process in order to forecast the nature and volume of future demand. Not all organizations make this information available to their staff. **Consequently, in order to carry out our third and final step you will need to do one or more of the following:**

- Use your employer's published report and accounts to find out its view of the opportunities and threats facing it.
- Pay attention to internal publications like a staff newsletter to gain the same insight.
- Find out if your organization runs a marketing customer awareness or TQM course at your level. If so arrange to attend it!
- Gain access through your organization's policy development strategic planning or marketing team to future environmental and customer demand forecast.
- Find out who your organization views as its customers. Then read a quality newspaper regularly to see what informed outsiders believe is likely to affect them.

What's the point?

It would be foolish to pretend that the three steps we have described are simple or require no effort. The opposite is clearly the case. So you may be wondering why you should put yourself to the trouble and inconvenience of going through this discovery process. There are three answers to this. The first is painfully practical. The second and third are more philosophical and go to the heart of the nature of management.

Our first answer goes back to the principles of Total Quality Management. **Any operation in any organization should contribute ultimately to customer satisfaction.** And as we pointed out in Chapter 2* managers are responsible for ensuring that the operations they manage add value to the supply chain which results in customer satisfaction. This 'added value' concept implies that operations which do not add value are both unnecessary and

* See Chapter 2

redundant. Even in an organization which has not made its operations subject to outside competition, it will not be long before an operation which does not add value is removed from the supply chain. It costs money but contributes nothing.

Our second answer confirms a point made in previous chapters. Namely that for managers to be able to forecast and plan, they must understand the external environment in which their organization operates. Only then will they be able to make effective decisions about the future direction of their own operations.

And finally, success and progression in management involve the ability to take an increasingly wider view of the external environment. In 1983 Roy Strong, former Director General of the British Institute of Management, described qualities needed by the successful manager. One relevant example is:

'. . . awareness: the never ending strive to keep abreast of developments in technology, social conditions and financial legislative, political and international events that are likely to have an impact on managerial responsibility and success.'

Review

Now check your understanding of this chapter by completing these activities:

1 How would an organization benefit from investing in monitoring customer expectations?

2 Everybody has two types of customer – what are they?

3 Joseph Juran defines quality as:
   Fitness for **p** _____ or **u**_____.

4 List five factors which make up the external environment.

5 The supply chain (fill in the gaps).

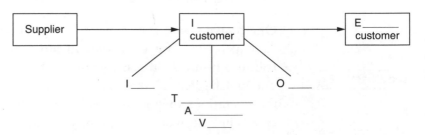

Figure 3.2

Workplace Activity

If you are currently doing a management job, relate this chapter to your own experience by answering the following questions:

1 How does your operation contribute to increasing customer satisfaction?

2 How much do you know about your organization's external customers?

3 How could you find out more?

4 What external factors affect demand for your organization's products or services.

5 Is that demand likely to increase, decrease or remain the same? Why?

6 How will this impact on your part of the organization?

References

1 Kanter, R. M. (1989) *When Giants Learn To Dance*, Simon & Schuster: London.

2 Oakland, J. S. (1989) *Total Quality Management*, Butterworth-Heinemann: Oxford.

3 Goldsmith, W. and Clutterbuck, D. (1985) *The Winning Streak*, Penguin: Harmondsworth.

4 Juran, J. (1951) *Quality Control Handbook*, McGraw-Hill: New York.

5 Crosby, P. (1979) *Quality is Free*, McGraw-Hill: New York.

6 Wild, R. (1983) *How to Manage*, Butterworth-Heinemann: Oxford.

MANAGING IN CONTEXT

4   Understanding the culture

- *How does culture affect an organization's performance?*

In an environment of rapid change such as we described in the previous chapter, organizational success depends on the ability to respond quickly and appropriately to changes in resource availability, demand levels and customer requirements.

We also suggested earlier that the best decisions are most likely to be made by those people who are close to the situation, affected by the decision and who understand the implications. It is for this reason that organizations are increasingly delegating decision-making, responsibility and accountability to lower levels of management and to non-managerial staff.

However, regardless of how desirable it may be, it is not possible to simply stick-on speed of decision-making and delegation like a first-aid dressing to improve effectiveness because the culture of the organization may prevent this from happening.

Working in an organization, whether private or public sector, at any level, means being part of the organization's culture. As a manager it is important for you to understand your organization not only in terms of its functions and procedures but also what its values and beliefs are, and how they underpin the organization.

What is organizational culture?

The following quotes provide a good starting point in helping us to understand the meaning of organizational culture:

'The glue that holds the actors together, it provides people with a continuing sense of reality. It gives meaning to what they do'.
(John Hunt)

'A pattern of beliefs and behaviours, assumptions and routines ... which are distributed across the organization, usually in an uneven pattern'.
(Charles Galunic and John Weeks)

So, culture is all about 'the way we do things round here'.

'The way we do things round here' will be the result of an organization's:

- History
- Size
- Ownership
- Purpose or function.

History

It is obvious that all organizations were established at particular moments in *history*. Each moment had its own prevailing philosophies or management. An organization set up a hundred years ago may have a tradition of making decisions centrally at a high level in the expectation that they will then be obeyed without question.

Size

Small organizations present different management challenges from large ones. A small organization will typically have a 'hands-on' style of management simply because it is not big enough to afford the luxury of managers who spend their time in offices away from the shop floor. Large organizations on the other hand, particularly those operating from several sites like retail chains, are likely to have books of formal rules and procedures to ensure consistency of decision-making.

Ownership

Differences in ownership have several implications. Publicly owned and funded organizations (government departments, schools, hospitals) usually place great emphasis on ensuring that taxpayers' money is not wasted. As a result, decisions are carefully monitored and controlled to check that they give good value-for-money. On the other hand, businesses owned by their senior managers have much greater freedom to take **entrepreneurial** decisions.

Purpose

Some organizations exist to provide largely routine and repetitive products or services. Think, for example, of simple manufacturing processes, or rubbish collection, or the processing of invoices. Any of these activities offers limited scope for creativity. But think now of an advertising agency, or a training department, or an architect's practice. All these functions depend for their success on creative and innovative thinking. In these cases it is essential for 'the way we do things round here' to allow freedom to experiment with the potential risk of expensive failure.

Many writers have attempted to define culture and in this chapter we introduce you to one of these.

Charles Handy's four cultures

Charles Handy, a well-known management thinker, described four main organizational cultures. He stresses that no one culture is preferable to the others. Instead, he points out that each brings its own advantages and disadvantages. The secret is to make sure that the culture of an organization is a suitable match for its size, stage of development and the external environment in which it operates.

The Power Culture

Handy illustrates the power culture, as a spider's web:

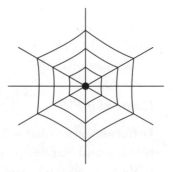

Figure 4.1

The spider at the centre of the web is a single senior manager or a very small group of them. Like a real spider, the managers at the centre will be sensitive to everything that happens in the organization. Faced with a problem or an opportunity, they will make quick decisions based on their own intuition or experience. They will be quick to reward or punish, often arbitrarily. A power culture has few or no rules and procedures. What happens, happens because the manager says so.

A power culture is responsive and opportunistic. Little or no power or **authority** is **delegated**. It can only work in a small, centralized organization because decision-making relies on managers 'walking the job' to keep up-to-date with everything that goes on. It also depends for its success on having a strong, capable leader at its centre.

- Power cultures are good at handling change because of this speed of response. But they are frustrating for staff who want to make their own decisions. They are often found in small, owner-managed businesses. However they cease to work so well as the business grows because managers lose touch with things happening at its edges. They also face crisis when the manager retires or moves on because it is often impossible to find a successor with comparable leadership qualities.

The Role Culture

The role culture is the total opposite to the power culture. Handy illustrates it as a Greek temple:

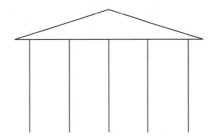

Figure 4.2

A role culture is the one you would find in a traditional bureaucracy. Each of the pillars in the temple represents a different function – production, sales, administration, personnel. Work in a role culture is controlled by formal rules and procedures, typically with large manuals which specify exactly what actions to take in every imaginable situation. Each function operates independently with co-ordination being carried out by senior managers at the top of the structure (represented by the temple roof).

The role culture is good at achieving consistent decisions based on its comprehensive set of rules. It is therefore well suited to large organizations like supermarkets where:

- Each branch carries the same merchandise
- Window displays present the same image
- Customer complaints are handled consistently
- Staff receive the same terms and conditions.

Role cultures offer significant job security. Their procedures do not allow them to operate on a 'hire and fire' basis. However, staff are rarely treated as individuals but rather as payroll numbers expected to carry out a specific task according to the rule book. As such they are easily replaceable.

It is also difficult for role cultures to respond quickly to change. Procedures are tightly defined. As a result nothing can change until new procedures have been worked out and the rule book re-written.

The Task Culture

The task culture is most frequently found in organizations which place a premium on innovation and creative thinking.

Handy's symbol for the task culture is a net:

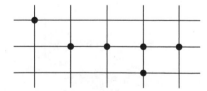

Figure 4.3

The net, with people where the cords cross, suggests that in a task culture people depend on each other. It is also **flat** indicating that

34

hierarchy or status are not issues. Instead people respect each other for their knowledge and expertise — their ability to come up with the right ideas to get things done.

To reiterate, task cultures are often found in creative businesses. They are also often the culture underpinning project teams where the development of innovative or revolutionary approaches are a primary requirement. Consequently task cultures work well in an environment of rapid change because their principal strength lies in finding different ways of doing things.

Task cultures are not all good news though. Because they are nonhierarchical and respect expertise rather than status, they are notoriously difficult to control. They are also expensive. Creative solutions may work — or they may not. Task cultures come up with more than their fair share of costly failures. That after all is the price of a culture founded on experimentation.

The Person Culture

In this culture it is the individual rather than the organization who matters.

Person cultures appear less frequently than the other three we have described. Handy's symbol is a cluster — a series of unrelated blobs representing the people in the organization.

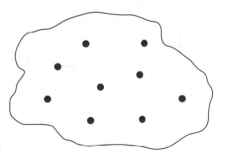

Figure 4.4

A person culture consists of a group of individuals sharing a limited range of common facilities like a suite of offices, a GP practice or a switchboard. Typical examples are a barrister's chambers.

Person cultures are hardly organizations at all. No-one is in charge, decisions can only be taken with the full agreement of all the members and there is no control: everyone can do their own thing without reference to others.

As we said earlier, none of these four cultures is ideal. As circumstances change each will seek to adapt by borrowing approaches from others. For example:

- As a power culture grows in size, it may well introduce formal performance monitoring procedures from the role culture.
- Faced with rapid change, a role culture may introduce change groups or project teams from the task culture.
- When money is tight, a task culture may introduce financial controls from the role culture.
- Faced with a crisis decision, a person culture may introduce a dynamic leader from the power culture.

Consequently the majority of organizations present uneasy cultural blends. A dominant culture may have bits of other cultures tacked on. Or different departments of the same organization may exhibit different cultures. As a result when the departments meet they negotiate from totally different sets of values and expectations.

Identify the cultures underlying the following situations:

Case Study

1 Peter is Managing Director of a metal forging company. He has strict rules and procedures, which he makes sure are enforced. He approves of staff that comply with his rules and disapproves of people who question his methods.

2 Alison is Creative Director in a large advertising agency. Her job is to lead her team in developing proposals for client promotions. The agency has recently been bought out by a major investment bank which has introduced systems to monitor how staff spend their time and how much is chargeable to clients.

3 Titchfield Brewery has decided to sell off its public houses to its tenants in order to concentrate on beer production.

> David, one of the tenants, has decided that the brewery's old ways of doing things are out-of-date. He is sure that he and his staff can work out a range of new approaches to increasing turnover and profit.

Here are our suggestions:

1 Peter's organization is a role culture governed by rules and procedures. Peter has created an environment of fear and by using his status and authority has turned his operation into a power culture.

2 Alison's job makes it reasonable to assume that she has historically worked in a task culture. But, as we pointed out, these can be expensive. The investment bank is looking to introduce control mechanisms borrowed from a role culture.

3 With a network of public houses, Titchfield Brewery has almost certainly maintained consistency by operating them as a role culture. Now David will be able to make his own decisions. By involving his staff it looks as though he wants to develop task culture.

Changing organizational culture

Different cultures are better suited to different contexts. For example:

- Power and task cultures are better able to adapt to change.
- Role cultures are better suited to larger organizations.
- Task cultures make a better job of developing individuals.
- Power cultures are better at managing crises.
- Person cultures give greater freedom to the individual.
- Role cultures are easier to control.
- Task cultures make more expensive mistakes.
- Person cultures take longer to make decisions.

As Charles Handy said originally no one culture is ideal. Unfortunately an organization's environment and situation do not remain constant. Consequently organizations need to adapt their cultures over time. However, culture is derived from history and tradition among other things. As a result it is deeply rooted in an organization and therefore difficult and time consuming to change. Consider the following situation:

Insight

Alpha Industrials is a manufacturer of electrical components. Owned for several years by a multinational company and now on the edge of financial collapse, the business has been sold to its managers. Previously, instructions were issued by the multinational company owner, and Alpha Industrials obeyed. In order for the business to survive the new owners want to involve their staff in proposing and implementing some revolutionary changes to operating methods.

What culture changes will this involve?

How difficult will they be to introduce?

Here are our ideas:

In recent years, Alpha Industrials has probably been either a power or a role culture. Its multinational owner may have issued instructions and expected obedience. Or else it will have been a role culture with operating methods contained in a procedures manual. In either culture, staff will have been expected to do as they were told.

Under its new management Alpha Industrials wants to introduce a task culture with an emphasis on managing change, innovation and problem solving. In the past suggesting a different approach may well have been frowned upon. Now it is going to be welcomed. Cultural changes like this do not happen overnight. Staff will need to be encouraged, rewarded and probably trained to view their jobs differently. Alternatively the new owners could decide for themselves the new operating methods they wanted and give the orders (a power culture but with a new centre of power) or else issue a new set of procedures (a role culture). Of course both of these alternatives raise a range of issues. Neither involves staff in the decision-making process. Both assume that the new owners know exactly what operational changes need to be made. It may be that following the buy out staff have been looking forward to involvement in making improvements. Either alternative will disappoint them if this is the case.

Successful cultural change is likely to require:

- Time to implement
- A visible change in management attitude
- Explanation and training for staff
- Willingness to accept confusion and misunderstanding
- Some expensive mistakes.

Nevertheless it is worth repeating that Handy's four cultures are descriptive. He *does not* say one is better than another and therefore should be adopted. Also, no organization falls neatly into one of these cultures in practice. Instead, the model offers a useful way of looking at organizational culture. His aim was to describe what he saw not what ought to be in an ideal world. One of the tasks of any manager is to assess whether the culture of their operation fits:

- The needs and future direction of their organization;
- The capability of their staff;
- The extent to which the controls to which they are subject allow for mistakes, experimentation and waste;
- Their own ability to make decisions and give instructions;
- The changes taking place in the environment in which they operate.

| **Review** | **Now check your understanding of this chapter by completing the following tasks:** |

1 Organizational culture means:
   'The way we d _ t _ _ _ _ _ r _ _ _ _ h _ _ _.'

2 List the four factors which determine an organization's culture:
   H _ _ _ _ _ _   O _ _ _ _ _ _ _ _
   S _ _ _   P _ _ _ _ _ _

3 What does a role culture do well?
   And what does it do badly?

4 What does a power culture do well?
   And what does it do badly?

5 List three things which staff are likely to need in order to implement cultural change:

Time to i _ _ _ _ _ _ _ _
Change in m _ _ _ _ _ _ _ _ _ a _ _ _ _ _ _ _
T _ _ _ _ _ _ _

<table>
<tr><td>**Workplace Activity**</td><td>If you are currently doing a management job, relate this chapter to your own experience by answering the following questions:</td></tr>
</table>

Workplace Activity

If you are currently doing a management job, relate this chapter to your own experience by answering the following questions:

1 Which aspects of Handy's classification of culture fit with your organization?

2 Obtain a copy of your company's mission statement. What does the statement tell you about its purpose and core values?

3 How does the culture of your organization impact on the day-to-day operation?

References

1 Hunt, J. (1995) *Managing People at Work*, McGraw-Hill: New York.

2 Galunic, C. and Weeks, J. (2001) A Cultural Evolution in Business Thinking: Mastering People Management, *Financial Times* (London), October 29, pp. 2–3.

INTRODUCING MANAGEMENT

40

5 Understanding the environment

Chapter Objectives	• *What affects an organization's success – or failure?*

Organizations do not exist in a vacuum. They are subject to a wide range of external factors and influences which will have an effect – either positive or negative – on:

- The cost and availability of resources, including raw materials, equipment, staff, property and money;
- The demand for the organization's products or services;
- Its turnover and profitability;
- How cheaply and efficiently it can run its business.

These factors and influences are commonly called the 'PESTLE' factors for short. The initials stand for:

Political
Economic
Social
Technological
Legal
Environmental.

It would of course be a mistake to assume that each of these categories is watertight and has no influence on others. For example:

- Political decisions can have an impact on economic conditions;
- Changes in technology can affect the physical environment;
- Legal judgements can change people's working conditions as part of the social environment.

MANAGING IN CONTEXT

41

Nevertheless, for the remainder of this chapter we shall attempt to keep the six categories separate, simply pointing out where one is heavily influenced by others.

Political factors

It is under the political heading that this overlap of categories is most apparent. Directly or indirectly, political decisions can influence the economy, society, the law and the physical environment. In fact there can even be a political impact on technological development when governments decide to put public money into specific research and development initiatives.

Political decisions may make specific markets more or less attractive. For example, the French and German governments' actions in banning the import of British beef during the recent outbreak of foot-and-mouth disease resulted in the closure of many farms and the subsequent loss of farming and related sector jobs within the UK.

In the Budget the Chancellor may introduce or remove opportunities for organizations to make tax savings. Recent budget proposals in the UK have focused on giving incentives for businesses to **invest,** and lowering the levels of **corporation tax.**

Governments may offer financial incentives to encourage firms into areas of high unemployment (a good example of a political decision with social consequences). Such incentives may take the form of reduced local taxes, the offer of property at artificially low rents or even a subsidy to cut the cost of wages. Other political initiatives with social consequences include:

- Government sponsored training schemes
- Job-seekers' allowances
- Publicly funded careers guidance
- Equal opportunities legislation.

If central banks keep interest rates high borrowing becomes more expensive both for consumers (buying things like cars and houses) and for businesses planning to invest.

Governments can take alternative views on the benefit of offering public support to businesses.

- Some seek to encourage competition.
- Redistribute wealth.
- Encourage enterprise.
- Lower taxation.

The implications of a government's philosophies upon business could include:

- Higher or lower investment in technology and new products.
- More or less emphasis on efficiency.
- More or less encouragement to enter foreign markets.
- Less or more state intervention in the decisions made by organizations.

All of these considerations affect an organization's long-term strategy and its day-to-day operations. As a country approaches the time of an election, any uncertainty about the philosophy of the next government will cause a marked slowdown in economic activity.

- Individuals will delay purchase decisions.
- Businesses will put investment decisions on hold.
- Public services will draw up alternative plans for the use of resources.

Economic factors

The state of the economy depends in part on political factors. It is affected by political decisions such as:

- **The level of individual taxation**
  Income tax in the UK has been reducing for the last two decades. In order to maintain government income, successive administrations have increasingly taxed expenditure through VAT and excise duties on things like alcohol and petrol. This has had a major effect on businesses in the transport and beverages markets.

- **The level and nature of corporate taxation**
  Increasingly, UK governments have tried to give firms incentives to invest in technology and research and development. This has

been done through the granting of tax relief on profits re-invested in the firm. Such tax relief has made it more attractive to retain and reinvest profit therefore paying less out to share-holders.

- **The government's attitude to unemployment**
High unemployment nationally leads to reduced consumer demand.

However, in recent years writers on politics, economics and management have argued that governments have far less impact on a nation's economy than they would like to think. There is significant logic in this argument. Governments have little or no influence over:

- The economies of other countries.

- Levels of demand from other countries.

- The level of competition from businesses at home or abroad.

- Social change and consequent shifts in demand. For example, divorce rates, numbers of children in families, where people choose to live, the age of the population.

- The overall rate of technological development.

- Customer preferences.

- Customer confidence and willingness to spend money.

As a result, although we realize that political decisions have some impact on the economic environment, we can see that it is reasonable to treat economic factors as independent and worthy of separate consideration.

Economic Cycle

When individuals and organizations have a high level of confidence in the economy they are prepared to spend and invest, and the economy will boom. In other words demand will grow to the point where eventually it exceeds supply. A booming economy makes inflation rise because excess demand pushes up wages and prices so costs rise. Recent governments have sought to keep inflation below 3 per cent in order to keep in line with other major trading nations. This overriding objective has meant UK governments have sought steady growth rather than a 'stop, start' or 'boom and bust'.

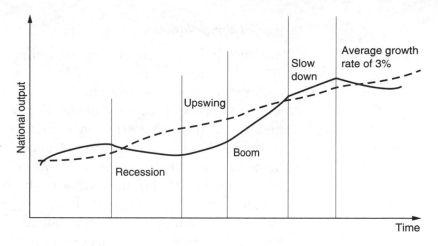

Figure 5.1

However, even with government efforts to control the upward and downward swings in the economy we still encounter good and bad economic periods.

It would be wrong to assume that economic conditions are the same for all organizations and all geographical areas. At any one time the economy may be more or less favourable to:

- Private rather than public organizations.
- Service rather than manufacturing industries.
- Food producers rather than house builders.
- Businesses serving private individuals rather than other businesses.

Equally, retailers in an area of high unemployment will enjoy less demand than others in areas of low unemployment as spending money is less readily available.

Social factors

Society is made up of people – individuals, families, communities. Sociology is the study of people – which means that it includes a very wide variety of topics! The following is a representative list of the social factors which influence an organization's customer base, nature and level of demand, staff availability and expectations.

Age of the population

Throughout Europe populations are getting older. In Germany, by 2010 there will be more pensioners than those in work! At a national level, this is resulting in serious concerns about who will be available to earn the money to pay for state pensions for the retired. At a local level, there is an increasing need for smaller properties, both for couples whose families have grown up and left home and for people who now live alone because their partners have died. Predictably the nature of the products and services people want and need is influenced by age. For example, a younger population has a greater need for maternity services while an older population has more need for hip replacements and elderly care. With an ageing population employers who traditionally recruited school-leavers are now having to be prepared to take on older staff.

Education and training

The standard of education which people receive influences their lifestyle and their leisure activities. Higher standards of education tend to increase demand for specialist books and the arts like theatre, ballet and opera. Currently in the UK schools and universities are placing greater emphasis on giving students the skills necessary for work. The quality and quantity of training available have increased, partly in recognition of the need to compete in the international marketplace. At both local and national levels standards of education and training influence the nature of demand and the availability of qualified and competent staff.

Family composition

Twenty years ago a typical UK family was made up of husband, wife and 2.4 children. That stereotype no longer applies. This has resulted from a range of social changes, including:

- Increased divorce rates.
- Couples deciding to live together rather than getting married.
- Increased numbers of homosexual couples.
- More people living alone.
- Working women delaying the starting of a family.
- Single parent families.

The organizational impact of these changes has included an increased need for part-time working and workplace crèches, a further need for smaller housing units, increased demand for labour-saving devices like microwaves and dishwashers and for convenience foods.

Wealth and status categories

Traditionally we have separated society into simple categories like working class; middle class; upper class. Today, social researchers use more sophisticated methods of analysis and separation. Nevertheless old-style and new-style social categories both recognize that people's lifestyle, purchasing power and the nature of the things they buy are dependent on their wealth and status. Over time the size and importance of different social categories change. A hundred years ago it was the nobility who had most money and, as a result, products and services were largely designed, produced and priced to appeal to them. A combination of the expense of maintaining their family homes, extravagant living, death duties and the growth of the middle classes has turned the nobility into a minor and specialist market.

Insight

> Alan Thornton has decided to use his experience of computer manufacture to start a business making electronic components. He has found a possible factory site on a light industrial estate outside a small town in Northern England. What questions should he ask about political, economic and social factors before finalizing his plans for the business and its location?

It would be sensible for Alan to find out:

- Whether there are any financial incentives from local or national government available for his chosen location.

- Whether the components he plans to make are the subject of severe competition, either from the UK or abroad.

- Whether the markets he intends to service are experiencing fast, slow or negative growth.

- Whether there are enough people available in the local job market to satisfy his recruitment needs.

- Whether they have the right training and experience.

- How easily and cheaply he will be able to buy the raw materials he needs.

- Whether most of his sales will be to national or overseas customers.

- If to overseas customers, the export regulations he will be required to obey and the cost and inconvenience of doing so.

Technological factors

Improvements in technology significantly affect:

- Production and distribution methods
- Customer demand and expectations
- Product desirability and price
- Administrative efficiency.

This can be illustrated in the following examples:

Example	**Production methods**
	The introduction of computer control into manufacturing and stock management has reduced the need for people to do repetitive, semi-skilled production-line jobs; improved production control and output quality; given scope to change product specifications more easily and quickly; improved the accuracy of stock control and thereby reduced stockholding.
	Distribution technology
	This has mainly affected information transfer and mechanical handling. Orders are now often placed and processed using electronic data links. Most warehouses of any size are now operated from a central control point, using computer systems and electronic switching to move products around.
	Customer demand and expectations
	These change as new technology becomes available. Professor Theodore Levitt in 1960 describes the American buggy-whip manufacturer who had for many years made good profits from supplying whips to owners of horse-drawn buggies. His business folded with the introduction of the Model T Ford as customers switched to the convenience of the petrol engine. More recently, the accessibility of the World Wide Web to the domestic market

has led to a significant reduction in sales of compact discs (CDs) as customers can download and copy music directly from the Internet.

All of the above are examples of product desirability rising and falling as competition changes in response to technological development. As technology becomes more sophisticated and widespread, so it becomes easier and cheaper to produce highly specified products. Now for example most pocket calculators have several memories, an electronic diary, clock and scientific functions because basic calculators are too cheap to be worth marketing.

Conversely, new technology may lead to simpler products which respond to the buying public's environmental awareness (a theme we shall return to a little later) and making new types of product available to developing countries. Examples of this are wind-up radios and torches which are powered by a simple mechanical action and have no need of batteries or mains electricity.

Legal factors

In Europe, America and increasingly in the Far East there is a large body of legislation which governs the decisions managers are allowed to take concerning their organizations. In the UK one well-known business law textbook lists no fewer than 120 separate legal statutes which have organizational implications!

Legal controls on organizations can be divided into three main categories:

Company law

Company law lays down rules which specify how different types of organizations – charities, partnerships, private companies, sole traders, public limited companies – must behave. It affects such things as the preparation and publication of accounts, the issue of shares, liability in case of bankruptcy and the actions needed in order to set up an organization legally.

Issues like these are normally handled by the company secretary and we have included them here simply for the sake of completeness.

Contract and trading law

This category of law on the other hand is likely to have much greater impact on you – either as a manager, or as a customer, or both.

UK **contract law** is based on two assumptions: that everyone is free to choose which contracts they enter into and the terms on which they do so. Fundamental to this philosophy is the idea that if two parties cannot agree an acceptable contract, they are free to take their business elsewhere. It is this idea which has led to competition law in the UK and anti-trust law in the US, both of which are designed to ensure that no single business controls so much of a market that customers cannot go to another supplier. Contract law also sets out to ensure that if one of the parties to a contract is in a weak bargaining position (for example a single member of staff negotiating with a big employer), their rights are strengthened.

A legal contract must have six ingredients. It must involve:

- **Agreement** (one party makes an offer; the other accepts it).
- **Consideration** (each side must promise to give or do something to the other's benefit).
- **Intention** (the parties must intend their agreement to have legal consequences).
- **Form** (some contracts must be in writing).
- **Genuineness of consent** (no-one can be forced into a contract).
- **Capacity** (the parties must be legally capable of entering into a contract). For example, many contracts with young people under 18, those with recognized mental health problems, or those under the influence of alcohol, cannot be legally enforced.

Some examples of the day-to-day implications of contract law are as follows:

Example	
	- Businesses intending to expand their operations may find themselves prevented from doing so by competition law.
	- A bankrupt organization may not be entitled to continue trading.
	- Employees cannot be forced into accepting changes to their contracts of employment.

Trading law relates primarily to the supply and sale of goods and services. Legally goods and services must be:

- **of satisfactory quality** (in other words they must do what might reasonably be expected of them).

- **fit for the purpose** (they must meet the customer's needs if the customer has specified these needs and relied on the supplier to provide something suitable).

- **in accordance with their description** (a 'leather suitcase' must not be made mainly of plastic).

- **consistent with a sample** (for example, if you inspect a display table in a furniture store and the store then orders one for you from the manufacturer, the table you get must be of the same specification as the one you inspected).

These legal requirements are of particular relevance to marketing and advertising (description); sales (fitness for purpose); but also to manufacturing and production (merchantable quality) and to quality assurance (samples and specification).

Employment law

It is this category of legislation which is likely to have the greatest and most frequent impact on you as a manager. In Europe and the US, the following are all against the law:

- Discrimination on the basis of sex, race, religion, disability
- Sexual harassment
- Providing unsafe working conditions
- Unfair dismissal.

Other requirements which apply in some countries but not others apply to: written contracts of employment; rights to paid holidays and sick leave; union recognition; redundancy procedures; age discrimination; minimum wages.

This diverse range of employment law requirements have implications for one-off events like the recruitment of a new member of staff; for regular events like appraisal and the provision of training; and for the day-by-day management of staff. Consequently all managers would be well-advised to ensure they know the law which applies to them and take early advice from human resources or personnel colleagues in cases of doubt or difficulty.

Environmental factors

This heading refers to society's concern for the physical environment. As we mentioned earlier, some governments have passed laws to, for example, reduce exhaust emissions from cars and lorries; protect natural resources like slow-growing hardwoods, limestone and peat; prevent the destruction of areas of national beauty by limiting the building of roads, houses and factories.

Public concern for the environment has resulted in demands for recyclable packaging; ozone-friendly cleaning products; improved public transport; reduced use of chemicals in food production; a more cautious approach towards developing genetically modified food.

Manufacturing responses have included the development of electric cars; emphasis on the use of renewable raw materials; more efficient use of energy; improved methods of waste disposal.

You may not be involved in the design and development of products or services. You will certainly not be involved in deciding the location of new premises for your organization. However since continuous improvement is a central part of a manager's job, you may well be able to introduce or influence:

- More energy efficient production methods
- Reductions in waste
- Reduced use of consumable items (even basic things like paper, cleaning materials, telephone usage)
- Simpler, less wasteful administrative procedures.

Review

Now check your understanding of this chapter by completing the following activities:

1 List six categories of external factor which affect an organization's performance.

P _ _ _ _ _ _ _ _ _
E _ _ _ _ _ _ _ _
S _ _ _ _ _
T _ _ _ _ _ _ _ _ _ _ _
L _ _ _ _
E _ _ _ _ _ _ _ _ _ _ _

52

2 'A strong currency makes exports cheaper.' True or false?

3 Choose two from the following social needs particularly relevant to single-parent families.

Faster cars   Crèches
More libraries   More part-time working
More churches

4 Falling demand leads to higher prices and contributes to inflation. True or false.

Workplace Activity	**If you are currently doing a management job, relate this chapter to your own experience by answering the following questions:**

1 How have your organization's products or services changed in recent years? What influence have external factors had on those changes?

2 Is your organization finding it harder or easier to recruit staff? Which external factor has brought about that change?

3 What impact have technological developments had on your organization?

4 How confident are you in your knowledge of employment law? How could you find out more?

5 What could you do to improve energy efficiency in your operation?

6 How could you reduce waste in your operation?

Reference

1 Levitt, T. (1960) Marketing Myopia. *The Harvard Business Review*, July/August, pp. 45–56.

Website addresses

www.bh.com
Business and management publisher providing a range of textbooks and flexible learning resources on related subjects.

www.businesslink.org
Provides impartial advice for small businesses.

www.FT.com
The *Financial Times* – provides UK and international business news and reports.

MANAGING IN CONTEXT

53

Section 2　Managing People

- *What is motivation?*
- *Why is motivation important?*
- *What motivates people?*
- *What is the difference between a manager and a leader?*
- *How do I get the best out of my staff?*
- *How do I develop an effective team?*
- *How do I manage conflict?*
- *How do I effectively review the performance of my staff?*
- *What are the processes involved in training and development?*
- *What do I do about under-performance?*
- *What makes change successful?*

MANAGING PEOPLE

6 Motivating people

Chapter Objectives	• *What is motivation?*
	• *Why is motivation important?*
	• *What motivates people?*

We can define motivation as:

getting people to *want* to do what *you* want them to do.

*See Chapter 1

Managers* obviously have to be able to motivate as they achieve results through other people. To succeed, managers need to:

- Know the results they want to achieve
- Ensure staff understand what is expected from them
- Check that work is completed correctly, and on time.

Until fairly recently the process was relatively straightforward to deliver. The manager's responsibility was to decide what work should be done and how. Achieving results was simply a question of:

- Giving instructions
- Ensuring they were carried out satisfactorily.

Until the 1970s the manager's job was to give orders and the workers' job was to do as they were told.

In the past, employees under management control would have to have taken and stuck with the work as ordered by their supervisor because of:

- Lack of power and
- Lack of choice.

MANAGING PEOPLE

57

Of course things have changed enormously. Employees today are protected by a large body of employment legislation, often by union representation and a general social expectation that workers will be looked after by their employers. They have greater access to training and education and, generally, jobs go to those best able to do them. Employees are expected to move from job to job and gain promotion.

We have also come to recognize the importance of the people within our organizations and the need to value their contributions and treat them fairly and as individuals.

The importance of motivating people comes partly as a result of the changes in the work environment. But it also results from the growth in numbers of 'knowledge workers'.

This phrase is used in recognition of the fact that many previously non-skilled jobs, which involved simply carrying out the routines designed by management, have now been automated. Consequently increasing numbers of workers are now employed for their ability to think and make decisions for themselves.

In recent years, organizations have stripped away layers of management and supervision. Workers at a quite junior level are increasingly expected to take responsibility for work previously done by their managers, resulting in increased **delegation** of responsibility.

Effective decisions and acceptance of increased **responsibility** will only come from people who are enthusiastic, skilled and knowledgeable.

The basics of motivation

The remainder of this chapter will describe a range of motivation theories. All of them start from two basic principles:

- All people are different
- Finding out what is important to people and structuring their work accordingly.

Case Study

Gwyneth Williams is an intelligent young woman who enjoys working with people. But she found school boring and left

58

without any qualifications. She is starting a job in her local branch of an estate agent office. The branch has front-office (dealing with customers) and back-office (administrative) functions. It is Gwyneth's first day and she is feeling overwhelmed at starting work.

As the Branch Manager, how would you introduce her to her new job, in order to maintain and, if possible, increase her enthusiasm for it?

The Case Study reminds us of how it was when we started our first job. The implication is that Gwyneth is likely to be feeling:

- Insecure
- Not capable of much
- Vulnerable
- In an alien environment
- Surrounded by strangers.

Nevertheless she is intelligent and therefore will probably learn quickly. She also relates well to people.

As her manager, you might have decided to start her in the front office, to make best use of her people skills. But, in order for her to operate effectively and to avoid making her feel more unsure, she will need to understand the:

- Products
- Systems
- Paperwork.

That means she will need some introductory or induction training before she starts, to boost her confidence. She is also new to the branch and knows nobody so she would also benefit from the chance to meet colleagues, not just to say 'hello', but also to find out something about each of them.

We have said nothing about pay or promotion. That is deliberate. We can assume that Gwyneth would not have accepted the job if the pay were not adequate. And, at the moment, she is likely to be more concerned with short-term survival than with long-term advancement!

The Case Study has mentioned the following factors relevant to motivation:

- Security
- Relationships with colleagues
- Training
- Confidence in doing a good job
- Pay
- Promotion.

All these factors are more or less important to different people. And each one is relevant at some points of an individual's career, but less so at others. You will find them cropping up repeatedly in the motivation theories which follow. The secret is recognizing which ones are significant to a particular individual at a particular time.

Maslow's Hierarchy of Needs

Abraham Maslow published his famous Hierarchy of Needs in 1943. The easiest way of understanding his theory is by putting yourself in the position of a survivor from a shipwreck.

Insight

Your ship sank several hours ago. Since then you have been swimming in a rough sea, supporting yourself on a piece of wreckage and swallowing unpleasant amounts of salt water. You see a desert island and manage to crawl ashore.

What will be your first priority when you land?
And your second priority?
And your third priority?

Maslow argued that we seek to satisfy five levels of motivational need. He suggested that someone would not seek to satisfy a need until more basic needs had been satisfied – hence he called it 'a *hierarchy* of needs'. We can show Maslow's hierarchy as a kind of pyramid.

If we apply Maslow's ideas to our desert island, we can assume that:

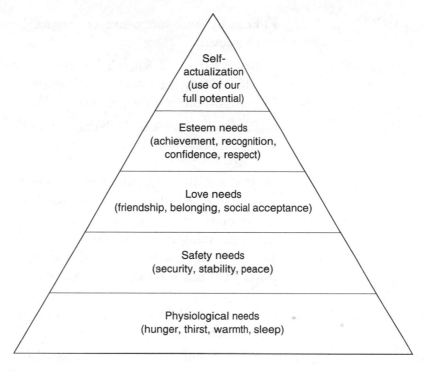

Figure 6.1

- Landing wet, cold, hungry, thirsty and exhausted, our survivor's first priority will be food, drink, a fire and sleep. These will be so important, says Maslow, that our survivor will risk personal safety – by fighting wild animals, for example, or venturing into the unknown – in order to achieve them.

- Our survivor's second priority, according to Maslow, will be shelter – a hut, perhaps, or a cave – to meet safety and security needs.

- After a while, though, our survivor will start to feel lonely. So, in Maslow's terms, the third priority will be companionship, a group of other people to belong to.

The use of this analogy works less well for the top two levels of Maslow's hierarchy. So we can translate his ideas back into work terms. In that context, Maslow is suggesting that:

- We will accept danger, loneliness and a boring job in order to earn enough to buy food and drink.

- When those needs are met, we will treat personal and job security as priorities.

61

- Friendly and supportive colleagues become important at the next level.

- Beyond that, the knowledge that the worker is doing a worthwhile job (self-confidence, self-respect) and praise from others (recognition) are the greatest needs.

- Finally, we will seek a job that makes the fullest use of all we are capable of.

Most, if not all, of us will be able to identify with the five elements that make up Maslow's theory of motivation. In fact, they provide recurrent themes in the various theories that follow. However, later psychologists – and probably our own experiences – have disagreed that one level of need does not come into play until the lower level has been satisfied. For example:

- How to explain an artist who is prepared to starve in order to produce a masterpiece?

- What about a policeman prepared to risk his life in order to protect members of the public?

- And, more personally, if you had no money to buy food, would you no longer be interested in respect and affection from your family?

- Many people satisfy the higher order needs – esteem and self-actualization – outside of the workplace, for example, through their leisure activities.

Although we can see the limitations in Maslow's theory, as indeed he recognized himself, it nevertheless serves as a starting point in understanding motivation. It also provides a valuable explanation of what people look for from their work.

Herzberg: motivators and hygiene factors

Frederick Herzberg's ideas stem back to when he wrote *The Motivation to Work*. His writing has had a huge influence on the way motivation theory is considered and taught.

Herzberg's research resulted in the discovery that there were two distinct categories of factors that influenced people's satisfaction with their work. He called one category maintenance or 'hygiene needs'. In this category he put:

- Company policy and administration
- Supervision
- Salary
- Interpersonal relations
- Working conditions

When these needs deteriorate below an acceptable level the employee will become dissatisfied. However if they are present they are not sufficient to provide motivation to work.

Herzberg called his second category 'motivators'. These were:

- Achievement
- Recognition
- The work itself
- Responsibility
- Advancement.

Herzberg found that these were the things which made people put more effort in. More importantly, the more of them people got, the more motivated they became.

The message Herzberg was trying to send was that employees should be motivated by the job and not through the use of the carrot and stick.

Later writers have called the job satisfiers 'intrinsic' factors and the dissatisfiers 'extrinsic' factors. In other words, if you as a manager give your staff a sense of achievement, recognition for success, satisfying and responsible work and promotion based on results, they will put in extra effort because they find their work motivating. On the other hand, enlightened company policy, effective supervision, high salaries, a friendly atmosphere and a comfortable workplace will stop people complaining – but will not make them work any harder!

Maslow and Herzberg use different terms, but it is worth noting that Herzberg's hygiene factors are similar to the factors contained in the first three levels of Maslow's hierarchy, while his motivators appear in the top two levels of the pyramid.

Expectancy theory

The two theories we have examined so far present a reasonably clear picture of what people want from work and what motivates them to try even harder. But that is only part of the story. Consider the following situation:

Insight

> Your team has been struggling to achieve their output targets. Sometimes they succeed. More often they fail. You offer them £1 million each if they can double their output next month.

How much extra effort will they put in?

Your team will almost certainly ask two questions:

- Based on history, how possible is it for us to double our output?
- If we do, how likely are you as manager to deliver the money?

The most probable answers to these questions are that it would be impossible to double the output, and you could not find the money anyway.

As a result, it is most unlikely that your team will try any harder when the target is unrealistic and the reward is almost certain not to appear.

Of course, the Insight assumes that money is a motivator. And, as we have seen, that may not be the case. However it does provide a good example of expectancy theory.

The Expectancy theory of Victor Vroom ('Work and Motivation') suggests that people will only put in effort if they are confident that:

- Effort will result in the required performance
- Performance will lead to the promised (or expected) reward
- The reward is of a nature that people want.

These ideas work best as a diagram (Figure 6.2) which indicates that:

- Motivation results in effort

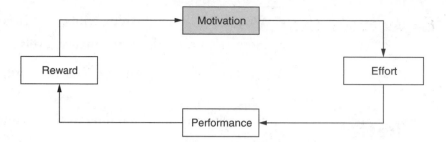

Figure 6.2

- Effort results in performance
- Performance results in reward
- Reward results in motivation.

But as our Insight indicated, there is no point in the manager asking for performance that is not achievable; promising unrealistic rewards is unproductive.

Our experience affects what we expect in the future. In most cases we expect that history will repeat itself:

I do this, then that happens.

Insight

> Richard has been told by his manager several times in the last three years that good performance will result in promotion. His performance has been consistently good but there is no sign of a better job. Richard's manager has asked him to take on a special project, with the promise of a promotion if he succeeds.

How likely is Richard to take on the project?

In our view, highly unlikely! His experience will have told him that his manager's promises are meaningless.

This chapter has provided an introduction to a subject that has much wider implications than we have covered so far. It has not given answers to several questions:

- What constitutes adequate supervision?
- How can a manager make jobs more satisfying?

- What makes relationships with colleagues work?
- How can I raise the performance levels of my team?

All of these are answered in Chapters 7–10.

Review

Now check your understanding of this chapter by completing the following activities:

1 What is motivation?
2 Complete the diagram of Maslow's Hierarchy of Needs.

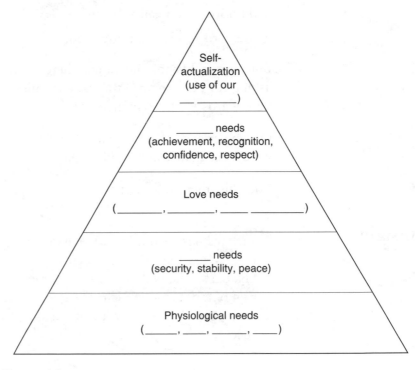

Figure 6.3

3 Which of these are motivators and which are hygiene needs, as described by F. Herzberg?
- Salary
- Opportunity for promotion
- Responsibility
- Status
- Working conditions

- Supervision
- Sense of achievement

4 In Expectancy theory,

motivation results in _ _ _ _ _ _

_ _ _ _ _ _ results in performance

performance results in _ _ _ _ _ _

_ _ _ _ _ _ results in motivation

5 Why is it important for managers to honour their promises?

Workplace Activity

If you are currently in a management position, relate this chapter to your own experience by answering the following questions:

1 What are the factors that motivate you at work?
2 What are the factors that motivate the individual members of your team?
3 What are the main things which dissatisfy them?
4 How could you reduce these dissatisfiers?
5 How will you use your understanding of the theories of motivation to improve your own performance, and that of your team?

References

1 Maslow, A. (1943) A Theory of Human Motivation, *The Psychological Review*, Vol. 50, pp. 370–396.
2 Herzberg, F. (1959) *The Motivation to Work*, Wiley: New York.
3 Vroom, V. (1964) *Work and Motivation*, Wiley: New York.

MANAGING PEOPLE

7   Leading and delegating

Chapter
Objectives

- *What is the difference between a manager and a leader?*
- *How do I get the best out of my staff?*

Is management the same as leadership?

Are leaders born or made?

Does being a good manager mean you will also be an effective leader?

The following chapter attempts to answer these questions.

Managers and leaders

The management task, as we have described it, involves the effective use of resources, including people, to achieve desired results. Therefore, managers are responsible for:

- Plant, equipment and machinery
- Quality
- Output volumes
- Costs
- Short-term and long-term planning
- Some investment decisions.

Many of these responsibilities relate to objects – such as equipment, money, and physical production. Others are related to *administration* – the processes of planning, organization, co-ordinating and controlling, in order to deliver output requirements and meet quality standards. As we have seen, these are all

68

essential, not only to the manager's job but also to the survival and success of the organization as a whole.

However they tell us little about the *people* side of management. This is where leadership comes in. **Leadership** is to do with:

- inspiring and motivating people
- making them feel good about themselves, their work and the organization
- encouraging their participation and involvement
- helping them to grow and develop.

And, since people are a manager's most important resource, these are clearly essential activities. That means that an effective manager has to be an effective leader too. But does it work the other way round? Is a good leader necessarily a good manager?

Case Study

Alice was the national sales manager of a specialist publishing company. Her sales team loved her. The atmosphere in a room seemed to warm when she walked into it. She knew all of them well, their family situations, their hopes, their strengths and weaknesses. Her selling skills meant that when she accompanied one of her team on a call, her presence guaranteed a major order. They would follow her anywhere, do anything for her.

Unfortunately, Alice became ill and had to take extended leave. During her absence the office manager came in to bring Alice's paperwork up to date. She found that:

- She had regularly authorized extra discount for new customers so that some sales had been made at a loss.

- She had been in the habit of passing her team's expense claims for payment without checking them. Some were extremely doubtful.

- She had promised her team bigger and better cars when they became due for replacement, although the company had taken a policy decision to move to more economical models.

Was Alice a good leader?

Was she a good manager?

Alice appears to have had the personality and popularity of a leader. She was interested in her team, supported and helped them. But she also made false promises to them and took several actions which, whilst increasing her popularity, threatened the business. She seems to have been flawed as a leader but definitely poor as a manager.

In the next part of this chapter we shall explore various ways of looking at leadership. There are of course differences between them. However, as you read through you should find a number of common threads which we shall return to later.

The qualities approach to leadership

This is the traditional view of leadership and comes closest to the idea that leaders are born not made. Countless research projects have been undertaken to identify the ten or twenty or more qualities that make an effective leader. As you would expect, the resulting lists vary — and the longer the lists, the more variety there is in them! Nevertheless there is reasonable agreement that leadership benefits from the following qualities:

- Decisiveness — the willingness and ability to take decisions, including difficult ones.
- Integrity — having and being known to have a set of personal values which you apply consistently.
- Enthusiasm and commitment — energy, effort and a clear belief in the value of your own work and that of your team.
- Fairness — treating other people even-handedly, without favouritism.
- Interest in people — a genuine liking for people, wanting to help and support them.
- Communication skills — particularly face-to-face, listening and speaking.
- Reliability — consistently delivering what you have promised.
- Confidence — inspiring trust both from and in your team.
- Open-mindedness — a willingness to try new ideas.
- Forward looking — considering and planning for the future.

Leaders: born or made?

The list of qualities above may be fairly daunting! In fact, in the past it has been pretty difficult finding enough people with these management qualities to the extent that people have been referred to as 'born leaders', which somehow implies that leadership is an inherited quality. However, the reality is more promising. If you look through the list again, you will find that most, if not all, of the qualities are demonstrated in normal day-to-day life — taking difficult decisions, for example, or listening carefully, or keeping promises. All of these are learnable skills — things we can all do if only we recognize why they are important and know how to apply them. That is why the qualities approach to leadership, though old, is not out-of-date. We are suggesting that leadership skills can be learned and managers can be trained to develop them although the rider to that view is as John Adair suggests:

'The common sense conclusion ... is that leadership potential can be developed, but it does have to be there in the first place.'

Situational leadership

Many of us will have encountered if not, heard of, company-sponsored team-building exercises. Many have been featured on TV. Imagine the situation. The Managing Director along with the Sales Manager and her team are stranded on an island in the middle of the Outer Hebrides. Together they have to build a shelter for the night and cook their food armed solely with cotton wool and a box of matches.

Would you expect the Managing Director to be the leader in this situation?

Is the Managing Director necessarily going to be the most qualified to lead this team?

The Managing Director may lead this team and be successful, but it is equally likely that someone else from the team will have superior experience and skill, and will therefore lead the group in cooking the food and building a shelter. The leadership here is situational.

There are two ways of interpreting situational leadership. The negative view is that, as different situations demand different

71

strengths and leadership styles, it is impossible for any manager to be an effective leader in all of them. The more positive view contains two elements:

- That managers should be prepared to allow members of their team to take the lead when the situation demands their particular strengths
- That managers should ensure that they have the expertise to command the respect of their team.

Which brings us to the topic of a manager's power.

Power and authority

In today's work environment, we will normally only accept the authority of our leader if we believe it comes from a valid source. French and Raven argued that there are five *possible* bases of power:

- *Charismatic power* – stemming from personality and personal magnetism.
- *Legitimate power* – deriving from the leader's position in the organization.
- *Expert power* – based on the leader's technical knowledge or expertise.
- *Reward power* – the ability to reward subordinates with pay, promotion, praise or recognition.
- *Coercive power* – based on the leader's ability to punish.

Our judgements will in all cases be influenced by the:

- Culture we come from
- Environment we are used to
- Colleagues we work with (their age, experience and job maturity).

The validity of each of those power sources will depend on the situation.

Functional leadership

Our final approach to leadership is the brainchild of one man, John Adair. Adair's approach goes under two titles. The first –

'functional leadership' – refers to the fact that Adair sees a leader as fulfilling three functions:

- Achieving the task
- Building and maintaining the team
- Developing the individual.

The second title – 'action-centred leadership' – emphasizes his belief that leadership involves a series of actions which can be learned.

Functional or action-centred leadership is usually presented as three overlapping circles as in Figure 7.1. The fact that the circles overlap indicates that the role of the leaders is to address all three groups of needs.

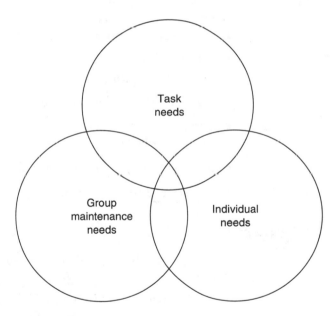

Figure 7.1

However, the separate, non-overlapping areas also indicate that there are times when the leader should focus *entirely* on only one or two groups of needs. The overlaps between the different circles *also* indicate that, for example, meeting team needs contributes to meeting individual needs, and meeting individual needs helps achieve the task.

MANAGING PEOPLE

Management/Leadership — is there a difference?

So can we conclude that management and leadership are synonymous? We hope that you agree that they are not! We can all think of excellent managers who are reasonably ordinary when it comes to leadership. On the other hand we may also know inspired leaders who have the ability to create confidence in others but who lack good management skills!

Common leadership themes

The various approaches to leadership we have described do, of course, have differences in emphasis. Nevertheless, they do tend to have common themes.

They all seek to identify: what leaders do and how they do it and answer by saying:

- leadership is about getting things done
- effective leaders have to be able to analyse situations and take relevant decisions
- leaders need to develop the trust and confidence of their team
- personality is not enough on its own the right to lead requires leaders to 'know their stuff'
- leadership skills can be learned
- leaders are made, not born.

Why delegate?

In today's workplace we find many middle managers are finding that their jobs have become uncomfortably big. There is too much to do and insufficient time in which to do it. There is just too much to do for one person.

How do you cope?

How would you respond to the following situation?

Case Study

Jim Ryan is the operations manager in a large warehouse, which stores and distributes a range of products throughout the UK and abroad. He has worked his way up through the company having started as a warehouse operative. Jim has always set high standards for himself and his staff and expects the warehouse to be clean and tidy at all times. He has three shift managers and twelve team leaders reporting to him. Although the shift managers are very experienced Jim insists on checking each loaded trailer before it leaves the warehouse. As he walks round the warehouse he continually checks on people's work and can often be found sweeping the warehouse floor. Jim complains that he works extremely long hours and that he often gets behind with essential paperwork. Jim justifies his approach by saying: 'If I want a good job doing then I have to do it myself.'

How would you answer Jim?

It would be difficult to fault Jim either for his high standards or for his dedication. But it is worth examining the effects of his approach, both on him and on his staff.

Jim is in a senior management position. Managers achieve results through people, so his approach means he is not making effective use of the people resources available to him. That is why he is too busy. And, despite his high standards, the harder he works, the more likely it is that he will overlook something essential, or rush a task and make a mistake.

As for Jim's staff, his standards no doubt mean that they do the basic jobs he gives them superbly well. But there is a limit to how much job satisfaction they will get from these mundane tasks alone. In terms of the principles of motivation we looked at in the previous chapter, they have neither the chance to learn and develop, nor make use of their full potential. This is likely to lead to boredom, frustration and dissatisfaction. Finally, although it is clearly not Jim's intention, he is blocking his staff's promotion opportunities because they are not learning the higher-level skills needed for the next job up the promotion ladder.

We can therefore say that effective **delegation**:

- helps managers to make the most productive use of their own time

- avoids managerial over-load
- improves *their team's* job satisfaction
- develops their knowledge and skills
- improves their promotion prospects.

Delegation – or abdication?

We have just said that delegation has to be *effective* to deliver these results. So what makes for effective delegation? Let us start with a definition:

Delegation involves giving a member of your team the *responsibility* for part of your job and the **authority** to carry it out, whilst retaining *control* and **accountability.**

The words in italics from that definition are the central elements of effective delegation.

Giving *responsibility* involves ensuring that the team member knows just what is required of them and the standards expected.

Giving *authority* means allowing the decision-making freedom to carry out the task and either providing the necessary resources or making sure your team has enough delegated power to gain access to them.

Retaining *control* involves avoiding two contrasting mistakes. The first is that of 'dumping' the task, walking away and forgetting about it. The second is that of appearing to delegate but staying so close to your team that they feel you are sitting on their shoulder. Control means setting-up a mechanism (regular reviews, perhaps, or progress reports) so that you can monitor what is happening without stifling initiative.

Retaining *accountability is* a key principle of delegation. You can delegate responsibility and authority but accountability stays with you. In other words if the task goes wrong you are not entitled to shrug your shoulders and simply blame your *team.* And if it goes well, you have a right to some of the praise – although it is good management practice to pass it on to your team and tell others who actually did the work.

76

What to delegate

Some aspects of a manager's job should not be delegated. These include:

- Confidential matters which relate to other members of the team
- Activities that go to the heart of a manager's job like setting performance standards or staff discipline
- Tasks which you have been specifically asked to do yourself
- Work which combines high urgency and high importance to the point where it is too risky and would take too long if delegated.

Nevertheless, those exceptions should leave significant scope for delegation. The sorts of tasks that can usefully be delegated are these.

Specialist, technical tasks

As you are promoted up the organizational hierarchy you will become increasingly distant from the technical content of your original job. You will become more focused on larger matters of managing people, resources, outputs, costs and standards. Consequently your staff will need to be more competent at the technical tasks and delegating to them will maintain and enhance that competence.

Development tasks

Delegation is also an important source of training and development as long as you strike a balance between giving authority and retaining control. In order to take on a new task, your team will need access to information, advice and possibly training. It is your responsibility to make sure that these resources are available to them. Equally, you will need to supervise quality and progress more frequently than you might otherwise do – and make yourself available to answer questions and discuss options and concerns.

Important but non-urgent tasks

These are ideal to develop your teams' skills. They give your team the opportunity to learn new skills and grow personally. The fact that they are non-urgent gives you time to brief the team and monitor their work, and also allows the task to take longer if it's done by inexperienced members of the team.

Bonus tasks

Few things damage a manager's reputation with staff more seriously than delegating all the mundane, tedious tasks and holding on to all of the interesting work like attending exhibitions, visiting clients or being elected to project teams. Of course any, or all of these, may require specialist knowledge or experience but careful selection from your team can ensure these requirements are met and delegating such tasks will contribute to your reputation for integrity as a leader.

Routine tasks

These are the kinds of work that may spring naturally to mind when you think about delegation. Remember though to avoid the trap that Jim in our case study fell into. Delegating does not just mean passing on all your boring work to someone else! It also means delegating the specialist, development, important and bonus tasks we have just described.

Insight

> Suzanne has studied the principles of delegation. With a relatively inexperienced team, she has been careful to delegate important, non-urgent tasks so that they have the chance to develop. She also delegates much of her interesting work. Unfortunately, she finds her time taken up with extended briefings, side-by-side training, progress monitoring and review meetings. She is also doing more routine, mundane work than before she was promoted.

What has Suzanne done wrong?

Suzanne's problem seems to stem not so much from a wrong application of the principles of delegation, but more from a failure to combine them with good practice in organizing work and managing people. It is likely that she will enjoy her own job more and develop her people better if she:

- Remembers that it is perfectly allowable to delegate routine tasks.
- Identifies the different levels of experience, ability and confidence her individual staff members are bound to have and avoids the attempt to develop them all at the same rate.
- Improves the balance of what she delegates, to whom and when.
- Recognizes that, as a manager, her right to enjoy her own job is as great as her duty to motivate and develop her staff.

How to delegate

So far, we have assumed your team would welcome the power to make delegated decisions. You are comfortable delegating decision-making and empowering your team.

However those assumptions do not apply to every manager. Douglas McGregor described two very different attitudes amongst managers. He called them 'Theory X' and 'Theory Y'.

Managers who believed in Theory X held the attitude that workers:

- Dislike work and responsibility and prefer to be told what to do.
- Work for money, not the desire to do a good job.
- Need close supervision and control in order to achieve the objectives of the organization.

Managers who believed in Theory Y on the other hand held the attitude that workers:

- Are only passive or resistant because the organization has made them so
- Are keen to develop, to accept responsibility and to support the organization's goals if encouraged to do so
- Have the potential to think for themselves and be creative but are rarely given the chance to do so.

Not surprisingly, McGregor argued that Theory X managers received Theory X responses from their staff and vice versa. He concluded:

'Delegation is not an effective way of exercising management by control. Participation becomes a farce when it is applied as a sales gimmick or a device for kidding people into thinking they are important. Only the management that has confidence in human capacities and is itself directed towards organizational objectives rather than towards the preservation of personal power can grasp the implications of this emerging theory. Such management will find and apply successfully other innovative ideas as we move slowly towards the full implementation of a Theory like Y.'

Clearly, McGregor disapproves of Theory X and recommends Theory Y!

Do you agree with him?

Could it be, that your attitudes are themselves causing the behaviour you experience from others?

McGregor suggests that there is a 'wrong way' and a 'right way' of managing people. Unfortunately it is not so clear-cut.

Tannenbaum and Schmidt, two American psychologists, developed a decision-making model.

The relevance of this model – which Tannenbaum and Schmidt call the 'continuum of leadership behaviour' – to delegation stems from the fact that your approach to decision-making will depend on the urgency of the decision and the maturity of your team. If

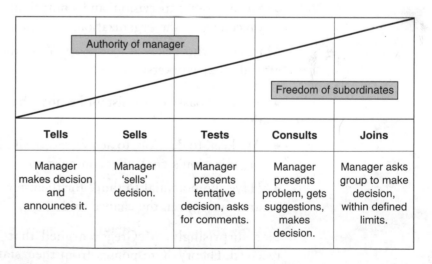

Tells	Sells	Tests	Consults	Joins
Manager makes decision and announces it.	Manager 'sells' decision.	Manager presents tentative decision, asks for comments.	Manager presents problem, gets suggestions, makes decision.	Manager asks group to make decision, within defined limits.

Figure 7.2

your team lacks skill and experience, you will need to give specific and detailed instructions, allowing little freedom for them to contribute. The more skilled, experienced and knowledgeable they are, the more you should seek their ideas and suggestions until you reach the 'joins' end of the continuum where you can simply explain the desired results and leave your team to decide how to achieve them.

Extending these ideas, it is obvious that, whilst you will need to closely monitor, supervise and control an inexperienced team, it will be possible and desirable to give a mature, capable team much more freedom.

Delegation, training and you

As you were reading about the principles of effective delegation, you may have been concentrating on your responsibilities towards your team. In that case, you will have recognized that:

Regardless of maturity, all of your team need to be carefully briefed about what they are to achieve; standards; time-scales; available resources; and limits of their authority.

When tasks are delegated, the manager should monitor progress and be available to give advice and guidance. In the case of familiar tasks and competent staff, monitoring can be less frequent, and less detailed. Guidance will be less necessary. With new tasks or less competent staff, the opposite applies.

How does your manager delegate to you? After all, managers should expect to be treated in the same way. That means that YOU should be seeking the same development opportunities as we have been recommending you should give to your own team.

The following checklist contains questions which you as a manager should be asking about your own development:

- What are the key areas of knowledge, skill and experience that I need for my job?
- How confident am I about my ability in each of them?
- If I cannot answer that question by myself, which of my colleagues (including my manager) would I consult?

81

- What does that analysis say about my strengths and weaknesses?

- What action is my manager taking to build on my strengths? (For example, delegating more demanding tasks; involving me in project teams; arranging formal training; giving me greater understanding of the department's work.)

- Are these actions sufficient?

- If not, what more should I be asking for?

- What are the mechanisms for asking? (For example, the appraisal process; regular performance reviews; informal discussions.)

Review

Now check your understanding of this chapter by completing the following activities:

1 'Managers must be leaders'
   'Leaders must be managers'
   Which of these statements do you agree with? And why?

2 Allowing members of the team to take the lead on occasions is an aspect of _ _ _ _ leadership.

3 Complete Figure 7.3.

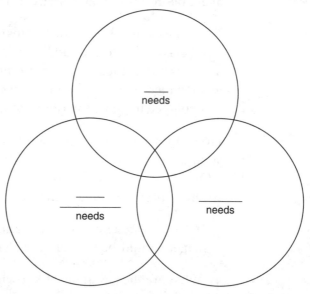

Figure 7.3

What is the model called?

4 List five benefits of delegation.

5 Which of Tannenbaum–Schmidt's leadership styles would you use with a member of staff who was competent at the task?

Workplace Activity

If you are currently in a management position, relate this chapter to your own experience by answering the following questions:

1 Compare your own leadership qualities with those listed on page 70. Which qualities and their associated behaviours need developing? Draw up an action plan, with the help of your line manager, of how you will go about developing these qualities over the next three months.

2 Which power bases apply to your situation and why?

3 What kinds of tasks do you currently delegate? And what kinds do you think you should delegate more of?

4 Are your attitudes to staff Theory X or Theory Y? What are their implications for delegation?

5 Using Tannenbaum–Schmidt's continuum, how could you improve your delegation?

References

1 French, J. R. P. and Raven, B. (1968) *Group Dynamics Research & Theory*, Harper & Row: New York.
2 Adair, J. (1983) *Effective Leadership*, Gower: Aldershot.
3 Adair, J. (1989) *Great Leaders*, Guildford: Talbot Adair Press.
4 McGregor, D. (1957) *The Human Side of Enterprise*, MIT: Cambridge, Mass.
5 Tannenbaum, R. and Schmidt, W. H. (1973) How to Choose a Leadership Pattern, *Harvard Business Review*, May/June.

8 Managing teams

Most people, when asked to think of a team, will typically come up with an example from sport — a cricket team, perhaps, or netball, hockey or soccer. It may not be famous, it may not be playing very well, but, in their minds, it is still a team. Ask them for an explanation of what makes that group of sports people a team though and they will find the question a lot more difficult to answer. So that is where we shall start.

What is a team?

Workplaces are full of lots of teams.

What makes some teams work whilst others don't?

In the teams that work members will:

- Have a common purpose
- Be interdependent
- Respect each other
- Be selected
- Have commitment.

All the members of a team should have a common purpose — they should be working towards common objectives. The individuals in a team that is not working will have few objectives in common.

The members of a team will depend on each other. An advertising account team will be made up of account managers, media planners, media buyers, art director, copywriter, account planners and more. Each will bring a particular set of skills and the team will not be able to function properly unless each makes his or her contribution. The members of a team who do not interact will not work effectively.

Team members should respect each other. They should carry that respect to the point where they also care for and support each other. In ineffective teams individuals are likely to know very little and care little about each other.

Members of a team are brought together deliberately. Selection should be on the basis of skills and knowledge. Someone must put effort into seeking and finding people who, together, have the ability to achieve the team's objectives.

Finally, a team is made up of members who are committed, both to each other and to achieving their common purpose. A group that lacks mutual respect and common objectives will not reap the benefits of team working.

You will certainly have been the member of a team at some point — a sports team, work team, a project team, team of volunteers. You may well have been thinking that not all the criteria we have been describing applied to it. That should not be surprising. Our descriptions relate to effective teams, working well together. When one or more of these criteria is missing, the so-called team is no more than a group of individuals who happen to be in the same place at the same time.

Building a team

So far, we have said nothing about teams having a leader. Of course sports teams usually have a captain, a coach or a manager who leads them. In the work environment this would have been true in the past — in fact, even nowadays, many teams still have a manager, supervisor or team leader in charge of them. There are exceptions, however. Current trends towards de-layering (removing layers of management) and empowerment (giving people the responsibility and authority to make decisions for themselves) have led increasingly to the formation of self-managed teams, teams which choose one of their members as the leader and teams where the leader changes on a project-by-project basis.

Nevertheless even if the team has no formally appointed leader, one is likely to emerge. In fact, teams without a leader are rarely effective because they tend to lack:

- Co-ordination and direction
- Focus on their objectives
- A sense of urgency
- Emphasis on outputs.

All of these factors are central to the process of team building. Psychologist B. W. Tuckman described one way of looking at this process.

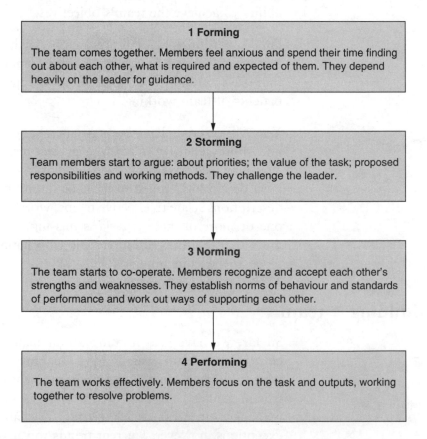

1 Forming

The team comes together. Members feel anxious and spend their time finding out about each other, what is required and expected of them. They depend heavily on the leader for guidance.

2 Storming

Team members start to argue: about priorities; the value of the task; proposed responsibilities and working methods. They challenge the leader.

3 Norming

The team starts to co-operate. Members recognize and accept each other's strengths and weaknesses. They establish norms of behaviour and standards of performance and work out ways of supporting each other.

4 Performing

The team works effectively. Members focus on the task and outputs, working together to resolve problems.

Figure 8.1

The role of the team leader:

- Is different at each stage of the process

- Is to recognize the stage at which the team has reached and the issues that need to be addressed
- Involves managing each stage so that it is properly completed before the team moves on to the next.

At the *forming* stage, the leader will be involved in:

- Explaining the task, the standards and the deadlines
- Setting the team's objectives
- Providing information and resources.

At the *storming* stage, the leader will be:

- Resolving conflict between individuals and factions in the team
- Dealing with emotions
- Clarifying and justifying the task
- Facing rejection and dealing sympathetically with it.

At the *norming* stage, the leader will be:

- Taking a less central or dominant position
- Working with the group to negotiate norms and standards
- Encouraging co-operation and mutual support.

At the *performing* stage, the leader will:

- Recognize that the team has reached maturity
- Allow members to make their own decisions and find their own solutions
- Encourage the team to manage itself.

Tuckman's team-building model concentrates on teams that come together for the first time. However, it is worth recognizing that the role of the leader is similar when a new member is introduced into an existing team.

In the same way as with a totally new team, the new member:

Forming will need to understand the task and the objectives to be achieved;
will need information and resources;
may feel anxious and insecure.

Storming	may experience rejection by, or conflict with, other members of the team; may decide that moving into the team was a mistake.
Norming	will need to be integrated with other members; will be establishing what team membership involves.
Performing	and, finally, will become a fully productive member of the team.

Now apply Tuckman's team-building model to the following situation:

Case Study

> Alya has just taken James, a recent school-leaver, into her team of switchboard operators. On James's first day, Alya introduced him briefly to the other members of the team, ran through details of start and finish times, meal breaks, how his salary would be paid and the basic emergency procedures, following the company's induction checklist.
>
> After a week, the problems started to arise. Other members of the team complained that 'the new boy' was much too slow at his job and continually interrupted them to ask for help. His clothes were too casual to meet the company standards and he was not responding to callers in the proper way. Alya took James aside for a short chat to point out what he was doing wrong.
>
> After a further week, James came to tell Alya that he was leaving. He asserted that 'it was an awful job, nobody talked to him or helped him, he had been stupid to take it in the first place.' Alya accepted his resignation.

After looking at Tuckman's model, what would you have done differently?

How satisfied are you with the company's induction procedure?

The information given in the Case Study suggests that:

Alya should have been more careful at the start to explain how James was to do his job and the standards (phrases to use, clothes to wear) expected of him. In other words, she rushed the forming stage.

Other members of the switchboard team did not accept James. They may have resented his arrival, or simply felt uncomfortable with a stranger. Alya could have prevented this, not only by spending more time on the introductions, but also by involving them in James's basic training. Such actions would have helped the forming stage, but also reduced the rejection and resentment that are part of storming.

James's resignation was an emotional response; partly to the treatment he had received and partly to the isolation, lack of support and personal incompetence he was feeling. These are all typical of the storming stage if it is not managed effectively. Alya could have lessened these negative effects by more attention to the forming stage, but even now it is not too late. Accepting James's resignation is simply accepting defeat. Alya could alternatively sympathize, acknowledge his criticisms and work with the whole team to integrate James properly this time.

As for the company's induction procedure, it appears that this consists of no more than a checklist. It would be far more effective if it took account of the human side of joining a team!

Effective and ineffective teams

We have already suggested that effective teams:

- Know, understand and are committed to their objectives
- Respect and support each other
- Have complementary skills
- Co-operate and work together.

From the performing stage of Tuckman's team-building model, we can add that effective teams also:

- Monitor their own performance

- Remain focused on task objectives
- Solve their own problems.

* See Chapter 7

Douglas McGregor* extended these characteristics and contrasted them with the performance of ineffective teams (see Table 8.1).

We have already said that effective teams should be made up of people with balanced, complementary skills. The obvious application of that is to technical skills. After all, in a road-laying team, there would be no point in having a member who could pour the tarmac if no one knew how to drive the roller! However, Meredith Belbin, a Cambridge psychologist, has extended the idea of complementary skills to a more general consideration of effective team working.

Table 8.1

Effective teams	Ineffective teams
Informed, relaxed atmosphere	Bored or tense atmosphere
Much relevant discussion with a high degree of participation	Discussion dominated by one or two people and often irrelevant
Team objective understood and commitment to it obtained	No clear common objective
Members listen to each other	Members tend not to listen to each other
Conflict is not avoided but brought out into the open and dealt with constructively	Conflict is either avoided or allowed to develop into open warfare
Most decisions are reached by general consensus	Simple majorities are seen as sufficient basis for group decisions which the remainder have to accept
Ideas are expressed freely and openly	Feelings are kept hidden and criticism is embarrassing
Leadership is not always with the formal leader but tends to be shared openly	Leadership is provided by the formal leader
The team examines its own progress and behaviour	The team avoids any discussion about its own behaviour
Low staff turnover and absenteeism	High staff turnover and absenteeism

Belbin identified nine team roles each of which embodies a function which is essential to team effectiveness. Of course not all teams have nine members, so in smaller teams members will have to take on more than one function for the team to be effective. Belbin's team roles, with a description of the contribution each makes to the team and the probable weaknesses each brings, are shown in Table 8.2.

Table 8.2

Role	Contribution	Allowable weaknesses
Co-ordinator	Mature, confident, a good chairperson. Sets the agenda. Delegates well.	Can be seen as manipulative. Delegates personal work.
Shaper	Challenging, dynamic, thrives on pressure. Has the drive and courage to overcome obstacles.	Can provoke others. Hurts people's feelings.
Team worker	Co-operative, mild, perceptive, diplomatic. Listens, builds, calms the waters.	Indecisive in crunch situations. Can be easily influenced.
Plant	Creative, imaginative, unorthodox. Solves difficult problems.	Ignores practical details. Too absorbed to communicate.
Implementer	Disciplined, reliable, conservative, efficient. Turns ideas into practical actions.	Somewhat inflexible. Slow to respond to new possibilities.
Completer	Painstaking, conscientious, anxious. Searches out errors and omissions. Delivers on time.	Inclined to worry. Reluctant to delegate. Can be a nit-picker.
Monitor–Evaluator	Sober, strategic, discerning. Sees all options – judges objectively.	Lacks drive and ability to inspire others. Overly critical.
Resource–Investigator	Extrovert, enthusiastic, communicative. Links team to outside world. Develops contacts.	Over optimistic. Loses interest once initial enthusiasm has passed.
Specialist	Single-minded, dedicated. Provides knowledge and skills in short supply.	Contributes on only a narrow front. Dwells on technicalities. Overlooks the 'big picture'.

(Adapted from R. M. Belbin, Team *Roles at Work,* Butterworth-Heinemann, 1993.)

Now apply Belbin's team roles to the following situation:

Case Study

> The technical project team of Ducati Motor Group has been working for eighteen months on the problem of how to develop a diesel engine which will provide better performance than an equivalent petrol engine, reduce environmental damage whilst retaining the fuel economy associated with diesel. To date, they have produced six alternative designs, three of which run on either petrol or liquefied gas. Two of the remainder are impossible to put into production. One looks promising but the team is too busy looking for better ideas to take it further.

Which roles are missing from the team?

The team seems to be well supplied with innovators (which explains the unorthodox ideas). However, they appear to lack a coordinator who would have reminded them that their task was nothing to do with petrol or gas engines. A shaper might have helped to avoid or overcome the production problems, supported by some specialist input. And an implementer would have turned their promising design into a practical prototype.

So far we have concentrated on what makes a team effective. Two final principles help to explain why teams are sometimes ineffective.

The first reflects a corruption of our earlier point that, in effective teams, members care for and support each other. Robert Blake and Jane Mouton suggested that teams show varying degrees of:

concern for people
concern for production

Their diagram, in the form of a grid, is shown in Figure 8.2.

Although expressed in management terms, the attitudes indicated at the five marked points of the grid are equally applicable to team thinking.

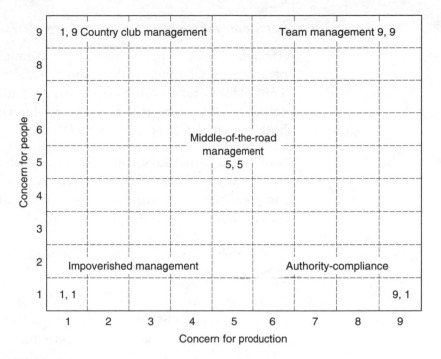

Figure 8.2

1,1 Impoverished management

Attitude: The work group expend the minimum of effort on the work in hand. They do just enough to keep their job.

9,1 Authority-compliance

Attitude: The team focus on efficiency in operations in such a way that human elements interfere to a minimum degree. Output is all that matters. There is minimal social contact.

5,5 Middle-of-the-road management

Attitude: Adequate organization performance is possible through balancing the need for morale and the need for output, i.e. moderate attention to both people and output.

1,9 Country club management

Attitude: Attention to the needs of people for satisfying relationships in work. This leads to a comfortable, friendly atmosphere and work tempo, i.e. keep people happy. Output is unimportant.

93

9,9 *Team management*

Attitude: Work is accomplished by committed people; interdependent on each other, with a 'common stake' in the organization. This leads to relationships of trust and respect, i.e. maintain an equally strong emphasis on task and human requirements and both output and people will benefit.

'Country club management' is the corruption of the idea that team members should care for and support each other. It is distorted to the point where the team spends so much of its time and effort looking after its members that nothing else is achieved.

'Team management' of course presents an alternative way of describing effective team working.

Another distortion of an idea that underpins effective teams is that of 'group think'. Effective teams are confident, committed and largely self-reliant. Taken to an extreme though, these positive characteristics turn into a set of attitudes that can be summarized as:

- Nothing can possibly go wrong
- We always know best
- Anything we do is infallible
- Nothing outside the team affects or concerns us.

Of course, these are extremes. However, it is interesting to note that many major organizations in both the public and private sectors, deliberately split up teams after they have been operating effectively for a time, specifically to avoid the onset of 'group think'.

Conflict in teams

Our instinctive first reaction is that conflict is negative and destructive − to be avoided if possible and dealt with firmly if it does arise. However, we saw earlier that:

- Conflict is a natural, even inevitable, part of the storming stage of team development
- In effective teams, members share ideas openly. This will often lead to disagreement, which will be resolved through discussion and debate.

Table 8.3

Productive conflict	Destructive conflict
Argument and debate to resolve problems and find improvements	Personal antagonism between members
Disagreement over the exact nature of tasks and objectives	Physical violence
	Refusal to co-operate
Conflicting expressions of real feelings	Lack of mutual support
	Bottled-up dislike or resentment

So we can say that conflict, at least in the form of disagreement and debate, is a sign of a healthy team. Of course, that does not mean that all conflict is healthy. Table 8.3 differentiates between productive and destructive conflict.

In the main, productive conflict centres on the task and ways of tackling it. It results in debate, leading to agreement on the best way forward. Destructive conflict is between individuals. It results in bad working relationships and poor performance from both the team and individuals.

Both kinds of conflict can arise from similar causes. It is the way the leader deals with it which differs. Those causes are:

Lack of information or understanding.
Debate over tasks, objectives and priorities arises from lack of clarity. This may be because they have not been properly explained or alternatively because they have not yet been fully defined. Personal antagonism or resentment often arises because one team member believes another is being treated more favourably.

Seemingly impossible or incompatible objectives.
Disagreement over the task and rejection of the leader may be caused by individual and team objectives that appear unachievable. Resentment towards other members may result if they appear to be working in opposition to the rest of the team.

Failure to follow team norms, principles or procedures.
Most often the cause of destructive conflict, this involves members of the team failing to meet its standards or follow agreed working practices. Nevertheless, it can also lead to a constructive review of

95

those standards and practices with the intention of making them more appropriate.

Latent hostility.
One team member may harbour dislike or resentment of another. This may be caused by something personal outside work; a past working relationship that went sour; a fundamental difference in personality, attitude or outlook. That hostility will be kept in check until a minor incident brings it to the surface. On the productive side, feelings can then be expressed and the issue resolved. On the destructive side, it may lead to a shouting-match or even physical violence.

Several techniques are available to the leader when dealing with conflict. Not all are suitable for every situation. The secret is to select those that address the causes and are relevant to the individuals, the team and the environment. Here is a menu of techniques which seem to work:

Communicate clearly and openly.
Misunderstanding and disagreement can often be avoided if you ensure the team knows as much as you do about the task, its objectives and standards. Make sure you explain in such a way that people understand properly.

Encourage discussion.
Give your team plenty of opportunity to debate issues, particularly at the start of a project when there are signs of disagreement or lack of clarity. Allow as much scope as possible for the team to establish its own objectives, standards, norms and working methods.

Focus on the task.
Keep conflict productive by preventing disagreement degenerating into criticism of the person.

Show respect and fairness.
Be seen to pay equal attention to everyone's ideas and suggestions. Avoid any sign of discrimination or favouritism.

Contribute without dominating.
Explain your own view clearly and carefully. If you disagree, say so. But be prepared to back off if the team has a preferred solution that is different from your own.

All of these techniques rest on the assumption that it will be possible to involve the team in reaching solutions and decisions that will resolve the conflict. But what if that is not possible? Here are three fallback techniques to use in extreme cases:

Be prepared to take the initiative.
Remember that an effective leader will be willing to take hard decisions. If team members fail to agree, they will expect you to decide on action yourself. They may not always like it, but you will gain more respect by taking a decision that is unpopular than by leaving the conflict unresolved.

Know the rules.
In most cases, serious conflict may need to be dealt with through disciplinary action. Be sure you know your organization's procedure and the law — and be ready to follow them promptly and accurately. This is likely to involve keeping written records at each stage of the procedure, informing the staff involved of their misdemeanour and their rights, and allowing them to be accompanied by a colleague or union representative at formal hearings.

Consult your manager.
If matters are getting out of control or look likely to do so, make sure your manager knows about it. Ask for advice and clarify your own limits of authority so that you know at what point you should pass responsibility to your manager.

Review

Now check your understanding of this chapter by completing the following activities:

1 Explain the five criteria which define a team.
2 Complete Figure 8.3 of team development (see page 86).
3 According to Belbin, what contribution is made to the team by the:

co-ordinator?

innovator?

monitor–evaluator?

4 Explain 'group think'. Why is it dangerous?

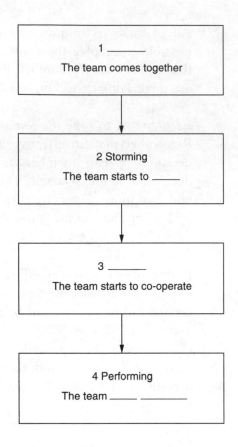

Figure 8.3

5 Complete the following four causes of conflict:

Lack of i _ _ _ _ _ _ _ _ _ or
u _ _ _ _ _ _ _ _ _ _ _ .
Seemingly i _ _ _ _ _ _ _ _ or
i _ _ _ _ _ _ _ _ objectives.
Failure to follow team n _ _ _ _ , p _ _ _ _ _ _ _ _ _
or p _ _ _ _ _ _ _ _ .
Latent h _ _ _ _ _ _ _ .

Workplace Activity

If you are currently doing a management job, relate this chapter to your own experience by answering the following questions:

1 How effective is your team in achieving its objectives?

2 What are the signs of ineffectiveness in your team? How can you improve the effectiveness?

3 Which stage of development has your team reached? How suitable is your behaviour to that stage and why?

4 Using Belbin's team roles as a benchmark identify the contribution individual members make to the team. Look at the overall strengths within your team, which are the areas that require development?

5 Which of Blake and Mouton's five descriptions best fits your team? What might you do to improve its effectiveness?

6 Is the conflict in your team productive or destructive? What more might you be doing to resolve it?

References

1 Tuckman, B. W. (1965) *The Psychological Bulletin*, Vol. 63, pp. 384–399.
2 Belbin, M. (1984) *Management Teams: Why They Succeed or Fail*, Butterworth-Heinemann: Oxford.
3 Blake, R. and Mouton, J. (1961) *The Managerial Grid*, Gulf Publishers: Houston, Texas.

MANAGING PEOPLE

9 Improving performance

Chapter Objectives	• *How do I effectively review the performance of my staff?*
	• *What are the processes involved in training and development?*
	• *What do I do about under-performance?*

In an ideal world:

- The workforce would remain unchanged
- All staff members would consistently achieve the standards and targets required of them
- Work objectives would stay the same
- Nothing outside the organization would change
- Nobody would have any ambition to gain promotion, extend their experience or move elsewhere
- Staff would neither grow older, nor retire.

Of course such a world is unrealistic — and the manager's job would be extremely simple, but very boring!

The reality is very different:

- Experienced staff are promoted, retire or resign
- Staff fail to perform
- Task requirements change
- Existing products and services are no longer demanded
- New expectations arise
- Job content changes as a result of new technology, increased competition or changes to company culture.

All of this may seem obvious. But it provides the background to this chapter which deals with the topics of performance assessment, training and development and discipline.

INTRODUCING MANAGEMENT

Performance review

Elsewhere, we have explored the need for staff to know the:

- Volume of output required of them
- Standards to be achieved
- Behaviour expected.

Understanding these is achieved formally through induction, regular briefing, target setting and performance reviews. We shall return to the last topic later. However, there are normally significant gaps of time between these events. Induction happens once only. Briefings take place at best weekly, usually less often. Targets are set and performance reviewed twice a year at best (once a year is more normal; sometimes not at all).

As a result, formal performance assessment is not enough. That does not mean it is irrelevant. On the contrary, most organizations depend on setting and monitoring objectives and performance standards in order to co-ordinate their activities and develop their staff. But the formality of these processes can get in the way. They cannot replace what is often known as 'management by walking about'.

This style of management means:

- getting to know your team
- finding out how they are getting on
- identifying their problems and concerns
- praising their successes
- being approachable and available for your team

and can contribute to the formal assessment of team performance. Performance review is a regular event that takes place in the majority of organizations. It involves the manager and team member sitting down together in order to review:

- the extent to which the team member has achieved the objectives set for the last period;
- any reasons for under-performance;
- resultant training needs;

101

- the team member's ambitions for the future;
- development needs to achieve those ambitions;
- objectives for the coming period.

In addition to this, in some organizations, performance review or appraisal is also designed to:

- determine future pay awards.

It is probably obvious that these two sets of objectives are contradictory. The first set requires team members to be open about failures, under-performance and future needs. The second set concentrates on how well the team member has done and the rewards potential arising from that performance.

In order to deal with that contradiction, many organizations separate performance assessment into two stages:

> the first deals with training and development needs;
>
> the second addresses performance against standards and objectives.

Nevertheless, even with a gap of time between the two stages, it is still likely that team members will be reluctant to accept past failures in case these result in loss of pay or disciplinary action. That is why it is so important for managers to know how well their staff are doing on a day-to-day informal basis.

Case Study

Andrew is conducting a performance review with Richard, a member of his staff, whose main responsibility is to maintain and update a computer database of customers. He has noticed on several occasions when using the database that records are either incomplete or inaccurate. Andrew raises this point with Richard, who claims that the records he has looked at must have been entered by his predecessor, and that any inaccuracies must have been caused by incorrect information from the customers themselves. The interview degenerates into a 'Yes, I did – No, you didn't' argument.

How might Andrew have avoided this situation?

Why do you think Richard is behaving defensively?

Andrew appears to be basing his judgements on second-hand evidence: the records he has looked at. He seems unable to justify them from personal observation of Richard's work. Consequently, he cannot tell whether:

- the missing information and inaccuracies resulted from someone else;

- Richard has a careless attitude;

- he has a training need (does he know what information should be included on a customer record? Have the mistakes crept in because Richard is not using the software properly?).

In summary, Andrew does not know enough about how Richard does his job to appraise his performance effectively.

Of course, one way of dealing with this lack of knowledge would be to get Richard to talk honestly about his work during the review. But he is not prepared to do this. The most likely explanation is that he fears a report that identifies weaknesses will have a negative effect on pay, job security or promotion. This may be the case or he may simply not understand the organization's appraisal philosophy. Whatever the reason, Richard clearly does not trust Andrew sufficiently for the interview to succeed.

There are several reasons why a performance review system may fail:

- Staff may distrust the intention behind it

- Staff or managers, or both, may not understand it well enough to use it well

- One or both sides are ill prepared

- The paperwork is so complicated that it becomes simply an exercise in form filling

- The process is rushed, either by the manager to get it out of the way, or by the organization setting unrealistic deadlines for completion

- Different managers apply different standards

- Managers show bias in favour of staff they like.

Some of these problems arise from the way the system is designed or administered. You are unlikely to be in a position to influence either of these although some organizations with a culture of consultation do regularly ask their managers and staff to comment on the effectiveness of the system and to suggest improvements. If the system you operate is imperfect (and few are totally faultless) the only advice is to get to know it well enough to make the best use of it, despite the imperfections.

The majority of the problems though occur because either managers, or staff, or both, do not put enough time or energy into making the system work. This is what should happen.

Before the interview

Allow time for you and your team to prepare. Some systems include a preparation sheet, others a log for managers and team members to complete independently during the year. Even if your organization does not have these, it is helpful for both parties to make notes of the strengths and areas for improvement, with examples of past events to support them, potential training needs and how they could be met. Staff should also record short-term and long-term personal objectives and career plans. A fortnight should be long enough for this preparation.

Set aside a formal time for the meeting and advise your team members. Be realistic about the length of time required. This will vary according to the individual and the complexity of the system, but it is advisable to make a judgement on the time your longest meeting will take and allocate the same amount for each of them. This is particularly important if members of your team work closely together, to avoid them jumping to conclusions about the nature of the meeting, based on the time allocated. It is also rarely successful to fill a whole day with reviews. You will find them exhausting and will be unable to give of your best in later ones. It is a good idea to conduct just one meeting in a morning and one in an afternoon, to give yourself breaks from them by doing other work.

Book a private room for the meeting. Make sure it is arranged informally, ideally with easy chairs. At very least avoid being separated by a desk.

Ensure you will not be interrupted.

During the interview

- Explain the purpose and structure of the meeting
- Encourage staff to talk more than you do by asking questions and listening to the answers
- Avoid generalizations about strengths and weaknesses. Be specific and quote examples
- Focus on behaviour not personality
- Agree performance, training and development objectives and how they will be met
- Maintain a relaxed, convivial atmosphere.

After the interview

- Complete the paperwork while the interview is still fresh in your mind
- Arrange any training or development activities you have agreed
- Monitor progress.

Remember that formal performance review only succeeds if it is supported by regular informal feedback.

Performance reviews are one way of giving feedback to your staff. In fact, staff often say that they are the only opportunity they get to find out from their managers how well they are doing! Of course, managers who act in this way are running counter to the principles of effective performance assessment, which should be an ongoing, day-by-day process. As you would expect, the same applies to giving feedback.

Feedback involves informing your staff of their performance against the standards required of them. Unfortunately, it is a process with which many of us feel uncomfortable. This is especially true of managers, particularly if they have established friendly, working relationships with their team. And, at least in the UK, giving praise for good performance does not come naturally, either!

Nevertheless, giving feedback is an essential part of improving performance. As you will have gathered, much of this chapter is as relevant to you as it is to you as a manager. So ask yourself these questions.

Discussion	How insecure would you feel if your manager never told you if your work was good, bad or indifferent?
	What chance would you have to build on your strengths and overcome your weaknesses?
	How could you decide what your future career plans should be?

Your staff feels the same way. The reasons why we find it uncomfortable to give feedback appear to be that:

- It seems too personal
- Negative feedback feels like an attack
- We are reluctant to let our emotions show.

All these concerns are reduced significantly if we recognize that effective feedback addresses performance, not the person. Compare these two statements.

Insight

> 'There, you've done it again. I don't think you've got it in you to ever get this right.'
>
> 'Could you adjust the margins to 2 centimetres on each side please. It will look better as it will be in line with our standard format.'

Which of these two is more effective feedback?

What are the differences between them?

The first statement sounds exasperated, rude and aggressive. It makes a personal attack on the listener, gives no detail about the error and no suggestions for improvement.

INTRODUCING MANAGEMENT

106

The second statement is assertive but supportive. It gives specific guidance for improvement and explains the need for it.

Table 9.1 summarizes the differences between effective and ineffective feedback.

Effective feedback

- Shows respect.

  It assumes that performance can be improved and that the staff member wants to improve. It values the person.

- Is immediate.

  This is why feedback is ongoing. That allows you to address weaknesses when they arise and the staff member will be in the right frame of mind to deal with them.

- Is limited.

  Staff performance may show scope for several improvements. Effective feedback is restricted to a limited number of priorities, to avoid overwhelming them.

- Puts the improvement into context.

  It explains the need and stresses the benefits.

- Is two-way.

  It allows the staff member to explain what went wrong and, where possible, involves the person in suggesting alternatives.

Table 9.1

Effective feedback	*Ineffective feedback*
Is supportive and constructive	Is aggressive and critical
Is specific	Makes broad generalizations
Suggests improvements for the future	Focuses on past failures
Looks for solutions	Allocates blame
Addresses behaviour	Attacks the person

Approaches to training and development

We have already identified in previous chapters that the people within our organizations are a crucial resource and an essential part of the role of the manager is to develop individual members of staff as well as the team as a whole.

So is there a difference between training and development?

Training is a short-term systematic process, which improves and develops the knowledge, skills and attitudes of employees to meet the current and the future needs of the business.

Development is a longer-term process, which enables individuals and organizations, through time, to reach their full potential.

What are the benefits of training?

Training brings a number of benefits to an organization; it is a process that can:

- Improve current skills.

  Training can be used to achieve and maintain performance ensuring high quality work from your team. It can be used, for example, to improve poor performance and reduce accidents and absenteeism.

- Increase range of skills.

  It provides people with the opportunity to develop their potential.

- Develop future skills.

  Training is the key to ensuring that people are prepared for the changing demands of the workplace, for example, new technologies and working practices.

Overall, training can increase the commitment, confidence and motivation of staff, which can be directly linked to the success of the organization not only in its ability to change, but also in increasing its competitiveness in the marketplace. However, it is important to stress that training for training's sake will not bring about these benefits. It needs to be part of the overall culture of the organization and be relevant to the needs and objectives of the business.

The aim of development is to improve an individual's overall knowledge and confidence and so broaden their opportunities for career progression. This may result in transfer to a specialist department and/or a management position within the company. Table 9.2 includes possible development methods. A word of caution – some companies are reluctant to encourage development, as they fear it will encourage staff to think about moving on!

A systematic approach to training

Training is an investment in people and, as with any investment, there are costs attached to it. So it is important to gain the maximum benefit, and to ensure that it does not become a wasteful expense, by taking a planned and systematic approach to managing the training.

There are simple steps in this process.

1 Firstly identify the training needs – what are the current skills, knowledge, attitudes and behaviours?
2 The next step is to identify what future skills, knowledge, attitudes and behaviours are required to move the business forward.

The difference between points 1 and 2 is often referred to as the 'learning gap'.

3 Design and plan the appropriate training to meet the 'gap' (Table 9.2 gives you suggestions for possible methods).
4 Deliver the training.
5 Validate the training to determine if it has been successful in achieving its aims and review how the learning will be applied in the workplace.
6 Evaluate the training in terms of the cost compared with the financial benefit gained by the improved performance of the staff. Examples of this may include a reduction in accidents, fewer customer complaints and increased productivity.

Table 9.2

Training and development method	Description
Formal courses	The traditional 'classroom' based approach usually involves presentations, case studies or practical exercises. Can be residential, delivered on company premises or non-residential. Can be costly to the organization but usually popular with delegates if well designed and relevant to their job roles.
Open or distance learning	Usually text based, such as the Pergamon Flexible Learning Super Series. Designed to be used in the workplace, they contain case studies, examples and activities to reinforce learning.
e-learning	Learning via communications technology. Learning materials are delivered online, reducing costs and increasing access.
Demonstration	Skills are demonstrated by the trainer and then practised by the learner.
'Sitting with Nellie'	A form of on-job training where the learner is trained by an experienced colleague. Can be effective if the colleague has the skills and ability to transfer knowledge but can result in the transfer of bad habits.
Coaching	One-to-one training by a colleague or manager to pass on skills and knowledge, answer questions and review work.
Projects	Involvement in company and/or department projects provides an opportunity to address a work-related problem or issue. Develops company knowledge, decision making and presentation skills.
Secondments	The staff member is transferred to a different position on a temporary basis to gain new knowledge, skills and experience.
Job rotation	Giving people the opportunity to work in other sections or departments. Care should be taken to match the learning needs to the job.
Visits or working with other companies	Exposure through visits or working with other organizations provides an effective way of broadening perspectives and benchmarking work practices.

Discipline

An organization's disciplinary procedure often conjures up pictures of punishment and ultimate dismissal. However, these are false. Under UK law, instant dismissal is only allowed in cases of gross misconduct (events like theft, serious violence to other employees, drunkenness, which the British courts define as 'striking at the root of the employment contract'). Instead, an organization's disciplinary procedure is intended to address under-performance by providing means of bringing it to the required standard.

In order to achieve that, a disciplinary procedure should ensure that:

- People know what they should do and to what standard
- If they fail to meet the standard, they should be given the opportunity to improve
- The organization should help by providing any training, support or guidance needed.

Firms use a three-stage process, as advised by ACAS (the Advisory, Conciliation and Arbitration Service), which is made up first by a verbal warning, *and* followed by two written warnings.

Each warning should specify:

- in what ways performance has been inadequate
- the nature of the improvement required
- the time allowed to make that improvement.

There will be a time-gap after each warning, varying from a few weeks to several months, depending on the nature of the work, the help to be provided and what the courts describe as 'the principle of reasonableness'. In other words, taking account of the improvement necessary, how long should it reasonably be expected to take?

Viewed in this way, discipline is an extension of the process of standard setting, performance assessment, training and review we described earlier.

Case Study

> Paul is a difficult man and he is often late for his job at the warehouse. Ian, his boss, has just been promoted to his first management position. He would dearly like to get rid of Paul, whom he sees as disruptive and a bad influence.

111

What advice could you give to Ian?

We can understand Ian's frustration but he should focus on the need to identify specific issues, for example poor time keeping or attitude. Firstly Ian should tackle the issue of poor time keeping, assuming that Paul is required to commence work at a clearly stated time, Ian needs to ascertain from Paul reasons for his lateness, e.g. family or transport problems, whilst restating the time Paul should be available for work.

Ian could then discuss Paul's attitude, again restating the company's expectation in terms of behaviour from its employees.

These do not appear to be training issues so Ian would be advised to give Paul a specific period, e.g. two weeks, to improve both his time keeping and/or attitude. Following this period Ian should review the situation with Paul.

Training, development and you

You will probably have realized that everything in this chapter about training and developing your own staff applies equally to what you should expect for yourself. So let us summarize from your viewpoint.

Do you know the objectives and standards expected of you? More specifically, do you know what is set out in your job description? If you do not have one or it is not clear, have you asked your manager?

Do you know how well you are performing against those standards? Do you regularly seek feedback from your:

- Manager?
- Colleagues?
- Staff who will be in the best position to tell you how effective you are as a manager?

Have you identified your own training needs? Firstly, by comparing your performance with the expected standards. Secondly, by looking ahead to see how your job will change and isolating any new knowledge and skill requirements arising from the changes.

Have you decided what your career ambitions are? Where do you want to be in, say, two years and five years? What development will you need to get there?

Are you making the best use of your organization's performance review process? Do you prepare effectively for your review? Can you give relevant answers to your manager's questions about your training and development needs?

How much thought do you give to how these can be met in practical terms? What knowledge and skills do you need? What additional experience? Would further qualifications help you achieve your career objectives?

<table>
<tr><td>

Review

</td><td>

Now check your understanding of this chapter by completing the following activities:

1 List the benefits to your team of you managing by walking about.
2 List five of the reasons why a performance review system may fail.
3 What makes feedback effective?
4 Explain the difference between training and development?
5 What is the main purpose of a disciplinary procedure?

</td></tr>
<tr><td>

Workplace Activity

</td><td>

If you are currently in a management position, relate this chapter to your own experience by answering the following questions:

1 How could you improve your contribution as manager to the performance review process?
2 What changes are taking place in your organization that will lead to training needs for your staff?
3 Of the training methods listed in this chapter, which might be worth exploring as possibilities for your staff?
4 How effectively does your organization evaluate training? How could it be improved?
5 Which of your staff have the potential to develop? How could you help them do so?
6 What more could you do to develop yourself?

</td></tr>
</table>

113

10 Managing change

- *What makes change successful?*

Change can be:

- Exciting
- Challenging
- Stimulating

yet be:

- Frightening
- Threatening
- Unsettling.

*See Chapter 5

Change can evoke positive or negative emotions. Yet, as we saw from Section 1*, change in the external world is something organizations can neither influence nor resist. And, as a result, organizations themselves have no choice but to change in order to adapt, improve and survive.

So why are some people excited, challenged and stimulated by change, while others feel frightened, threatened and unsettled? And, if change is inevitable, how do we ensure our team is positive about it?

The answers to these questions can be summarized in one word: ownership.

The evidence is overwhelming that people dislike and resist change if it is simply imposed on them, without explanation or consultation, as a set of new requirements they cannot influence and must accept.

INTRODUCING MANAGEMENT

114

By contrast, people will be more positive about change if they are:

- Informed about the reasons for it
- Helped to understand the benefits that should result
- Involved in planning and designing the change
- Encouraged afterwards to recognize what they have gained from it.

The rest of this chapter develops these suggestions in more detail and offers some practical techniques for achieving them.

The change process

Kurt Lewin started his analysis of change by presenting a diagram (Figure 10.1) which showed why change does not take place easily.

Figure 10.1
'Force feed analysis'

Lewin's argument was that situations remain constant when they are subject to two sets of equal and opposite forces: driving forces and restraining forces.

Case Study

> Atlas Engineering manufactures sub-assemblies which are bought by a small number of customers making domestic appliances. Atlas operates a rigorous but traditional quality control system. One of its main customers has now insisted that all suppliers must have ISO 9002 registration. Atlas recognizes that failure to obtain ISO 9002 will result in a major loss of business straight away and, potentially, a decline in reputation and further lost business in future if other customers introduce similar requirements. On the other hand, to achieve ISO 9002, the firm will need to develop quality assurance procedures, may need to revise its operating methods and will experience disruption, cost and lost output as this goes ahead.

Draw a force field diagram showing Atlas's situation.

Without expanding the information given, we thought the diagram would look something like the one in Figure 10.2.

Figure 10.2

Whether Atlas now decides to go for ISO 9002 will depend on whether management decides that the driving forces in favour are stronger or weaker than the restraining forces against.

Although a force field diagram is a helpful way of visualizing change, Lewin goes a lot further. First, he presents two types of strategy for achieving change.

A push strategy involves making the driving forces stronger. In our example, this would happen if:

- More pressure was added to the existing forces, perhaps by another customer demanding ISO 9002 now
- Additional driving forces were introduced, for example if the Managing Director expressed his support for the initiative.

'Push' strategies have the best chance of success when restraining forces are practical or financial. They are far less likely to work when the restraining forces are people's attitudes or concerns. Under these circumstances, if the driving forces get stronger, the restraining forces will push back harder and nothing will change.

Lewin's second strategy is *a pull* strategy, which involves reducing the pressure of the restraining forces. In our example, this might be done by:

- Reducing the likely level of disruption
- Finding ways of lowering the costs
- Bringing down potential lost production.

In most cases though the pressures against change have a strong human element. Lewin strongly recommends a 'pull' strategy in these cases and much of his book is devoted to implementing one.

Successful change, Lewin argues, involves three stages:

Unfreezing

For change to take place, the old ways have to be unfrozen and the need for change accepted. To achieve this requires confronting people with the risks of not changing, making them aware of the benefits of change, explanation and involvement. These are the themes of the next part of this chapter.

Changing

The second stage is a process of finding alternatives, defining and allocating responsibilities, implementing and troubleshooting. These are central activities in the 'implementing change' part of this chapter.

Refreezing

When changes have been made, they are still not established. People will feel tentative about them, problems will arise and it is possible that things will slip back. At the refreezing stage, it is important to highlight the successes, reward those involved and deal positively and effectively with any snags. These topics are covered in the final part of this chapter.

Shaping attitudes to change

Resistance to change often results from a combination of:

Fear of the unknown

People do not understand the implications of change and feel more comfortable with past routines (however unsatisfactory they may have been).

Fear of loss

Change may involve: loss of status; loss of income; loss of a job. Such fears may be unfounded but will still be present.

117

Ambiguity

People will wonder: what the change will involve; whether they will be able to cope; what the consequences may be.

Insecurity

We tend to fear the worst! Not knowing what will happen leads to the assumption that the worst may happen.

Loss of control

When people believe that change will mean they will have to sacrifice control over their own work, responsibilities or destinies, change will be unwelcome.

Of course change may, in reality, result in:

- Better working practices
- A more comfortable environment
- Greater rewards
- More satisfying work
- A more secure future.

But — and this is the significant point — the less people know, the more anxious they will feel and the more resistant to change they will be.

Viewed from the manager's perspective, the process of unfreezing people's attitudes so that they accept the need for change will require action in three areas, which can be summarized by the acronym ICE. These three letters stand for:

Information

Most of the listed reasons for resistance to change result from a lack of knowledge or lack of understanding — and a consequent belief that the worst will happen.

Consultation

Consultation is the opposite of imposed change and encourages people to feel that they are still in control of the process.

Enthusiasm

If the manager appears to lack belief or confidence in the proposed change, it is unlikely that the team will feel any more committed. But it goes further than that. To develop enthusiasm in team members will also involve providing them with the necessary knowledge and skills to cope effectively with the change.

It is worth looking at each of these three processes in a little more detail.

Information answers the questions:

- What is going to happen?
- Why is it going to happen?
- When and how will it happen?
- What will the consequences be?
- How will I benefit?

If the change has already been decided and planned in detail, the team will have little influence over the 'what', 'when' and 'how'. More often though change decisions are taken in broad terms and it is left to those closer to the work to decide how they will be implemented. Under those circumstances, team members will feel more in control and less insecure, because they will be able to determine how to make changes more effective and less disruptive.

The reasons, consequences and benefits though are a different matter. As a manager, if you announce that a change is taking place but cannot explain why or what will happen as a result, you will generate greater fear and anxiety than if you had waited. Consider the following situation:

Case Study

Rumours of a merger had been rife in the office for weeks. Finally, senior management issues a bulletin confirming that merger terms have been agreed. (In fact, the news was published in last night's local paper.) Rashid, the office manager, calls his team together to announce that the two operations will be merged in three months' time. He is bombarded with questions:

Will we keep our jobs?

What about redundancies?

How will our jobs change?

Will we be paid more or less?

But he cannot answer them.

119

What should Rashid have done differently?

Rashid has done no more than confirm what his team could have read in the papers yesterday. It is easy to understand his wish to keep them informed but there was really no point in holding a formal meeting until he knew enough to answer his team's questions.

Consultation has been a central theme of other chapters in this book. As far as change is concerned, your approach to consultation will vary according to the amount of freedom delegated to you in implementing it.

As we have pointed out elsewhere, lack of consultation is bad practice, resulting in dissatisfied and insecure staff and, usually, the imposition of systems which do not work as well as if they had been designed by those responsible for implementing them. Nevertheless if change is to be imposed, the best you can do is to attempt to gain a little more flexibility by making representations to your own manager. Failing that, you will need to use all your skills of leadership and persuasion to convince your team.

One of these skills will be your ability to demonstrate and provoke enthusiasm. The first step is to make sure that you find out enough about the proposed change to understand properly why it is essential, the consequences of not changing and how your team will benefit. You will then be in a better position to gain their commitment.

Implementing change

The implementation process involves both logistic and people considerations.

* See Chapter 11

The process of managing resources to achieve results is covered in Section 3* of this book. We can summarize its relevance to change by pointing out that implementing change requires:

- Clear objectives for the change
- An action plan with deadlines
- Milestones and responsibilities
- Resources and a budget

- A system for monitoring achievement against the objectives, deadlines and budget.

* See Chapter 9

The people side of implementation takes us back to some of the topics we covered in the last chapter*. It will involve:

- Individual and team briefings related to tasks, standards and output
- Training to accommodate job changes
- Regular communication
- Continual checking on progress, problems, concerns and complaints.

Beyond these activities, it may also require:

- Decisions on promotion and transfer
- A critical examination of the structure of your team
- The design of new working methods
- New definitions of your own and your team members' responsibilities.

Consolidating change

This is the final stage of the change process, which Kurt Lewin calls 'refreezing'. The problem associated with the thought that change should be refreezed or cemented, is that organizations are now subject to a continuous stream of minor and major changes.

'Refreezing' — setting new processes in stone — cannot be seen as final. Major, discontinuous changes are still necessary. And, if they are not consolidated, they will fail.

There are three aspects to consolidating change. They answer the questions:

- How well did it work?
- What further action is necessary?
- How are people feeling?
- What can we learn for the future?

The *first* aspect is to review the outcome of the change. It is most unlikely that the change was a totally unqualified success. Now everything is up and running, there are bound to be:

- Things overlooked or forgotten
- Opportunities for improvement.

If change is to be accepted, people will need to see evidence of its success. The more action is taken to smooth any remaining rough edges, the more persuasive that success will be.

The *second* aspect is to confirm ownership of the change. Some people will need further help to gain the new knowledge and skills required. Otherwise they will lose confidence and try to return to their old ways. Work teams may have been separated. New teams will need to be built, following the techniques we explored in Chapter 8. Pay schemes will need to reflect new work demands. But it also means ensuring that performance receives praise and that, for example, review systems are revised to incorporate new objectives arising from the change.

The *final* aspect is evaluation of the change. It is in place, it has worked, and people will have learned some valuable lessons; some of them painful. Evaluation means working out what can be learned from those lessons and recording them so that they can be applied to the next major change that comes along.

Review

Now check your understanding of this chapter by completing the following activities:

1 What is the one-word secret of successful change?
2 Complete the diagram of Kurt Lewin's force field analysis (Figure 10.3):

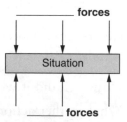

Figure 10.3

3 What does Lewin say are the three stages of the change process?

_____ _____ _____

4 Complete this acronym for the factors necessary to shape people's attitudes:

I _ _ _ _ _ _ _ _ _

C _ _ _ _ _ _ _ _ _ _

E _ _ _ _ _ _ _ _

5 What are the three actions necessary to consolidate change?

Workplace Activity

If you are currently in a management position, apply this chapter to your own experience by answering the following questions:

1 Identify a change taking place in your organization at the moment. How do the people involved feel about it? Why is that?

2 Think of a change you would like to make to improve your operation. What restraining forces would you face? What could you do to lessen them?

3 What mechanisms do you use to inform and consult with your team? How could they be improved?

4 How much do you know about the reasons for the changes taking place in your organization? How could you find out more?

5 How relevant is your organization's reward system to the way it operates today? What changes would you make to it?

6 How effective is your organization generally in managing change? How could it improve?

Reference

1 Lewin, K. (1951) *Field Theory in Social Science*, Harper & Row: New York.

Website addresses

www.acas.org.uk
The Advisory, Conciliation and Arbitration Service. Provides information and publications on all aspects of employment law.

www.belbin.com
Information on continuing research into team roles. Online team analysis and reports.

MANAGING PEOPLE

www.managementandleadershipcouncil.org
Provides information, publications and resources including a good
practice guide for managers.

www.trainingzone.co.uk
Online network for training and HR professionals includes advice,
guides and briefings.

Section 3 Managing Activities

- *What are outputs?*
- *Who wants quality?*
- *Are customers important?*
- *Who monitors results?*
- *Who controls results?*
- *Health and Safety – so what?*
- *When is improvement necessary?*

MANAGING ACTIVITIES

11 Changing inputs into outputs

Chapter Objectives	• *What are outputs?* • *Who wants quality?*

In Section 1 of this book we introduced the idea that managers are responsible for, among other things, transforming inputs into the products and services that people want. This process is the subject of a major body of management literature under the common heading of 'operations management'.

Operations management is not just the responsibility of a few specialist managers. Unlike decisions concerning major investment, or pay and reward structures, or product design, or the choice of target markets, all of which require specific technical expertise, operations management can only succeed if it is treated as the responsibility of all managers at all levels in all organizations.

Managing Operations defines operations as:

'The activities carried out by an organization to provide the service to customers or clients which is its basic reason for existing.'

Of course that definition is very broad but its breadth is deliberate. Going back to the principle of added value which we introduced earlier, it is worth emphasizing that:

- All products and services cost money;
- Customers will only pay for things they value;
- All organizations have customers (whether they are voters, taxpayers, patients, individuals or other organizations).

Every function in an organization costs money. All organizations receive limited revenue in the form of prices paid by customers,

127

budgets or subsidies from local or national government. Consequently any organization will work hard to ensure that it makes the most effective use of the revenue it receives. That means that any function must be able to justify its existence on the basis of the value it adds to the products and services provided by the organization it serves.

As economies become increasingly dependent on international trade and therefore need to compete with other countries, so the importance of adding value becomes more obvious.

So where does operations management fit into this big economic picture? Earlier references to inputs, transformation and customers hint at the answer to this question.

- All organizations have customers;
- Customers will only pay for things they value;
- Organizations exist to add value by transforming inputs into products and services that customers want;
- Every function contributes to that transformation process.

Therefore the role of operations management is to ensure that every function in an organization adds as much value as it can making the most efficient and effective use possible of the resources at its disposal. As a result we can confirm the statement made by Professor Ray Wild of the Henley Management College:

'Virtually everyone with a management responsibility is involved in managing operations – because almost every management job requires the efficient use of resources to achieve the defined outcomes, which in most cases relate to the needs of customers.'

Figure 11.1 illustrates the fundamental of operations management:

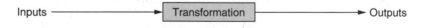

Inputs ⟶ Transformation ⟶ Outputs

Figure 11.1

Outputs are what go on to the next link in the **supply chain.** That next link may be the final customer or an **internal customer** in the organization (a theme we shall return to in the next chapter).

Outputs do not necessarily bring added value.

128

Insight

The Management Statistics Unit of a biscuit manufacturer takes cost and output data for each production line and uses them to prepare information which is intended to show the supervisors of each line how well their operations are performing. However, the resulting information is bulky, difficult to analyse and leaves the reader to work out comparisons.

What are the inputs, transformation and outputs of this process?

Do you think it adds value?

The inputs to this process are the cost and output data produced by each line. In theory these are then transformed into management information which represents the output. However to be useful, management information should present easily identifiable comparisons — with previous performance, for example, with budgets and between lines.

The insight suggests that individual line supervisors might do better to compare the raw data (which is prepared anyway as inputs to the Statistics Unit) and make their own comparisons. The process certainly produces outputs but appears to add little or no value.

Inputs consist of the resources used in a process — consumable resources like raw materials, time, energy, budget; and renewable resources like premises, machinery, tools and expertise. Outputs should ideally be the products and services that customers want — in the right place and at the right time.

Transformation is the process of changing inputs into outputs. However, since operations are every manager's responsibility it is not possible to give a simple definition of what that change involves. You will get a feel for the transformation process by answering the following questions:

What transformation takes place when:

1   A retailer collects a box of chocolate bars from the cash-and-carry warehouse and displays them on his shelves?

2   A dentist drills and fills your tooth?

3   A gardener cuts your lawn?

MANAGING ACTIVITIES

4 A bricklayer mixes concrete?

5 A secretary types a report?

6 Your local garage fixes your car?

Transformation may involve a change in:

- Form
- Content
- Location
- Presentation
- Efficiency.

- Question 1 involves changes in form (single bars not a whole box) and location.
- Question 2 may involve a change in form or content but certainly involves a change in efficiency!
- Question 3 involves a change in presentation.
- Question 4 involves a change in both form and content (a combination of water, sand and cement).
- Question 5 involves a change in presentation.
- Question 6 involves a change in efficiency (and possibly content if the repair required, for example, is a new gearbox).

Economy, efficiency, effectiveness

Added value is not an absolute. Of course it is relatively easy for customers, both internal and external, to decide that a product or service adds value at all. Over time they may come to the realization that they can happily do without it completely.

However this is an unusual situation. Consider these two insights.

Insight

Alpha Assemblies buys iron strip which they use as a major component in the manufacture of industrial shelving units. The price of strip from their current supplier is making the units too expensive to compete with those of other manufacturers.

Can the company do without this component completely?

If not what else might they do?

Insight

> Wexford Local Authority provides a weekly refuse collection service to the local traders who are complaining about the prices it charges for the service. Refuse collection is currently carried out by staff employed by the local authority.

Can the traders do without the service completely?

What could it do to reduce the price?

Iron strip is obviously an essential component for Alpha Assemblies – no strip means no product. However they are not permanently tied to their current supplier. A relatively simple alternative would be to find another supplier able to provide strip of a suitable specification at a lower price.

Wexford's local traders are unlikely to be able to do without refuse collection completely. But the local authority charges separately for it so there appears to be nothing stopping them from taking their business elsewhere. They might choose to:

- Form a co-operative to buy the service from a commercial provider;
- Or even make individual arrangements to that each store is serviced by a different refuse collection business;
- Or else band together to recruit their own refuse collectors.

The local authority could choose to withdraw the service but it would lose a valuable source of income. Less extreme alternatives would be to reduce the cost of the service by:

- Raising the productivity of its existing refuse collectors;
- Finding a commercial provider who could offer the same service for less.

Either approach would then allow it to reduce the price of the service whilst maintaining its income.

Implied in these insights are three concepts which are central to the process of operations management and adding value.

Economy is the term used to describe how cheaply inputs can be bought. By finding a supplier of the iron strip at a lower price, Alpha Assemblies would be improving the economy of its purchasing. So would Wexford's local traders if they found a commercial provider prepared to offer a cheaper deal.

Efficiency relates inputs to outputs. Increased efficiency comes from achieving greater outputs using the same or fewer resources. This is what Wexford Local Authority would be doing by improving the productivity of its existing refuse collectors. Other ways of increasing efficiency include:

- Reducing waste;
- Increasing production speed;
- Making more efficient use of equipment and machinery;
- Introducing equipment and machinery which is better suited to the job;
- Improving staff capability through better training, instruction or management.

Effectiveness describes the extent to which outputs achieve the objectives set for them. That means the extent to which outputs satisfy the needs and wants of the next customer in the supply chain. The closer outputs come to meeting their needs, the more customers will value them.

However, improving effectiveness does not necessarily mean providing a better product or service. The emphasis here is on achieving a match between outputs and customer needs. The next insight illustrates this point.

Insight

Weston Couriers offers a delivery service to local businesses. It guarantees collection and delivery within 4 hours in a 50 mile radius of its depot and charges a premium price for the service. However, many of its customers want packages delivered outside the 50 mile radius and are content for this to take up to 24 hours. They also complain about paying a premium price for non-urgent deliveries.

What are the customers' needs and wants?

How could Weston Couriers improve its effectiveness?

The problem for Weston Couriers is that they are providing a fast, guaranteed service at a high price to customers who, in many cases, want a cheaper, slower service.

Contradictory as it may seem, the company could improve its effectiveness most easily by lowering its standards, thereby reducing its input costs so that it can offer lower prices. In everyday language, this would result in a service of poorer quality but in the terms of quality management the quality would actually improve because it would be a closer match with customers' needs.

The theory and practice of quality improvement

Both in this chapter and earlier in the book, we have stressed that quality means meeting customer needs (the Total Quality message). In the next chapter we shall describe various ways of finding out what those needs are. But it is important to avoid getting carried away by grand ideas of consumer savings, customer consultation and sophisticated research studies.

In many cases, managers and staff alike are perfectly aware that the economy and efficiency of their operations are not as good as they might be and that their outputs do not fully meet customer requirements. They also have a good idea of what is going wrong and, perhaps even more importantly, what should be done about it. This is totally consistent with the idea of delegated decision-making we mentioned earlier.

The practice of quality improvement therefore involves both you and your staff looking out continually for ways of improving operating methods. Peters and Waterman quote a senior manager for the Dana Corporation who explains the benefits of this approach:

'Until we believe that the expert in any particular job is most often the person performing it, we shall forever limit the potential of that person, in terms of both his own contributions to the organization and his own personal development. Consider a manufacturing setting: within their 25 square foot area, nobody knows more about how to operate a machine, maximize its output, improve its quality, organize the material flow and keep it operating efficiently than do the machine

133

operators, materials handlers and maintenance people responsible for it'.

This philosophy may not match your experience or the culture of your organization (for an explanation of organizational culture see Chapter 4). Nevertheless it is fundamental both to improving the economy, efficiency and effectiveness of an operation and, as we explained in Section 2, to gaining staff commitment and helping them to develop.

In most organizations, managers have the right to decide how they will manage their staff. There are usually also mechanisms for passing suggestions for improvement up the line even if managers do not have the authority themselves to implement them.

Review

Now check your understanding of this chapter by completing the following activities:

1 Fill in the gaps in Figure 11.2.

Inputs

Figure 11.2

2 Give a definition of 'operations'.
3 Match the terms to their respective definition.

1. Economy

2. Efficiency

3. Effectiveness

(a) achieving greater output with fewer resources

(b) the extent to which outputs meet desired standards

(c) how cheaply resources can be bought.

4 Who should you consult when seeking quality improvement?

Workplace Activity

If you are currently doing a management job, relate this chapter to your own experience by answering the following questions:

1 Describe the inputs you use, the transformations and outputs for which you are responsible.

Inputs:

Transformations:

Outputs:

2 Who are the customers you service as the next link in your supply chain?

3 How economical are the inputs you use?
What improvements could you make?

4 How efficient is your transformation process?
What improvements could you make?

5 How effective are your outputs?
What improvements could you make?

6 What more could you do to involve your staff in quality improvement?

References

1 Johnson, B. (1998) *Managing Operations*, Butterworth-Heinemann: Oxford.
2 Peters, T. T. and Waterman, R. H. (1982) *In Search of Excellence*, Harper & Row: New York.

Chapter Objectives	• *Are customers important?*

You may have seen on a company notice-board a notice which says something like:

'Customers are our most important asset. They are the life-blood of our business and their satisfaction is the ultimate objective of all that we do.'

'Our customers have the right to expect the highest possible standard of service. They are not interruptions to our work but the reason for it.'

'Without customers we could not exist.'

Such a statement should come as no surprise at this stage of the book. It fits in neatly with everything we have said about operations management, **total quality** and the **supply chain.**

But we ought to be realistic about:

• What customers expect and the way they behave;
• The difficulty of staying close to final customers if customer contact is not part of your job;
• The attitude to customers of many staff in many organizations.

Increasingly management literature places heavy emphasis on the need to be responsive to customers. To the authors we quoted in Chapter 3* we could also add:

* See Chapter 3

INTRODUCING MANAGEMENT

'In the search for productivity the correct starting point is the marketing concept. *Productivity is* not *an end in itself but one of the* means *to an end; and that end is consumer satisfaction.'*
(Ray Wild)

'The purpose of a business is to create and keep a customer.'
(Theodore Levitt)

'A business must first find out what its market is — who the customer is, where he is and what he buys, what he considers value, what his unsatisfied wants are. On the basis of this study, the enterprise must analyse its products or services according to the wants of the customers they satisfy.'
(Peter Drucker)

All of these quotations place an uncompromising emphasis on the need to satisfy customers' wants and expectations. And yet those wants and expectations are often unreasonable and sometimes impractical. If your operation sits a long way down the supply chain and away from the final customer, it may well be difficult to know just what their wants and expectations are. And in many organizations staff could agree wholeheartedly with the old retail complaint that:

> 'This would be a great place to work if it weren't for the customers.'

In all cases the solution to these problems is one of attitude. Of course customers are unreasonable! They expect products and services of too high quality and complain when they do not get it; they expect delivery too soon, to pay an unreasonably low price and to receive immediate personal attention. Nevertheless in an organization which views customer satisfaction as its principal objective, everything will be geared to meeting unreasonable expectations on the basis that it cannot survive unless it does so. W. Edwards Deming, commonly regarded as the founder of the quality management movement, confirmed this point when he wrote:

'In the future there will be two kinds of company — those who have implemented total quality and those who have gone out of business. You do not have to do this — survival is not compulsory.'

As we pointed out in Chapter 3, a total quality approach brings final customers closer to all links in the supply chain, because at all stages, managers and staff should be responding to the needs of those internal customers who make up the next link in the chain. Ultimately that chain should lead to the final customer.

Nevertheless if customer focus has not traditionally been part of an organization's culture it will require both time and significant management effort to change that attitude. There have been several examples in the UK of organizations, particularly in the not-for-profit sector, attempting to introduce customer focus simply by issuing a new set of instructions to staff.

Needless to say, the change needs more than that to be successful. Prime requirements are:

- *A re-education programme*
  Telling people why the organization is adopting a marketing approach. Saying what is necessary and what staff will get out of it.

- *Introduction of processes to identify customer wants, needs and expectations.*

- *Review and adjustments to systems and procedures.*
  In an organization which has traditionally lacked customer focus, these are likely to be designed principally for internal convenience.

- *Management commitment and example.*
  The culture will only change if managers are seen to support the new focus on customers.

Identifying customer needs

Finding out what the end customers want, need and expect and how satisfied they are with what they get is a standard marketing technique. The process may involve:

- *Telephone interviews*
  These are quick, relatively cheap to conduct but not suitable for in-depth research.

- *Postal questionnaires*
  Take longer than telephone interviews before the results are received but can include more questions. The questions must

138

be carefully designed to avoid misunderstanding. The major problem associated with researching via questionnaires is that only a small number are ever returned completed. An average of only 2–5 per cent will be returned unless some form of incentive is given.

- *Face-to-face interviews*
  Are costly and time-consuming to conduct but do allow a more in-depth exploration of issues and give scope for the interviewer to use visual prompts and to show physical products.

- *Focus groups*
  These involve a small group of people meeting, often for a whole evening, to discuss complicated issues like buying motives and personal preferences, under the guidance of a skilled researcher. Expensive and time-consuming they nevertheless provide complex research information which could not otherwise be gathered.

- *Customer response cards*
  Included with products or sent specially to selected customers these provide a way of finding out why customers made their purchase and their level of satisfaction.

These are all specialist market research methods although you may be able to gain access to the information they bring in. They are used mainly for final customers. They all result in what is known as 'primary data' because they collect facts, figures and opinions for the first time and for a specific purpose.

'Secondary data' is the phrase used to describe information on statistics already collected for a different purpose. Sources of secondary data include:

- Internal records like past sales records, customer complaints or letters of praise.

- Industry data available from trade magazines, trade association reports and academic journals.

- Government statistics related to topics like car ownership, numbers of students attending school and university, how old people are and where they live.

Although these are generally used to find out more about external customers, it is worth pointing out that several of these methods are equally applicable to internal customers.

139

Many organizations adopting a total quality approach and realizing their lack of knowledge about internal customers' needs have used:

- Telephone and face-to-face interviews
- Questionnaires
- Focus groups
- Internal records.

Another approach which is equally relevant to both external and internal customers is what is known as *customer—supplier partnerships*. The principles on which this approach is based are that:

- The closer customers are to suppliers, the more they can influence the products or services they receive.
- The greater their influence, the more likely it is that products and services will meet their needs.
- Customers and suppliers should work together in co-operation rather than opposing each other as enemies.

In practical terms, customer—supplier partnerships involve customers developing accurate and comprehensive specifications for what they want and communicating those specifications to the supplier. But the process goes further than that. Partnerships also involve customers and suppliers working together to design and develop the product or service and, where necessary, modifying the original specification, or production methods, or quality standards to the point where the final output is acceptable to both parties.

There may appear to be nothing revolutionary in this approach. Surely it is no more than common sense?

Nevertheless the fact that it was hailed as a radical new approach in late twentieth century business dealings shows how wide the traditional gulf has been between customers and suppliers. And that applies to internal as much as it does to external customers!

140

Satisfying customer needs

The Chartered Institute of Marketing defines marketing as 'the management process for identifying, anticipating and satisfying customer requirements profitably'. That definition suggests that at our peril we ignore the needs of our customers. Satisfying customer needs is not simply about providing a product or service, it is also about doing it in the right way. Marketing involves providing:

The *right* product
In the *right* place
At the *right* time
At the *right* price
In the *right* way.

What constitutes *right* in each case will of course depend on the individual customer's needs. And the extent to which customers can find an exact match with their needs will depend on how specific they are. In most cases however customers, whether they are internal or external, will have to make a compromise choice depending on which of the five rights are most important to them. (See Case Study on page 142.)

What are the *five rights* in Alan's case?

What compromises may he have to make?

For Alan the:

Right **product** is a traditional, dark grey, three-piece suit that fits him
Right **place** is in Birmingham
Right **time** is ready for him in three weeks
Right **price** is no more than £200
Right **way** is with reliable advice from the salesperson.

MANAGING ACTIVITIES

Case Study

> Alan's daughter is getting married in three weeks' time. He has gone out to buy a new suit for the wedding. Ideally he wants:
>
> A dark grey, three-piece suit
>
> In a traditional style
>
> Costing no more than £200.
>
> He does not usually wear a suit so he wants some reliable advice from the salesperson. The suit may need some minor alterations so he wants to order it this afternoon. He has gone into Birmingham where he knows there are several shops which stock suits.
>
> He soon finds that most suits are only two-piece and their styles are far too modern. He finds one in a traditional style which fits perfectly but the waistcoat will have to be specially made. It may be ready in three weeks but could take a month. Another is exactly what he wants — but is only available in blue. Finally the local branch of a national men's clothing chain appears to have the answer. The colour, style and fit are right. The trousers can be shortened in a week. Unfortunately the nearest jacket in his size is in London. The salesperson is helpful. It could be transferred. The transfer will take ten days. But of course Alan will only be able to try it on when it arrives. The total price of the suit is £230.

None of the available alternatives is an exact match with his needs. He may choose to compromise on product (give up the waistcoat, accept a different colour, risk a jacket that does not fit) or on price. He cannot compromise on time — the wedding is not going to be delayed for the sake of his suit! — nor on place. He is in Birmingham so he will have to buy his suit there. But if he could find the perfect suit which fitted him at the price he wanted to pay, he could probably do without reliable advice from the salesperson.

In Alan's situation, time is the prime driver in his buying decision. For other customers in other situations it may be product, price or location. It is rare for the way in which a sale is made to be the main consideration and then only in situations where competing alternatives are identical in all other ways.

Improving customer satisfaction

We can group the *five rights* under just three headings:

Product factors (the right product at the right price)
Convenience factors (in the right place at the right time)
Human factors (in the right way)

In most organizations the staff who have direct contact with final customers are in a minority. They are typically limited to:

Sales staff

Telephone staff and receptionists

Accounts staff who prepare invoices

Customer service staff.

Using our three headings these are the staff who constitute the human factor for final customers, whose attitude to the organization will depend on their:

Promptness of response

Friendliness and courtesy

Knowledge and expertise.

However, it is worth recognizing that these frontline staff have little or no control over product and convenience factors.

Case Study

> Sally is a reception nurse working in an outpatients' clinic of a major London hospital. The clinic is busy and patients are having to wait at least an hour before seeing a doctor. Many are cross about the wait and complain to Sally.

What action can she take?

Which of our factors can she control?

What changes would be necessary to improve the situation and who would be responsible for them?

Sally's scope for action is very limited. She can sympathize, direct patients to the magazine rack and the coffee machine and give them as accurate information as possible about how much longer they will have to wait. These are all human factors – important to get right but not central to the problem.

There appears to be nothing wrong with the product factors – we assume that the doctors are prescribing suitable treatment and patients rarely complain about price in a National Health hospital.

The problems stem from convenience factors – primarily availability and time. They could be solved by:

Scheduling more doctors into the clinic rota;

Allowing more time for each appointment so that they do not over-run;

Booking fewer patients in at the same time.

However none of these are Sally's responsibility. They are all administrative decisions which, once taken, will be set into formal procedures. Unfortunately it is unlikely that the administrator responsible for them will ever experience the impact they have on Sally. She and the clinic doctors along with the patients are all their customers – but the customers' needs seem to have been ignored.

This takes us back to the supply chain concept. To improve customer satisfaction it is important for everyone working in the organization to understand the needs of the final customer so that they are aware of how they contribute to satisfying them. Some organizations arrange for all staff, as part of their induction or other training, to experience frontline contact with final customers.

If that is difficult or impossible, the total quality principle of internal customers achieves a similar objective. But both approaches go no further than identifying needs.

Improving customer satisfaction requires the manager to take the lead in asking and answering some fundamental questions. John Oakland listed these questions as:

Who are my immediate customers?

What are their time requirements?

How do I, or can I, find out what the requirements are?

Do I have the necessary capability to meet the requirements? (If not then what must change to improve the capability?)

Do I continually meet the requirements? (If not then what prevents this from happening when the capability exists?)

How do I monitor changes in the requirement?

To this list we would add five further questions:

How much scope do I have to make changes?

What organizational constraints may prevent me from making changes?

How do I encourage my team to contribute to improving customer satisfaction?

How effective am I in persuading others to be involved?

How can I gain the agreement of my line manager?

These questions raise issues related to managing change, a topic covered in Section 2 of this book, and informing, persuading and influencing which is dealt with in Section 4.

Review

Now check your understanding of this chapter by completing the following activities:

1 What does W. Edwards Deming say is the alternative to Total Quality?

2 List three requirements to bring about a change to customer focus.

3 Explain what is meant by a customer–supplier partnership.

4 Fill in the gaps in this sentence:
Customers need the right _ _ _ _ _ _ _ in the right _ _ _ _ _ at the right _ _ _ _ at the right _ _ _ _ _ provided in the right _ _ _.

5 Who is responsible for improving customer satisfaction?

6 Name two primary and two secondary potential sources for identifying consumer needs.

Workplace Activity

If you are currently doing a management job, relate this chapter to your own experience by answering the following questions:

1 List your main internal and external customers.

2 How do you and your team identify their needs?

3 How could you use the techniques described in this chapter to find out more about their needs?

4 How can you involve your team in improving customer satisfaction?

References

1 Wild, R. (1982) *How to Manage* (quoting Sir Donald Barron, former Chairman of Rowntree Macintosh), Butterworth-Heinemann: Oxford.

2 Levitt, T. (1983) *The Marketing Imagination*, Free Press: New York.

3 Drucker, P. (1954) *The Practice of Management*, Butterworth-Heinemann: Oxford.

4 Deming, W. E. (1982) *Quality, Productivity and Competitive Position*, MIT Centre for Advanced Engineering Study, MIT: Cambridge, Mass., USA.

5 Oakland, J. (1989) *Total Quality Management*, Butterworth-Heinemann: Oxford.

INTRODUCING MANAGEMENT

13   Planning, organizing and controlling work

Chapter Objectives

- *Who monitors results?*
- *Who controls results?*

Managers achieve results – through people and other resources. That is our summary (though over-simplified) of the first chapter of this book*. It leaves several basic questions unanswered. It does not explain:

*See Chapter 1

What results managers should achieve

How to make the best use of people

How to use other resources

What to do to ensure that work achieves the desired results.

This chapter provides answers to all of these questions.

Setting management objectives

People at work must know what is expected of them. Otherwise they have no way of telling whether they have succeeded or failed. Even more importantly they cannot decide what to do, what their priorities are or where to focus their effort. There would be no point in getting into a cab and not telling the driver where you wanted to go!

Most organizations tackle this issue by ensuring that managers have a set of objectives to achieve. Traditionally those objectives were set using a **cascade system.** In other words, the organization would decide its corporate objectives through the strategic planning process, then pass those down, translating them at each level into objectives which would contribute to the achievement of the organization's corporate goals (see Figure 13.1).

147

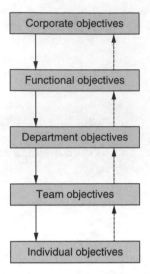

Figure 13.1

A lot of organizations still follow this traditional approach. Others though use what is known as a 'bottom-up, top-down' approach: this is in line with the trend towards greater staff consultation and involvement. This approach involves the organization setting broad corporate aims then asking managers and staff at lower levels to specify what they can do to achieve them. The 'bottom-up, top-down' approach can be messy and time-consuming because it involves several cycles of consultation and amendment before final objectives are agreed. Nevertheless it is far more effective at ensuring that objectives are realistic, achievable and gain commitment from those responsible for delivering them.

You may have objectives imposed on you, you may set them for yourself, or you may sit somewhere between those two extremes. Regardless of your situation you will need to ensure that your objectives are sufficiently detailed and complete for you to know exactly what you are expected to achieve. To be truly useful objectives should be SMART:

Specific
Measurable
Agreed
Realistic
Time-based.

In other words the outputs should be clearly defined such that performance can be quantified, agreed between you and your manager, achievable within the constraints of time and resources and with a target date so that achievement can be measured.

There are obvious motivational and practical reasons why objectives should be agreed and realistic. But you may be wondering why the SMART definition places so much emphasis on quantified and measurable objectives. That is because objectives are of little value on their own. They only become valuable as a basis for measuring performance.

This brings us to the idea of the control loop: a mechanism developed originally for engineering applications but now extended for use in management. A central-heating thermostat is a good example of how a control loop works. Imagine a thermostat at work. It measures the temperature in a room, recognizes when it is not warm enough and then triggers the boiler to send hot water through the radiator. When the room is warm enough the thermostat switches off the boiler.

There are various elements operating in this process:

Input – heat from the boiler

Process – heating and circulating the water

Output – a warm room

Standard – the desired room temperature

Comparator – a way of comparing actual with desired temperature

Actuator – a mechanism for turning on the boiler (see Figure 13.2).

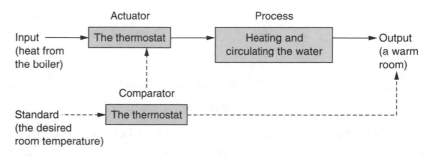

Figure 13.2

149

In more general terms, a control loop is a system which recognizes when output performance does not meet the required standard (quality, quantity, time, cost) and then triggers action to correct the process so that the standard is achieved. That is why it is so important for objectives to be specified, measurable and time-based.

Being in a position to set your own objectives may sound desirable but is actually both fraught and complex. Your objectives should take account of:

Corporate direction

Long-term survival

Current financial position

Available resources

Customer requirements.

But not necessarily in that order!

* See Chapter 12

Long-term survival* depends ultimately on customer satisfaction so your objectives should come as close as possible to meeting customer requirements within the limits of available budget and resources. These considerations come next.

Organizing your team

People are the only resource which:

Do not wear out over time

Can be developed to achieve more than when they started.

Unfortunately they are also the only resources which disagree with you and cannot be relied on to perform properly when you press the button!

In order to achieve results through people you need to ensure that your team:

Knows what to do

Knows the standards to which it should be done

Is motivated to do it.

* See Chapter 6

Staff motivation was a key theme of Section 2*. This chapter will concentrate on the other two themes of giving instructions and setting standards.

The basic principles of organizing staff are common sense and can be summarized in the following questions:

What are the objectives – what do we need to achieve?

What resources do we have?

What are the requirements in terms of quality and quantity?

What are the time-scales for achieving the objectives?

How can I get the best out of the team to achieve these objectives?

Members of your team should not be expected to help you achieve your objectives if they do not receive the necessary pay, praise, recognition and development to compensate for their efforts.

Shop-floor staff used to be known as *operatives*. The word somehow gives the impression that they were pieces of machinery – there to follow commands in the same way as an industrial lathe or a conveyor belt. This way of thinking can be traced back to the last century and the writing of F. W. Taylor. Taylor invented worthwhile modern techniques like time-and-motion study, functional specialization and technical training. Taylor intended all of these to improve productivity and efficiency by ensuring that each worker was doing the job best suited to him, had the necessary skills to do it and was doing it in the most efficient way. The drawback though is that 'in Taylor's system there was a strong element of dehumanising the workforce' (Clutterbuck and Crainer). This is because the emphasis on the 'one best way' of carrying out every task suggests robotic obedience to it.

Managers now recognize individual differences, acknowledge people's right and ability to influence the nature of their own work and therefore consult and involve staff.

Insight

All production-line and administrative staff at Premier Plastics are selected on the basis of rigorous ability tests. They punch a time-clock when they arrive. All production-line jobs are given a daily output target and workers receive a bonus for exceeding it. In recent years, the factory's profitability has declined. Senior management are seeking ways of improving efficiency and have set up small groups of staff to review and recommend changes to operating procedures.

What examples of Taylorism can you see in this case?

What examples of a modern approach to management can you see?

What difficulties would you expect in moving from one to the other?

Selection on the basis of ability-testing, time-clocks, output targets and production bonuses are all Taylorist techniques. Involving staff in changing procedures is a modern approach. The main difficulty in moving from one to the other is likely to be that staff who have previously had no chance to think for themselves will now find themselves expected to 'do management's thinking for them'. As Adam Smith pointed out in 1776:

'A man who spends his life carrying out a small number of very simple operations with perhaps the same effects has no room to develop his intelligence or to stretch his imagination so as to look for ways of overcoming difficulties which never occur. He therefore loses quite naturally the habit of using these facilities.'

Consequently, as we said about improving customer satisfaction in the previous chapter, a culture of consultation needs to be supported by a programme of staff education, management encouragement and example.

Organizing other resources

In an ideal world (as seen in Chapter 9):

1 Customer demand would always be predictable
2 Equipment would never break down or need maintenance
3 Staff would never go sick, take holidays, resign or retire
4 Raw materials would always be available.

Under those circumstances, organizing resources would be a one-off event. It would be possible to calculate resource requirements once only, make those resources available and continue to meet customer needs completely from them without making any adjustments.

1 Unfortunately reality is very different. The demand for an organization's products or services varies according to:

- Customer confidence, disposable income and other external factors).

- Seasonal patterns (e.g. garden furniture in summer, Christmas trees in winter).

- Levels of local, national and international competition.

2 Equipment needs maintenance. All equipment requires 'down time' in order for staff to carry out checks and maintenance.

3 Staff availability will vary for the reasons given. Of course those who resign or retire will normally be replaced but there will be a delay before new staff reach the performance standard of those they are replacing. Gaps resulting from sickness or holiday can be filled by temporary staff, but these are unlikely to have the relevant experience or expertise to achieve the same level of productivity.

4 Raw materials should be readily available but at times demand for them may outstrip supply, or there could be a transport strike, or an increase in price, or a fall in quality may necessitate a search for an alternative supplier.

Of course you could just shrug your shoulders and say 'not my problem'. But we would suggest that is not an acceptable response from a manager, for three reasons:

- Your team looks to you to provide the resources and support they need to do their jobs. Your credibility as a manager would suffer if you fail to do so.

- Other customers in the supply chain depend on you.

- Leaving others to make your decisions means you get no practice in a key management skill.

The physical resources available to a manager are:

- Stock or inventory (raw materials)

- Consumable items which are used up in the production process

- Tools and equipment.

153

Forecasting demand

The first stage in organizing resources to achieve results is to calculate demand for the outputs you produce.

The organization's strategic plans and objectives

Part of **strategic planning** involves analysing customer expectations, competitive pressures and overall changes in the market. Some of this analysis will be based on informed guesswork, but it will result in a set of quantified objectives which will then become the organization's targets for the planning period.

Historical demand

It would be a mistake to assume that future demand will be an exact repetition of past demand. Many organizations have gone out of business as the result of making that false assumption! Nevertheless an intelligent examination of past demand patterns can give a good indication of likely future demand. Consider Alice Hay's situation.

Insight

> Alice Hay is a dental surgeon. The average number of patients she treated daily is shown in Table 13.1, split between NHS (public) and private patients, for each of the twelve months of last year and this year to date.

What trends and patterns can you see in these figures?

How many public and private patients would you expect Alice Hay to treat in August of this year?

What are the resource implications of this analysis?

Last year and this year both show a seasonal pattern. The number of patients treated drops in the summer (perhaps as people go on holiday) and in December. A comparison between last year's and this year's figures shows a further trend – numbers are consistently higher this year, and the proportion of private patients rose steadily last year and continues to rise this year. (Alice may have decided to accept no new public patients.)

154

Table 13.1

Last year			This year to date		
January	Public	14	January	Public	15
	Private	4		Private	6
February	Public	15	February	Public	16
	Private	3		Private	5
March	Public	16	March	Public	17
	Private	4		Private	7
April	Public	17	April	Public	18
	Private	4		Private	6
May	Public	17	May	Public	18
	Private	5		Private	7
June	Public	16	June	Public	17
	Private	5		Private	6
July	Public	13	July	Public	14
	Private	5		Private	5
August	Public	11			
	Private	4			
September	Public	15			
	Private	6			
October	Public	14			
	Private	4			
November	Public	13			
	Private	7			
December	Public	10			
	Private	6			

The seasonal pattern suggests that Alice's patient numbers will again drop in August but the steady increase in both overall numbers and private patients makes it likely that she will treat twelve public patients and five or six private patients in August of this year.

With this information, Alice can:

Ensure she has enough raw materials to carry out the treatments which will require more detailed analysis of average usage.

Negotiate holiday arrangements for herself, her nurse and receptionist.

Work out likely revenue and profitability for the month.

Make decisions about equipment maintenance.

Decide whether, in view of the rising trend in patient numbers, she should take on extra staff or find a partner to join her in the practice.

Quantitative production

Historical demand data is an accurate reflection of what actually happened. However, as the last insight shows, it rarely repeats itself exactly. Quantitative production provides a fairly accurate picture of short-term demand and can be used either as an alternative to historical data, or as a complementary technique. It normally involves a basic form of market research — asking customers what their needs will be for the following week or month. Customer–supplier partnerships are a useful source of quantitative production. Regular internal production meetings attended by supplying and receiving departments are another good example.

Qualitative prediction

Forecasting from historical data and quantitative production rely on the assumption that future demand will be fairly similar to past demand. But in the case of new products and services where there is no historical data, and in environments where external factors are going through major change, such assumptions are not safe. Qualitative prediction, otherwise known as the *Delphi technique* because it involves 'asking the oracle' is a matter of finding a team of experts and asking them to make a best guess about levels of future demand, based on their expert analysis of customer expectations and environmental change.

Smoothing demand

Regardless of the sophistication of the techniques used, demand forecasting can only be an approximate science. New customers, changes in customer requirements or external influences and seasonal patterns will all make demand uneven: higher at some periods, lower at others. Organizations can take certain actions to smooth demand by:

Offering price reductions and discounts at periods of low demand.

Producing 'summer goods' and 'winter goods' to reflect seasonal fluctuations.

Manufacturing products at a consistent level throughout the year but warehousing excess production when demand is low and supplying from stock when demand is high – although risky and costly.

Encouraging customer loyalty by providing, for example, loyalty discounts, season tickets on the railways, or offering retail incentives like saver stamps or supermarket saver cards.

Adjusting capacity

However none of these techniques will totally remove the inconsistency and unpredictability of customer demand. It is therefore important for organizations to be able to adjust resource capacity in line with demand. They can do this by:

- Maintaining excess capacity
  This involves forecasting peak demand and making resources available to meet it. For example, holiday resorts and airlines have more capacity than they need except at peak holiday times but offer discounts and other incentives to off-set this excess capacity out-of-season.

- Automation
  This involves the adoption of automated, computer-controlled methods to allow easier adjustments to the nature and volume of output.

- Flexible staffing
  As the name suggests, this involves techniques like overtime and part-time working, flexitime and the use of temporary and agency staff.

- Multi-skilling
  Ensuring that staff have a range of skills which will enable them to move between tasks according to market demand.

- Revising maintenance patterns
  This involves bringing forward equipment maintenance and staff training when demand is low and deferring them when demand is high.

157

- Subcontracting

  This involves keeping operations in-house when demand is light but buying-in from subcontractors when it is heavy.

Peter King owns and operates a motor business where he sells used cars and offers a repair and maintenance service. His peak periods for car sales are at the beginning of the summer (when customers replace their cars for holidays) and in March or August when many people sell their old cars in order to buy new ones registered with the bi-annual number plate. Peak periods for service work are again at the start of the summer, preparing cars for holiday trips and at the start of the winter, so that they are reliable during the bad weather.

In practical terms how could Peter: smooth demand?/adjust capacity?

Peter could smooth demand by:

- Promoting discounts at quiet times of the year;
- Finding additional products and services with different seasonal sales patterns (although it is difficult to picture what these might be if they are to be consistent with the motor-trade image of the business and the technical skills of his staff);
- Offering special deals to existing customers.

In order to adjust capacity he might:

- Arrange for staff to work overtime;
- Negotiate more flexible working patterns so that staff work long hours during busy periods but take time off at slack times;
- Train workshop staff to sell cars or salespeople to carry out repairs (difficult but not impossible);
- Use quiet periods for maintenance, refurbishment and training;
- Bring in temporary staff;
- Use subcontractors and accept a lower profit margin (perhaps to prepare used cars or carry out specialist repair work like tyre or exhaust fitting).

Managing stock

Stock or inventory provides a buffer between variations in demand and supply. But holding goods or stock is expensive. The physical and administrative processes of monitoring stock levels, re-ordering and replenishing stock are expensive, as is the stock itself. Efficient inventory management involves a balancing act between ensuring availability and keeping costs to a minimum. The past few years have seen an increase in high street retailers for example, using distribution and warehousing companies to manage their stock/goods. Instead of storing large quantities of goods in a stock room, the stores order and receive goods on a daily basis ensuring they have adequate supplies to meet production or customer demands.

This has proved a more cost-effective way to manage the stock and has reduced the need for large stock rooms, which in turn has increased the floor space available in which to promote and sell goods.

Organizations use a number of differing techniques and systems, many of which are now computer based, to ensure they are managing the supply and demand of their goods or stock in the most cost-effective way. One such technique is called *ABC Analysis.*

ABC Analysis works on the recognition that consumable resources can be divided into three categories, based on the volume of items and the value compared with total stockholding.

Category A items represent a small proportion of total volume but a high proportion of total value (typically 10–15% of volume, but 70–80% of value). These items will be tightly controlled, frequently re-ordered in small quantities.

Category B items represent a higher volume (say 20% of the total) but a lower value (maybe 15% again). These items will require a less sophisticated stock control system and will be held in greater quantities.

Category C items represent high volume but low value. They do not justify the expense of tight control and are typically ordered by the box or container load and held in large quantities.

MANAGING ACTIVITIES

The following Case Study shows how a furniture manufacturer uses ABC Analysis:

Case Study

Riley and Sons is an old established company, which manufacturers high quality furniture. The furniture is then sold through a limited number of shops on a 'made to order' basis. Customers can choose different finishes, including upholstery fabric for each style of furniture.

As each item of furniture is made following the customer's order, Riley's only carry a small quantity of, for example, upholstery fabric and solid brass handles (*Category A*). The solid wood, which is used in all the furniture, is imported from Scandinavia at a substantially discounted price to Riley's (*Category B*). Hidden castors are fitted to most of the furniture cabinets and tables, which are 'best sellers' for Riley's (*Category C*).

Do you consider Riley's is managing its stock in the most cost-effective way?

You have probably answered yes to that question. Riley's makes a good profit from the fabrics and such items as brass handles but despite this they are still costly for Riley's to buy. However, it is more cost-effective for Riley's to buy in the fabric for special orders rather than storing rolls of fabric just in case it is to be used. All of Riley's products are made from the imported wood so they purchase and use large quantities hence their good discount. The factory is kept busy on a fairly constant basis throughout the year so it makes sense to buy-in large quantities of wood. The castors are one of the cheapest components, made and imported from abroad and are supplied in boxes of 500.

Many organizations, not just manufacturing, have adopted the Just-in-Time (JIT) principle. Originally from the automotive industry, JIT is a simple concept that ensures that stock is delivered at precisely the time it is needed to be transferred into finished products or services. Stock levels are kept to a minimum but are always available when required. As you can see the principle depends on working closely with suppliers to ensure that quality goods — there is no time to replace faulty items — arrive at precisely the right time.

Materials Requirement Planning (MRP) is the general name for computer software that is increasingly available for organizations, which enables them to more accurately calculate their purchasing needs based on their current stocks and expected future requirements.

Organizations may use one or a combination of these techniques to ensure that they achieve the balance of meeting customer demand whilst keeping the cost of stockholding to a minimum.

Monitoring and controlling results

An effective control mechanism not only measures performance against standards, but also initiates corrective action when these standards are not being met. Typical standards are likely to include:

- Budget;
- Quality;
- Timeliness;
- Use of renewable resources;
- Use of consumable resources.

In order to monitor performance successfully, you will need:

- Quantified standards;
- Systems to compare performance with standards;
- Regular and timely feedback to enable corrective action.

Case Study

Kevin is a Business Link advisor. He compiles and receives weekly reports on the numbers of consultations he has performed which are compared with monthly targets. His performance is also assessed on the basis of how much trade is generated as a result of his work. His success rate is set by Business Link

How effective are these monitoring systems?

Will they work as control mechanisms?

161

The feedback Kevin receives on the number of consultations is quantified regularly and quick enough for him to take corrective action in order to meet his monthly targets.

His assessment on the basis of the amount of trade generated is a different matter. Again, it is quantified and regular. But once he has put companies in contact with each other he can do nothing. The ball is in their court. A deal could be done, on the other hand the deal could fall through. There is little corrective action he can take after he has introduced the firms to each other. Each deal between firms will take time to come to fruition, so there are sometimes very long delays before he is able to clarify how much business he has created.

Monitoring results costs money. But failure to detect errors or variances also costs money. To be cost-effective the frequency of monitoring should balance the cost of the monitoring with the cost of failing to take necessary corrective action in time.

Assuming that monitoring takes place early enough and frequently enough for you to take corrective action, what form might that action take? Consider Adam's situation:

Case Study

> University education in the UK is now paid for mainly by students and their parents, often by taking out bank loans. Adam Parker supervises a team in the regional office of a High Street bank. Their task is to process loan applications. It is the end of August and Adam has received a flood of applications for loans to finance university courses. They must all be processed by the end of September so that students know if they can afford to accept places on courses starting in October. Adam has four weeks, 1000 applications to process and five staff. By the end of the first week his team has dealt with 200 applications

What corrective action might he take?

Adam has several choices:

- He could bring in more staff, either temporary staff from an agency or by borrowing them from elsewhere in the regional office. That is provided that his budget is sufficient and the new staff can be trained quickly enough.

162

- He could ask his staff to check the applications less carefully and spend less time on each one. However, this will lower quality and the bank risks losing money if they make wrong decisions.
- He might adjust work priorities. If his staff are also processing other applications which are less time-critical he could put these on hold and concentrate on student loans.
- He may be able to make the checking procedure more efficient, thus saving time and maintaining quality.
- It is too late to help this year, but he could learn for the future by putting in a bid for more sophisticated equipment — a computer program, for example, to automate part of the process.

Failure to achieve results may be because:

- Output volume is too low;
- Output quality is not good enough;
- Output costs are too high;
- Output is too slow.

Any of these may be subject to correction by:

- Increasing resource inputs;
- Improving process efficiency;
- Changing the input specification;
- Changing the output specification.

However, all these corrective actions are dependent on budget constraints and customer requirements. The next chapter looks in more detail at process improvement. The remainder of this chapter will concentrate on quality issues.

Controlling quality

There are three main approaches to controlling quality. They are very different in:

- Their objectives
- The operational stages to which they apply

163

- The systems necessary to support them
- The actions resulting from them.

Nevertheless they all have one thing in common – they start by defining quality as 'conformance to customer requirements' or 'conformance to specification', that specification in turn being derived from what the customer requires.

Quality control is the traditional and most basic approach. It compares outputs with customer requirements, in order to identify which outputs meet, and do not meet, the quality standard. Typical quality control systems include:

- Quality inspection where inspectors assess whether the outputs meet the desired standard.
- Sampling the output which reduces inspection costs by assessing only a proportion of outputs (e.g. testing every other one).
- Statistical process control which identifies the causes of changing output quality.

Quality control is applied to outputs after they have been finished. In a manufacturing context, it is applied to finished components and completed products. Elsewhere it might involve:

- Trying on a coat to see if it fits after alteration;
- Checking the CO_2 emission from a car after it has been serviced;
- Proof-reading a letter after it has been typed.

As a result of quality control we either accept or reject the output.

Quality assurance differs from quality control in that it concentrates on processes rather than outputs. It is designed to ensure that the methods used to transform inputs into outputs achieve the required output quality.

Typical quality assurance systems include:

- **ISO 9000**, 9001/2/3;
- Process reviews and flow-charting.

Since quality assurance places an emphasis on monitoring *processes,* it is likely to involve:

- Process redesign

- Clarification of procedures
- Implementation of new systems
- Improved control documentation.

Such a system is therefore likely to prevent quality problems rather than solve them after they have occurred.

We have already referred to *Total Quality Management*. It is an all-embracing philosophy intended to put customer satisfaction at the heart of every organization. It makes every individual, team, activity and operation responsible for achieving quality and extends the idea of quality to include delivery, customer relations and added value, among other things.

Because TQM applies before, during and after the transformation process, the systems which support it cover such widely-diverse activities as:

- Customer consultation and feedback
- Staff training
- Systems design
- Process improvement.

The outcomes of TQM are more diverse and have an effect not only on processes, procedures and controls but also on the overall culture and attitudes of the organization.

Therefore the success of TQM is dependent on the commitment and involvement of everyone throughout the whole organization.

Review

Now check your understanding of this chapter by completing these activities:

1 What do you understand by a 'top-down, bottom-up' approach to objective-setting?

2 Objectives should be:

S _ _ _ _ _ _ _

M _ _ _ _ _ _ _ _ _

A _ _ _ _ _ _ _ _ _

R _ _ _ _ _ _ _ _

T _ _ _ _ _ _ _

3 A control loop is a system which compares o _ _ _ _ _ _ with
s _ _ _ _ _ _ _ _ and initiates c _ _ _ _ _ _ _ _ _
a _ _ _ _ _ when these are not being met.

4 Why do organizations seek to smooth demand?.

5 In ABC Analysis:
Category A items represent _ _ _ _ _ _ volume
but _ _ _ _ _ _ value.
Category B items represent _ _ _ _ _ _ volume
but _ _ _ _ _ _ value.
Category C items represent _ _ _ _ _ _ volume
but _ _ _ _ _ _ value.

Workplace Activity

If you are currently doing a management job, relate this chapter to your own experience by answering the following questions:

1 How SMART are your objectives? How could they be improved?

2 What systems do you use to compare outputs with standards? How effective are they and why?

3 What techniques does your organization use to smooth demand?

4 How much scope do you have to adjust capacity to demand? What more would you like?

5 How does your organization assess the quality of its outputs? What more could it do?

6 How could you improve the quality control of your team's outputs?

References

1 Clutterbuck, D. and Crainers, S. (1990) *Makers of Management*, Macmillan: Basingstoke.
2 Smith, A. (1776) *The Wealth of Nations*, Penguin Classics: London.
3 Taylor, F. W. (1911) *Principles of Scientific Management*, Harper & Row: New York.

INTRODUCING MANAGEMENT

14 Managing the workplace

<table>
<tr><td>Chapter
Objectives</td><td>● Health and Safety – so what?</td></tr>
</table>

Most of us go to the same place of work every day. As a result, over time we stop seeing it – we simply take for granted that it is the way it is and come to accept its imperfections. The purpose of this chapter is to encourage you to take a fresh look at the workplace and to be critical about the way its design and layout affects the efficiency of production and the health and safety of your staff.

Operational design and efficiency

Work flows. Depending upon your industry raw materials may flow through a manufacturing process, information may flow through an administrative process being analysed, interpreted and applied as it goes or guests may flow through a health club using sports equipment and leisure services.

Work flow is subject to a host of potential inefficiencies. Consider this situation. (See Case Study on page 168.)

What are the inefficiencies in this system?

How could they be removed?

We spotted the following inefficiencies (you may have recognized others):

● Waiting time
  The management accounts department needs to monitor sales values and production costs, but these arrive at different times and at different frequencies.

Case Study

> Wanda and her team produce monthly management accounts for a firm assembling computer hardware systems to individual customer orders. Sales information comes monthly from the sales force, normally arranged during the first week of the following month so that the sales force can claim all the commission due on sales made that month. Customer orders are identified by a unique job code, although members of the sales force are careless about getting the code right. As soon as a sale is made, individual salespeople also send details through to the production facility so that assembly can start. These details include a technical specification but not the value of the order. Production costs for each job come to the management accounts team as soon as the job is finished. The production facility uses a different system of job coding from that used by the sales force.

- Inconsistent systems

  The sales force and production facility use different job coding systems. Wanda and her team, or someone else in the firm, will need to make the two incompatible systems consistent with each other.

- Double-handling and repetition

  The sales force produces two incomplete sets of data but with common elements (customer details, for example). In other words, they are providing some data twice.

- Inaccuracy

  Not only are the job codes different for sales and production but the sales force sometimes get their codes wrong, which will make reconciliation even more time-consuming (or, at worst, impossible!).

Managers are responsible for ensuring, as far as they can, that the operations they control are efficient. Most of the inefficiencies we have identified are not directly under Wanda's control. However she and her team are still internal customers of the sales force and production staff. She needs to make them aware of her need for:

- Information inputs at the right time, to reduce or avoid waiting;
- The right inputs (no inaccuracies, consistent information).

She could point out that such inefficiency could be reduced by simplifying and streamlining the system.

The process of identifying and removing inefficiencies is part of *operations scheduling*. Operations scheduling involves analysing the flow and sequence of operations to ensure that they are logical and efficient. It needs to take account of:

- Activity duration
  How long the activity takes to complete, the resources currently used and its impact on the next activity in the sequence.

- Activity frequency
  The more frequent the activity, the more important it is to identify and remove inefficiencies because of their cumulative effect.

- Activity sequence
  The analysis of activity sequence involves a critical examination of the whole chain of activities which make up an operation, in order to identify inefficiencies like double-handling, repetition, waiting time and excess distance between activities.

The most helpful technique for analysing activities is the use of an activity flow-chart, otherwise known as a network diagram. Figure 14.1 shows an example for the preparation of a meal:

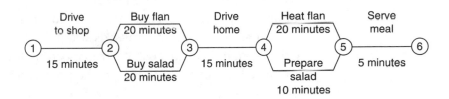

Figure 14.1

The conventions of a network diagram are as follows:

- All activities start and finish with a circle (called a 'node').
- Nodes are numbered for ease of reference.
- Activities are described in action words above the line with the duration below.
- Durations can be in anything from seconds to months, provided they are all consistent.

- 'Burst' nodes are points where several activities can start when one is completed (the later activities are said to 'depend' on the completion of the preceding one).

Network diagrams contribute to operations scheduling by:

- Enabling you to identify the sequence of activities which determines the minimum duration of an operation (called the 'critical path') through the network;
- Encouraging you to think critically about the duration of individual activities as a first step in improving efficiency;
- Helping you to streamline an operation by finding activities which could be carried out simultaneously (like preparing the salad whilst the flan is being heated, in our example);
- Highlighting waiting time.

Workplace layout

We referred earlier to inefficiencies caused by the need for work-in-progress to travel excessive distances. Picture an office-worker who has to refer frequently to the contents of a manual filing system. If the filing cabinets are at the other end of a large openplan office, each reference will require several extra minutes which could be eliminated by repositioning them close to the desk. Similarly, if Just-in-Time deliveries are made to a manufacturing business where goods inwards are a long way from production, the frequency and cost of transporting the deliveries could be reduced by holding stocks on the production line.

If you have the authority to re-arrange your team's working area you will need to start by putting together information about:

- The location of fixed structures like walls, doors and windows;
- The position of equipment which cannot be moved, including items like radiators and extractor fans;
- Where services like water and electricity are located;
- Typical flows of people and materials.

And, of course, you will want to ask your team for the sources of inefficiency they are experiencing and their suggestions for improvement.

An efficient workplace layout should provide:

- Easy accessibility to all parts of the work area;
- Maximum flexibility so that it can be changed easily to accommodate, for example, temporary staff, meetings or changes to the work flow;
- Maximum productive use of space, including wall-height for storage and avoiding 'dead space';
- Minimum distances for people and materials to travel, to save on time and handling;
- Maximum comfort and safety, ensuring adequate lighting, heating, ventilation, access to emergency exits and avoidance of hazards;
- Efficient work flow avoiding cross-traffic by ensuring that people and materials move only in one direction as far as possible.

Insight

Trish Walker is supervisor in the accounts office of Bricks Etc., builders' merchants. Figure 14.2 shows the arrangement of the office.

Trish receives and distributes work from her desk. The filing cabinets and photocopier are used by everyone.

What is wrong with this office layout?

How might it be improved?

The obvious problems with the layout are:

- The photocopier blocks the door, obstructs access to three desks and the electric cable is a safety hazard;
- Much of the centre of the office is unproductive space;
- Access to the filing cabinets involves covering long distances and obstructs Trish's work area;
- There is no natural light to Trish's desk;
- Distributing work involves a considerable walk round the office.

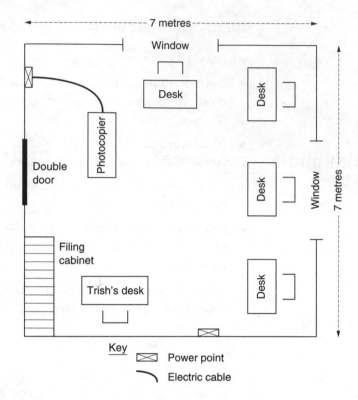

Figure 14.2

Possible improvements, based on the limited information given, might involve:

- Moving the photocopier to the top left corner of the office;

- Re-organizing files and relocating cabinets closer to individual desks;

- Moving Trish's desk to a more central position with better light.

Of course, these are only tentative proposals. A more detailed analysis of work flow and staff movements could result in more suitable changes.

Health and Safety — so what?

There are three reasons why a manager should treat health and safety issues as priorities:

- A manager's responsibility for staff is generally accepted to extend to caring for their welfare;

- UK law makes health and safety a legal duty of managers, individual staff members and of organizations;
- Sick and injured staff significantly reduce productivity.

We will look briefly at each of these three considerations in turn.

Health and Safety – part of a manager's job

Health and safety in the workplace is everyone's responsibility. The workplace is a potentially dangerous environment – you may be working with machinery, heavy loads, hazardous material, you and your team may be under pressure and have to work at speed to complete tasks in the required time. An office may have trailing cables, drawers left open, boxes poorly stacked – any of which has the potential to cause serious injury. Organizations need to actively plan for safety to prevent accidents and injury from occurring.

As a manager you have a key responsibility to ensure that your team works in a healthy and safe environment. Fortunately the law is there to assist you in this process.

Health, safety and the law

Legislation reflects society. As social attitudes change, so new legislation is introduced to ensure that the law keeps up with society.

Health and safety legislation culture is an example of this trend. In the UK, the first tentative steps to protect workers were introduced in the latter part of the nineteenth century. The Factories Act was passed in 1937, followed by a series of further Acts in the 1960s and early 1970s.

It is important to recognize that health and safety are vital issues – and failure to take them seriously can have significant legal and financial implications.

The Health and Safety at Work (HASW) Act 1974 is an unusual piece of business legislation in that it places obligations on both employers and employees. The Act sets out the duty of every employer with five or more employees, as:

'. . . to ensure, as far as reasonably practicable, the health, safety and welfare at work of all his employees.'

The nuts and bolts of legislation indicate that this should involve:

- The preparation of a written health and safety policy which must be communicated to all staff contractors who work regularly on the employer's premises.
- Consultation with safety representatives or a safety committee appointed by a recognized trade union.
- Informing employees about health and safety law and providing them with the local addresses of the authorities which enforce that law, by displaying approved posters or circulating leaflets.
- Reporting all fatal accidents and cases of major injury.
- Keeping records of reportable injuries for at least three years.
- Providing adequate first-aid facilities.

In addition to the 1974 Act, the Workplace (Health, Safety and Welfare) Regulations 1992 set standards for temperature, ventilation, lighting, workspace, seating, windows, escalators, toilet and washing facilities. All this is on top of an employer's general duties to provide:

- Safe work systems;
- Training and supervision;
- The maintenance of sites and premises;
- The provision of safe ways into and out of places of work;
- The provision of a safe and healthy work environment.

The HASW Act makes it the duty of employees to:

'Take reasonable care for the health and safety of himself and of other persons who may be affected by his acts or omissions at work.'

This includes responsibilities to:

- Co-operate with their employers and others to enable them to comply with the law;
- Avoid the intentional or reckless misuse of equipment or materials;

- Follow health and safety instructions;
- Report to the employer any dangerous situations in the workplace or any shortcomings in health and safety arrangements.

In addition to the HASW Act there are a number of key Acts that control health and safety at work. Many of these have derived from Europe. As a member of the European Union the UK has adopted, for example, a set of Regulations that affect both general and specific health and safety requirements. These Regulations, often referred to as the 'six pack', are more specific in their requirements, supplementing and reinforcing the HASW Act.

The Regulations are as follows:

Management of Health and Safety at Work Regulations 1999;

Workplace (Health, Safety and Welfare) Regulations 1992;

Manual Handling Operations Regulations 1992;

Health and Safety (Display Screen Equipment) Regulations 1992;

Personal Protective Equipment at Work Regulations 1992;

Provision and Use of Work Equipment Regulations 1998.

So far, we have described an employer's responsibilities and those of an employee. But where do you as a manager fit in? As a manager you should make sure that you are familiar with your own company's Health, Safety and Environmental policies and procedures and ensure that these are adhered to effectively. Whilst you are not expected to know everything about the law you should, however, have sufficient knowledge to ensure that you and your team comply.

From the viewpoint of health and safety legislation, managers are in the uncomfortable position of needing to fulfil both employers' and employees' responsibilities. As representatives of their employer, managers have a duty to:

- Monitor the extent to which the work environment meets the requirements of health and safety legislation;
- Identify and take remedial action;

- Instruct and train their staff on the health and safety policy and procedures;
- Encourage and provide opportunities for staff to identify short-falls and recommend improvements.

As employees, managers have a duty to:

- Point out shortcomings in their employer's approach to health and safety;
- Recommend improvements;
- Highlight remedial action which is outside their own authority.

All of these duties and responsibilities result from health and safety legislation. But there are others which stem simply from good management practice. These include:

- Looking after injured employees: perhaps by giving them comfort and support, taking them somewhere quiet to await medical attention and accompanying them to hospital if this is necessary.
- Managing the rest of the team: probably by getting them back to work in order to lessen shock or panic and by caring for anyone too upset to continue working.
- Learning from the incident: by identifying the cause, taking action to ensure it is not repeated and recording it for future reference.
- Planning processes with an eye to health and safety considerations.
- Making regular health and safety checks of all operations and activities under their control.

Much of this is fairly obvious though not always straightforward to implement. But what about situations where the manager's responsibilities as employer and employee appear to conflict? In other words, when the organization's demands cannot be met without damaging the health, safety or welfare of the workforce?

That raises some profound questions:

| * See Chapter 18 |

- How should you pass issues and concerns higher up the organization?*

- Are senior management aware of the consequences of their demands?
- Do they recognize the financial and practical costs of ignoring health, safety and welfare issues?

The costs of health and safety

In practical terms health and safety costs money because it involves all managers and staff spending part of their time in maintaining a healthy and safe working environment. The other side of the coin though is that an organization which turns its back on the health, safety or welfare of its staff is likely to incur additional:

- Legal costs;
- Recruitment costs;
- Productivity costs.

Legal costs may arise from the financial penalties incurred when an organization breaks health and safety law. In the UK because the Health and Safety at Work Act 1974 is a piece of criminal legislation, employers who break it are liable to fines or even imprisonment.

In addition, managers who fail to implement policies and procedures set up by their employers are also liable under the Act, as are employees who ignore their own health and safety responsibilities.

Also, if the employer has already been convicted under criminal law, it is likely that an employee will seek damages if he or she brings an action in civil law because the criminal conviction will provide proof of negligence.

Legal costs though are only the beginning.

Insight

Two light engineering firms in the same town are wishing to recruit staff. One has a history of injuries to staff and has been prosecuted under the Health and Safety at Work Act. The other has a better reputation for health and safety. The first pays higher wages.

Which, in your opinion, will find it easier to attract staff?

The answer to that question will of course depend on more factors than just health and safety.

Nevertheless assuming other things are roughly equal, it is unlikely that potential recruits will accept a higher risk of personal injury, or even death, in exchange for a little more pay. And they may well assume that a firm which pays no attention to health and safety matters is unlikely to care for its staff in other ways either.

In consequence an organization with a poor health and safety record will find it difficult to recruit and keep the staff it needs to meet its output and revenue targets. There will also be an ongoing impact on existing staff. In organizations where ill-health, accidents and injuries are commonplace:

- The workforce loses confidence in both the organization and its management

- Individual workers are more concerned about their own well-being than they are about that of the business.

And, of course, accidents and injuries cause disruption and loss of output, not only from the victims but also from their colleagues, from managers and from others with a first-aid responsibility.

| **Review** | Now check your understanding of this chapter by completing the following activities: |

1 What are the three factors related to an activity which operations scheduling should take into account?

    activity d _ _ _ _ _ _ _

    activity f _ _ _ _ _ _ _

    activity s _ _ _ _ _ _ _

2 A critical path is the s _ _ _ _ _ _ _ of activities which determines the m _ _ _ _ _ _ duration of an operation.

3 List four things which an efficient workplace layout should provide.

4 The UK Health and Safety at Work Act 1974 places legal duties on three groups of people. Who are they?

5 What costs could increase if you ignore health and safety issues?

Workplace Activity

If you are currently doing a management job, relate this chapter to your own experience by answering the following questions:

1 How could the work flows for which you are responsible be improved?

2 How could your workplace layout be made more efficient?

3 Are the members of your team aware of their health and safety responsibilities? If not, how could you change this?

4 Who is your local safety representative?

5 Are you aware of your own health and safety responsibilities? How could you find out more?

6 Carry out a safety audit of your workplace. What hazards can you find and how could you remove them?

15 Making improvements

The importance of adapting successfully to change is a frequent theme in today's management literature. Here are some sample statements which make the point:

'Every organization has to prepare for the abandonment of everything it does.'
(Peter Drucker)

'The status quo will no longer be the best way forward. That way will be less comfortable and less easy, but no doubt more interesting – a word the English use to signal an uncertain mix of danger and opportunity. If we wish to enjoy more of the opportunity and less of the risk we need to understand the changes better. Those who know why changes come waste less effort in protecting themselves or in fighting the inevitable. Those who realise where changes are heading are better able to use those changes to their own advantage.'
(Charles Handy)

'Today the idea of at least modest change everywhere in the corporation is becoming orthodoxy. Among the most promising 'themes' adopted by businesses to encourage incremental innovation are the concepts of 'total quality' and 'continuous improvement' – both predicated on the assumption that continual striving to reach higher and higher standards in every part of the business will provide a series of small wins that add up to superior performance. Such efforts point in the right direction

INTRODUCING MANAGEMENT

180

— towards organizations able to learn and adapt to the demands of a rapidly changing business environment.'
(Rosabeth Moss Kanter)

In fact, many authors now claim that a manager's primary role is managing change. They are eloquent about the need for 'creative dissatisfaction' which comprises:

- A continual search for better ways of doing things;
- And for managers to recognize that effective responses to change are the key to survival.

Improvement in context

Nevertheless, it would be naïve to assume that making improvements is a straightforward process. As we have pointed out earlier in this book:

- Ease of making improvements depends on the culture of your organization;
- People who are not used to change find it difficult and threatening to cope with;
- For change to succeed, managers – and particularly senior managers – need to give a positive lead;
- Even if your organization is geared to adapt to change and improvement, it is often not easy to identify the form that change should take.

* See Chapter 9

At this point, we need to distinguish between change and continuous improvement. Managing change* is a radical process. It is likely to cause short-term disruption and upheaval and may require significant inputs of time, money and other resources. It will, by definition, have a major impact on those involved:

- Their jobs may change, or even disappear;
- They may need to learn new skills, systems and routines;
- The work involved in implementing change will be significant.

Continuous improvement on the other hand is an incremental process of smaller changes. In other words it involves a continuing series of minor adjustments which are easier to incorporate than radical change and reduce the need for it.

MANAGING ACTIVITIES

181

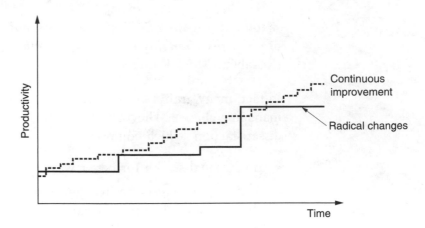

Figure 15.1

Interestingly, continuous improvement also prepares the way for radical change by encouraging people to accept and contribute to change. Vincent Nolan explains:

'The great paradox of innovation is that the biggest risk of all is not to innovate, never to do anything new, even at the experimental level. Yet it feels safe and comfortable to stick to the tried and tested.

Experiments are vital for several reasons:

- They identify new possibilities, some of which will probably be an improvement on what we are currently doing. Even if they are not, we have ensured that we are not missing anything – a valuable insurance in a changing world.
- A multiplicity of small risks is actuarially safer than one or two big ones – the risks are spread.
- The experiments are steps on a learning curve; the new knowledge obtained from each one can be used to minimize the risks of the next one.
- They keep the innovative muscles in trim; they provide practice in creating newness, taking new initiatives and handling the consequences. People who are used to doing new things are able to respond positively to unexpected new developments.'

The need for improvement

Continuous improvement involves a large number of detailed improvements, over a long period of time, and on an ongoing basis.

It works on the assumption that improvement is always possible, always necessary and always desirable. In many cases, all these are true. Continuous improvement may be necessary to:

- improve the contribution made to achieving the goals of the organization;
- Improve customer satisfaction;
- Reduce costs;
- Increase efficiency;
- Reduce or eliminate waste;
- Increase job satisfaction.

However, making improvements can only be justified if they are relevant and cost-effective.

Case Study

> Alan Studley's team of five assembly workers make components used in the manufacture of double-glazed window units. His output targets reflect the demand from the final assembly team (his internal customer in the supply chain). Their targets are in turn based on the firm's sales forecasts. His team are currently meeting their targets comfortably. A process review has shown that replacing a current piece of equipment with a more sophisticated version costing £5,000 would increase output by 10%

What questions should Alan ask before taking this proposal further?

We know from the Case Study that Alan's customers have no need at the moment for more outputs than his team are producing. But we do not know:

- What future demand there will be from them.
- Whether they are satisfied with output quality and whether the new machine will improve it.

- The firm's long-term plans (expansion? new technology?) and how the new machine fits in with them.
- The cost savings that might arise (for example, from maintaining current output levels but reducing staff).

Consequently, we cannot tell whether what is apparently a desirable improvement has any relevance either to current needs or future plans.

Equally we do not know whether it is likely to be cost-effective without more information about both overall costs and potential savings. We know how much the machine will cost, but:

- Will staff need re-training?
- Will other aspects of the assembly process need changing?
- If long-term cost savings can only come from making someone redundant, what will be the short-term cost and how will other staff react?

Whilst it therefore makes sense to be on the lookout for possible improvements, that does not always mean implementing them. The decision to take no action is a perfectly valid one, provided it has been made deliberately, following a careful comparison between the costs of the improvement and the benefits which will arise from it.

Designing improvements

A formal approach to continuous improvement involves regular meetings of improvement teams. This formal structure involves teams in:

- Assessing the need for improvement;
- Designing the improvement;
- Implementing the improvement.

Other types of improvement teams are:

- Project teams, brought together to deal with a specific issue, then disbanded when the issue has been resolved.

- Cross-functional teams with representatives from customer or supplier functions, or support or advisory functions like finance or purchasing.

Regardless of the nature of the team, it is always good practice to involve them as early as possible in the improvement process, in order to gain maximum commitment and to ensure that decisions are taken as far as possible by those who are responsible for implementing them. Which means that, even if improvement objectives are set by senior managers or by you as team leader, your team must be at least consulted about and preferably responsible for designing the improvement.

To be effective an improvement team needs:

- A clear statement of the objectives it is there to achieve (which may be set by others or the team itself).
- To understand the budgeting and resource constraints within which it is working.
- Knowledge of the organization's direction, its general aims and its values. These are all necessary in order to ensure that improvement teams are aware of the limits to the types and scope of improvement they can reasonably expect to make.

This is to avoid situations where the team is encouraged to make improvements, only to be told that their recommendations are too expensive, require resources which are not available or are not in line with wider organizational thinking, or have simply missed the point of the exercise.

In addition, teams should have:

Meeting guidelines
Giving a general idea of how often they will meet, at what time of day and for how long. Meetings will also need a chair, a note-taker, an agenda and some general principles concerning the degree of formality, the team's authority and how it will tackle problem-solving and decision-making.

Rules for allocating action
These will include: setting deadlines; a fair sharing of workload; and the recognition that delegated tasks are compulsory, not optional.

185

Team-working principles
These will deal with issues like: reliable attendance; time-keeping; listening to and involving others; conflict resolution*.

*See Chapter 8

Process and progress reviews
It is tempting for improvement teams to become so wrapped up in the problems they are addressing that they fail to keep track of their effectiveness. Regular process reviews should consider: individual commitment and contributions; interpersonal relationships; team co-operation. Progress reviews should assess achievement against deadlines, success to date and progress towards team objectives.

Implementing improvements

Permanent improvement teams will be responsible for the total improvement process — from assessing the need, through design and implementation, to monitoring its success. Project and cross-functional teams may disband after they have designed the improvement and leave its implementation to others. This may be a practical necessity but it is not ideal. Ideally, improvement teams should be responsible for implementing the improvements they have designed. This is because:

- Team members will have the best understanding of how they intend their improvement to work and the reasoning behind it;
- Team and individual motivation will improve as a result of seeing an improvement succeed;
- The knowledge that implementation will be down to them will keep an improvement team focused on what is practical and realistic.

However it is unusual for an improvement to have no consequences or implications for others outside the team. Its implementation may involve:

- The need for different inputs;
- Different outputs in terms of quality, quantity or scheduling;
- Changes to systems or documentation;
- The need for short-term support (equipment, advice, other resources).

Effective and trouble-free implementation will therefore depend on:

- Letting others know from the start why improvement is being sought, its benefits and likely consequences for them;
- Regular progress bulletins;
- Consultation on issues which will affect others;
- A clear action plan for implementation;
- Careful monitoring of implementation against the plan; Keeping disruption to a minimum.

Case Study

> The Foodstore is a cash-and-carry warehouse on the outskirts of a market town in Southern England. The warehouse is a free-standing building surrounded by its own car park. After several years' success the volume of traffic through the car park is becoming an issue. Customers park so that delivery trucks cannot get to the building and the car park entrance is so narrow that customers' vehicles and delivery trucks often block each other. Tom Dacre, the Warehouse Manager, has a plan to widen the entrance and clearly mark out entrance and exit routes, customer parking bays and delivery truck access in the car park. However Tom has been told by his contractor that this will require three days of disruption and two days when the car park cannot be used.

What action should Tom take to implement his plan?

We assume that Tom has senior management approval for his plan and that a budget has been allocated. These are certainly the first action steps he should take if he has not already done so.

Following those, he would be well-advised to check records of turnover and deliveries to identify the time of year and the five days in a week when traffic is lightest. It would then be a good idea to write to customers and suppliers explaining the benefits of the plan, his proposed timing for implementation and asking for comments. Of course, there is no point in doing that unless he is prepared to change his plan if there is a strong resistance, either to the plan or to the proposed timing.

When details have been finalized he will need to bring people up-to-date, asking them to keep visits and deliveries to a minimum while the work is going on. And if the plan changes he must communicate those changes urgently.

So now the contractor is at work but, as often happens, he finds he will need an extra day. It will now be important for Tom to:

- Negotiate with the contractor ways of finishing the job while keeping most of the car park free from obstruction;

- Display notices so that customers and delivery drivers know what is going on;

- Brief staff to answer questions and queries and deal with any complaints;

- And, finally, would it be clever marketing for the Foodstore to invite new and existing customers and suppliers to a celebration marking the successful completion of the project?

Monitoring improvements

Earlier we introduced the concept of the control loop. It referred to a process of:

- Setting performance standards;
- Initiating action to achieve those standards;
- Monitoring resulting performance or outputs;
- Taking further action as necessary.

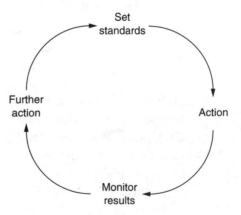

Figure 15.2

That process is central to just about every kind of management action. It applies to:

- Managing quality;
- Managing outputs;
- Problem-solving;
- Decision-making;
- Staff performance review;
- Training evaluation;
- Budget management.

So it should come as no surprise when we suggest that it is equally applicable to making and managing improvements!

Monitoring the results of the improvement process is apparently the final stage in the improvement cycle we have described. But, in fact, it would be a mistake to view it as coming at the end of the process. Instead, monitoring the results should be a consideration at the very beginning of the process and should continue to be a key issue as it unfolds.

At the start, any improvement initiative needs objectives and they should be set in quantified terms. This is easier in some cases than in others. It is relatively easy to say that an improvement initiative should:

- Increase output by 10%;
- Improve energy efficiency by 3%;
- Reduce waste by 5%;
- Cut overtime costs by £3,000 per month.

But it is less easy to quantify factors like:

- Customer satisfaction;
- Staff motivation;
- Team co-operation.

Difficult it may be, but it is nevertheless not impossible. It is usually possible, either to find quantitative measures of less obvious factors, or else to translate qualitative factors into numbers even if this is done in a somewhat arbitrary way.

For example:

- Customer satisfaction can be assessed on the numbers of customer complaints or the quality of rejected inputs.

- Staff motivation can be interpreted from numbers of resignations or applications for transfer.

- Team co-operation might be measured from a questionnaire, using a scoring mechanism as in Figure 15.3.

Question: How much confidence do you have in your colleagues' expertise

Total	A lot	Moderate	Not a lot	None
5	4	3	2	1

Figure 15.3

Although factors like these take more thought and creativity to turn into numbers, the process nevertheless remains essential. This is because improvement monitoring is a comparative process. It involves comparing actual results with:

- The original objectives;

- Historical performance;

- And, sometimes, external or internal benchmarks to identify whether there is need or scope for further improvement.

Such comparisons are only meaningful if they are based on numbers.

Earlier we linked monitoring with control. That is we suggested that monitoring performance against standards was of little use unless it was followed by corrective action if performance did not meet the standards. That principle applies equally to monitoring improvements.

Case Study

Elaine Wilson has been brought in to Premier Plastics as the new Personnel Manager. The firm's staff turnover is at an all time high of 27% – three times the average for the industry. She is given a free rein to improve the situation. She finds that:

- Wages and salaries are lower than in other firms

- Managers have not been trained to motivate staff

> - The business offers shorter holidays and longer working weeks than others in the area
>
> - Most local firms offer flexitime but Premier Plastics does not
>
> Armed with this information, Elaine receives approval to increase wages by 5%, introduce intensive training in staff management, make holidays and working hours more competitive and introduce flexitime.
>
> After six months, staff turnover has dropped to 7%.

How successful have Elaine's improvement initiatives been?

There are two answers to this question. At one level, they have been extremely successful. Staff turnover is now below the industry average, with the consequent reductions in recruitment and induction costs, and lost output. But, at a different level, it is not possible to identify how successful individual initiatives have been. Something has worked — but was it: the combination of all four initiatives? Only one, two or three? If so, which?

That in turn raises the very practical question:

Could Premier Plastics have achieved the same result by spending less?

That Case Study contains elements of: performance monitoring; performance comparison (against both historical performance and external benchmarks); and corrective action.

But it also throws up another consideration. If you work in an organization with a philosophy of continuous improvement, you are bound to find it difficult to know which improvements have led to which results. In order to be able to quantify the results of improvement initiatives, it is advisable to let the dust settle after each one, so that you can measure what happens without confusing the results through another initiative.

Review

Now check your understanding of this chapter by completing the activities below:

1 Vincent Nolan lists four reasons why 'experiments are vital'. What are they?

2 What does 'continuous improvement' mean and what does it involve?

3 Describe three kinds of improvement team.

4 Why do improvement teams need objectives?

5 In what ways might an improvement initiative affect others outside the team?

Workplace Activity

If you are currently doing a management job, relate this chapter to your own experience by answering the following questions:

1 How innovative is your organization in identifying problems and implementing solutions?

2 How could these processes be improved?

3 Think of an improvement initiative in your organization which has gone well. Why was that?

4 Think of an improvement initiative that has gone badly. Why was that?

5 How do you involve your team in contributing to continuous improvement? Could you involve them more?

References

1 Drucker, P. (1992) *The New Society of Organizations, Harvard Business Review*, September/October 1992, Vol. 7, Issue 5, pp. 95–104.
2 Handy, C. P. (1989) *The Age of Unreason*, Business Books: London.
3 Kanter, R. M. (1989) *When Giants Learn to Dance*, Simon & Schuster: Hemel Hempstead.
4 Nolan, V. (1987) *The Innovators Handbook*, Sphere: London.

Website addresses

www.bh.com
Publish a comprehensive range of Health and Safety textbooks including Health and Safety legislation, learning from accidents and risk assessment.

www.hse.gov.uk
Information, publications and downloadable resources from the Health and Safety Executive

www.quality-foundation.co.uk
British Quality Foundation provides help for organizations to improve their performance including best practice benchmarking.

Section 4   Managing Information

- *How should I solve problems?*
- *How should I make decisions?*
- *What management information do I need?*
- *How should I store and record information so that I can get to it easily?*
- *What makes communication effective?*
- *What are the best ways of informing, persuading and influencing?*
- *What information do others need from me?*
- *How do I make my written communication effective?*
- *How do I communicate effectively face-to-face?*

16 Solving problems and making decisions

Chapter Objectives	• *How should I solve problems?*
	• *How should I make decisions?*

An essential skill of a manager is effective decision-making. A considerable part of your working day will involve you making decisions, depending on the nature of your job some of these decisions will be more or less important.

'Making decisions and bearing the responsibility for them is one of the cornerstones of the manager's job.'
(Steve Cooke and Nigel Slack)

You may be finding that increasingly you are under pressure to make more complex decisions in reduced time-scales. So it is vital that you understand the processes involved in solving problems and making decisions.

In broad terms, solving problems and making decisions are two stages in the same process.

Solving problems answers the question 'What is wrong?'.

Taking decisions answers the question 'How do I fix it?'.

This is not always true however. Sometimes the problem is so obvious that its solving does not involve any decision at all. The analysis leads directly to the solution.

Decisions can also be linked to a search for a better way of doing things, even if there is nothing really wrong with the current way.

Nevertheless we can most usefully picture the process as a single cycle, although the relative importance of each stage will differ according to:

- The nature of the situation, issue or problem to be addressed.
- Whether the issue has operational (junior management), tactical (middle management) or strategic (senior management) significance.
- The complexity of the issue.
- The extent of the choice of alternative actions.
- The predictability of the outcome.
- The levels of cost and risk.
- The time-scales involved.

In the four parts of this chapter, we will look at two alternative attitudes to problem solving and decision making. We shall then seek to combine the best of each into a single **model.** We will then consider problem-solving techniques and finish by looking in detail at decision making.

You may be wondering why this topic of problem solving and decision making appears under 'Managing Information'. You may also be wondering why, if information is important to the process, we have not treated it as a separate heading. The reason is that, every stage of problem solving and decision making requires accurate and relevant information. Therefore we have included references to information which you need, where to find it and how to interpret it throughout the chapter.

Approaches to problem solving and decision making

In this chapter we look at two ways of approaching problem solving and decision making. The analytical approach which uses quantitative techniques to define and isolate problems. It originates from the work of Kepner and Tregor.

The creative approach which encourages us to throw off the limitations imposed by tradition, budgets or what we perceive to be possible in order to reach creative solutions. The creative approach originates from the ideas of Nolan and de Bono.

Taking an analytical approach, the problem is any 'deviation from the norm' In other words there is a right way and we can measure whether we are meeting standards using that way. If we are not, then we can amend it.

The creative school on the other hand sees a problem as 'the gap between where we are and where we want to be' (Nolan). This implies that there's no limit to our aspirations or what is achievable, provided we are prepared to use our imagination.

These two approaches to problem solving and decision making can be used together. Throughout the rest of this chapter you will find that one or the other school will be the most productive. One thing that is worth remembering though, is an analytical approach is likely to be better received in a formal, risk-adverse organization, whilst the creative approach brings greater risks, and greater potential rewards.

A problem-solving and decision-making model

There are eleven stages in the process of problem solving and decision making. The first five relate to problem analysis. Six relate to decision making. Each stage is expressed in the form of a question.

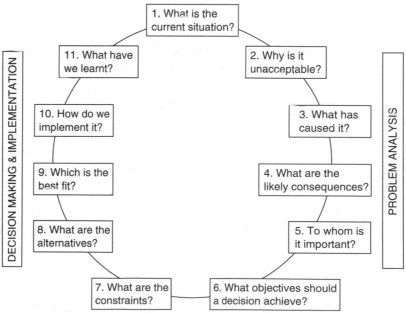

Figure 16.1

We shall now look briefly at each stage, before going on to examine them in more detail later.

1. *What is the current situation?*
   The analytical school would ask:
   What is the deviation from the norm?

   The creative school would ask:
   What is the gap between where we are and where we want to be?

2. *Why is it unacceptable?*
   The analytical answer will quantify the problem.

   The creative answer would emphasize that the situation is unsatisfactory and save quantification until later.

3. *What has caused it?*
   This is where the analytical approach comes into its own. An analysis of when the problem occurs, how often, under what circumstances and where, enables the problem to be isolated. Possible causes can be identified and each one assessed to see whether it is the likely cause.

   The creative approach is less concerned with causes. Creative problem solvers believe that too much attention to identifying the cause, limits our thinking about solutions, and results in minor improvements.

4. *What are the likely consequences?*
   Answering this question identifies both the urgency with which the problem needs to be solved, or whether the problem is big enough to warrant corrective action.

5. *To whom is it important?*
   Someone owns the problem. Someone will have to authorize action. Someone will have to take the action.

6. *What objectives should a decision achieve?*
   In analytical terms, the answer will be: the norm has been restored.

   The creative answer is more complex and far-reaching. Creative decisions may go far beyond the identified problem. In Vincent Nolan's words, we have to 'relearn how to wish for the impossible'.

7. *What are the constraints?*
   This question is more relevant to the analytical than to the creative school. The analytical school will expect to know:

What budget? What resources? What time-scale?

The creative school will take the view that the achievement of the impossible justifies a creative approach to eliminating constraints.

8. *What are the alternatives?*

Both analytical and creative approaches stress the importance of giving imagination a free rein at this point. However, the creative approach encourages freewheeling ideas.

9. *Which is the best fit?*

This is the point at which the creative approach takes on the techniques of the analytical school! Both stress the importance of comparing all the various alternatives with the objectives the decision should achieve and choosing the one that comes closest.

10. *How do we implement it?*

Implementing a decision uses the same techniques as project management. It requires an action plan, an analysis of necessary resources, budget and time, briefing and communication, monitoring and control.

11. *What have we learnt?*

The final stage, as with any project, is to review the success of the decision, make any final changes to cope with unforeseen snags and draw conclusions that can be applied to the implementation of future decisions.

A comparison of the analytical and creative approaches to problem solving and decision making appears in Figure 16.2.

Approach	Stage						
	Problem definition	Identification of causes	Analysis of consequences	Decision objectives	Idea generation	Cost and fit	Implementation
Analytical	Tight	Essential Measured	Quantitative	Restore the norm	Unconstrained	Objective Quantified	Planned Monitored
Creative	Loose	May limit creativity	Qualitative	Wish fulfilment	Unconstrained	Objective Quantified	Planned Monitored

Figure 16.2

Problem analysis

The questions that make up the stages of problem analysis combine the strengths of both the analytical and creative approaches. Together, they are designed to identify:

- The true nature of the problem.

- Whether it is serious enough to justify the effort, time and cost needed to put it right.

- Whether the people involved are sufficiently committed (can be bothered) to deal with it.

Problem definition

Identifying the nature of the problem may seem an obvious first step. But, surprisingly often, organizations are content to deal with the 'present problem' and do not look closely enough to find the underlying cause. As a result, the actions they take do not address the root of the problem. Let us look at this example.

Insight

> Petra's team has been moaning for a long time about the poor pay they get. But other teams in the same department are not complaining to the same extent, although no-one is ever totally satisfied with their pay.

If it were possible to award Petra's team a pay rise, do you think this would get rid of the real problem?

The clue in this Insight is the fact that Petra's team seems to be the only one really unhappy about their pay. That probably raised suspicions in your mind. It is clear that there is something else going on.

Two techniques will help to identify the real problem. The first is to keep on asking 'why?' until you reach the root of problem.

- *Why* are Petra's team moaning about pay?
  Because they are generally fed up with their jobs.

- *Why* are the jobs boring?
  Because they are all undemanding and routine.

- *Why* are the jobs routine?
  Because that is what the procedures dictate.

- Why are the procedures that way?
  Because they have never been challenged.

This brief set of questions and answers has redefined the problem. It is no longer: How to find a practical way of paying Petra's team more.

Instead, it has become: How to redesign their jobs so that they remain efficient while increasing job satisfaction.

The 'why' technique is adapted from what the creative school call 'backwards/forwards thinking'. This assumes that a solution has been found to the problem, then asks what extra benefits would come from the solution. In the case of Petra's team, higher pay should make them more satisfied, so the issue is one of satisfaction rather than pay.

Our second technique is taken from the analytical approach. It is designed to come up with a precise description of the problem by establishing the circumstances under which it does and does not occur. Table 16.1 shows this.

Both techniques depend on accurate information being available.

Problems can also be categorized according to whether they are:

- deviation problems
- potential problems
- improvement problems.

Table 16.1

When does the problem occur?	When does it not occur?
Where does it occur?	Where does it not occur?
Who is involved?	Who is not involved?
In what conditions does the problem occur?	In what conditions does the problem not occur?

Identifying causes

- Identifying the causes of problems is seen as critical by analysts and problem solvers.

A useful identification technique is the Ishikawa diagram, also known as the cause–effect or fishbone diagram. This technique was originally developed and used in the field of quality management but is now recognized for its wider application in problem solving and decision making.

You start by drawing the head and backbone of a fish, with a summary of the effect of the problem written into the head (Figure 16.3)

Figure 16.3

You then draw in a framework of potential causes as the main bones leading from the backbone. Standard headings are:

People, Environment, Methods, Plant, Equipment, Materials.

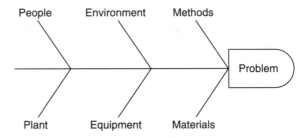

Figure 16.4

The next step is to apply creative thinking or brainstorming to the headings, using the prompts:

What, Where, When, Why, Who, How?

For example:

- How does the environment contribute to this problem?
- Why are materials not of the required standard?
- Who are the people involved?
- What is wrong with the equipment?

The answers to these questions provide smaller bones which you can add to each of the six main bones, resulting finally in a diagram which will look something like Figure 16.5, which is an analysis of the causes of late deliveries in a particular postal region.

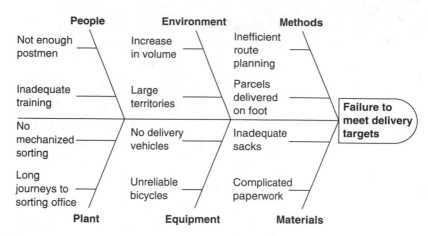

Figure 16.5

It is also worth noting, of course, that the 'why' technique of problem identification also helps to get to the causes of the problem.

Consequences

An analysis of future consequences should take both a short-term and a longer-term view. For the short-term, it is important to know what the problem is costing now in terms of productivity, standards and staff motivation. And then to compare these with the costs of resolving it. In the longer term, product or service changes, reorganization or a planned investment programme may indicate that it would be better to live with the problem until a larger initiative in the future resolves it. In other words, doing nothing is a perfectly valid response to a problem, provided you have made a conscious and reasoned decision to ignore it.

Again, information is important (current costs, improvement costs, future plans and their impact).

People

An identification of the people involved, or likely to be involved, in the problem is the last stage in problem analysis. They will fall into three categories:

203

- *Problem-owners*

  These are the people most affected by the problem; those who must be sufficiently inconvenienced or dissatisfied to want to resolve it. If this is you, ask yourself:

  > Do I care enough to take action?
  > What autonomy and resources do I have to act?
  > What are the limits to the action I can take?

- *Authority-holders*

  Answers to those questions may reveal that you need to seek support, permission or approval from someone higher up the organization. In that case, ask yourself: the problem may be important to me, but is it sufficiently important to my line managers for them to authorize the necessary action, resources and expenditure?

- *Implementers*

  These are the people who will take the action to resolve the problem. That is likely to be the members of your team. Ask yourself:

  > Do they understand the nature of the problem, its objectives and the benefits the solution will bring to them?
  > Will you involve them in designing the solution?
  > Have they the necessary skills and resources to implement the solution and make it successful?

Now bring the stages of problem analysis together by tackling this situation:

Insight

National targets have been introduced to reduce class sizes in primary schools. In response, Wellbourne School has recruited a new teacher, Lizzie Matthews, who will be teaching her class in a disused, prefabricated classroom on the school playground. Unfortunately, the classroom is cold, damp, draughty and generally in need of refurbishment.

What information will Lizzie need about this problem before considering what to do about it?

Concerning the current situation, Lizzie's *problem* is that her new classroom does not meet the standards in school classrooms and that there is a gap between what she has and what she would like. It is unacceptable because her own comfort and her pupils' motivation to learn will be affected by the conditions.

The ultimate *cause* of the problem was, indirectly, the new national targets. But Lizzie cannot influence those and, in any case, the intention behind them was positive. More immediately, the cause was the school's decision to make use of available resources to achieve the target. However, Lizzie may want to find out:

- What is the deadline for achieving the target?
- Was this a unanimous decision by the school governors or influenced by a few?
- Is any money available for refurbishment?

The short-term consequences will involve discomfort and reduced learning. Lizzie can calculate roughly what it would cost to put the classroom right, so she will need to find some way of costing the current disadvantages, in order to make a comparison.

For the longer-term, she will need to know:

- Is there investment planned to upgrade the classroom? If so, when will this happen?
- Does the school have any plans for new permanent buildings?
- Is there any intention for her class to move into a permanent classroom in the existing school?
- Is the increase in pupil numbers likely to continue?

As far as people are concerned, the problem-owners are Lizzie and her pupils; the authority-holders are the headteacher and the governors, who will need to authorize the work and the expenditure; the implementers will be mainly outside contractors. Although Lizzie and her class may be affected, Lizzie needs to decide:

- Is she willing to cause a fuss in the first months of her new job?
- Will parents take practical action by supporting her?
- Are the authority-holders more concerned about meeting the targets, protecting their budget or improving conditions?
- Will she and her class cope with any disruption?

As you can see, consideration of the five questions contained in problem analysis is essential in identifying:

- The real issue to be addressed;
- Whether it is worth dealing with;
- The people whose support is required and whether they will give it.

Only when you have this information will you be able to decide if you should take the issue further. If you do, you will have a firm basis for deciding on the action to take.

Decision making and implementation

Setting objectives

An important step in the decision-making process is the clarification and setting of objectives. These will obviously vary according to the situation you and your team face at any one time. Objectives of the decision need to be clear, unambiguous, agreed and understood by everyone concerned.Without this clarification you will be in danger of embarking on a journey with little knowledge of where it is leading and therefore will have difficulty knowing if you have arrived! As a manager you need to be able to make a judgement as to whether a particular decision that was made was effective or not.

Identifying constraints

This involves a thorough analysis of all the factors that are involved in the decision that may limit the scope. The following questions may help you in the process:

- How long have I got before this decision must be fully implemented?
- What staff can I use to put it in place?
- Do they have the necessary skills and experience to enable the decision to work?
- How much budget do I have?
- What will be the impact on other teams/departments of this decision?

This process recognizes the importance of working within the constraints of an organization. We often need to be creative in identifying ways of working with these constraints and generating alternatives.

Generating alternatives

This is an important stage in the process and involves considering all possible alternatives. This is the stage where creating ideas and involving other people will benefit you in several ways:

- The more people, the more ideas.
- Involve colleagues and managers and learn from their experience.
- Involve your team, who may well have a better understanding, as they are closer to the issues. Involving them is also likely to increase their ownership and commitment to ensuring success-ful implementation.

The culture of your organization together with the nature of the problem will determine how creative you can be in generating ideas. The more unstructured a situation is increases the need for a creative approach. There are a number of techniques that enable individuals and groups to creatively generate ideas. Brainstorming can be extremely effective. The focus with any of the techniques is to ensure that all ideas, even those that are apparently unworkable or off-the-wall are considered equally.

Evaluating the alternatives

Finding the best fit involves two steps:

Discarding from your list of alternatives those which are irrele-vant, clearly unworkable, illegal or at odds with the values of the organization.

Then making a careful, objective comparison between each on the basis of the objectives you have set for your decision and the constraints under which it must operate.

This stage is easier using the analytical approach to objectives and constraints because these will have been carefully quantified and are not subject to question. The creative approach on the other

207

hand will have lesser objectives and constraints that could be challenged if there is justification for doing so. Nevertheless, it is still possible to choose the best alternative on the basis of:

Which alternative addresses most of the problem with the least cost, upheaval and disruption?

Case Study

> Each summer, Candlewick Farm hires students on a temporary basis to pick the fruit crop. In the past, they have slept on straw in the barn. This year, the local health inspector has insisted they must have beds to sleep in.
>
> Neil, the farm manager, has decided that the beds must:
>
> - Cost less than £500 in total (he needs twenty of them);
>
> - Be delivered to the farm;
>
> - Satisfy the health inspector;
>
> - Not be too comfortable – he wants the students out of bed early in the morning;
>
> - Require no more than one day of his time to arrange.
>
> With some of his permanent workers, Neil has brainstormed the following alternatives:
>
> - Buy new beds;
>
> - Hire beds;
>
> - Buy a job lot of second-hand beds (perhaps old ones from a hotel or hospital);
>
> - Buy individual second-hand beds locally.

What information will Neil need to make a final choice between these alternatives?

Making any necessary assumptions, which would you choose provisionally as the best fit?

Neil should first find out:

- The cost of new beds;

208

- The cost of hiring beds for the summer;
- Whether anyone has twenty second-hand beds for sale at the moment and, if so, at what price?

However, we can make a provisional choice:

- New beds will cost more than £25 each;
- Hired beds will probably be too comfortable;
- Neil will have to collect individual beds himself.

A job lot of second-hand beds looks to be the best-fit alternative (assuming they are available and cheap enough).

Implementing the decision

This stage makes use of techniques which will already be familiar from our discussions of project management, managing change and **continuous improvement.** In summary, it involves:

- An action plan, perhaps in the form of a flow-chart or critical path analysis.
- A calculation of required resources, costs, time-scales, milestones and deadlines.
- Identifying and allocating responsibilities.
- Communicating reasons, standards and targets.
- Designing and installing some form of control loop to monitor progress and initiate remedial action.
- Carrying out a risk analysis.
- Formulating contingency plans in case something goes wrong.

Strictly there are two steps in this stage. The first is the plan, the second is the implementation. Even when you plan how to carry out your decision, you could still find that:

- Detailed calculations show your decision does not fit the constraints;
- Your plan needs more resources than you have;
- The plan is too risky.

Careful planning, by highlighting issues like these, will avoid the plan collapsing when you try to implement it. That will allow you to revise your plan to make it achievable. As a last resort, you might even decide that, as we mentioned earlier, the current situation is preferable to a high-risk plan to deal with it.

Review and evaluation

This stage works similarly to that we described as the final step in managing discontinuous change. It involves:

- A final check on how successfully the decision has been implemented.
- Action to deal with any remaining snags.
- Learning and noting lessons, which can be applied to the implementation of future decisions.

Review

Now check your understanding of this chapter by completing the following activities:

1 There are two approaches to making decisions:

   C _ _ _ _ _ _ _ managers try to irradicate constraints in order to find creative, off-the-wall solutions to problems.

   A _ _ _ _ _ _ _ _ _ _ managers use quantitative techniques to identify, analyse and evaluate alternatives within set constraints.

2 Why is it important to know the likely consequences of a problem?

3 Fill in the six main headings in Figure 16.6.

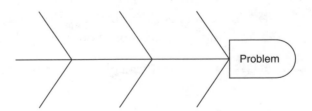

Figure 16.6

4 Why do you need to set objectives in the decision making process?

5 Complete the following:

'Identifying best-fit involves comparing each alternative on the basis of _ _ _ _ _ _ _ _ _ _ _ _ _ and

_ _ _ _ _ _ _ _ _ _ _ under which you operate.'

<table>
<tr><td>**Workplace Activity**</td><td>**If you are currently in a management position, relate this chapter to your own experience by answering the following questions:**</td></tr>
</table>

1 Which approach to solving problems and making decisions does your organization's culture favour?

2 Which approach do you prefer? How well does it match the problems and decisions facing you?

3 Think of a problem you faced recently. What more could you have done to establish its root cause?

4 Who would you consult for ideas on solving:

A people problem?

A quality problem?

A budget problem?

5 How careful are you to evaluate the success of your decisions? What more could you do?

References

1 Cooke, S. and Slack, N. (1991) *Making Management Decisions*, Prentice Hall: London.
2 Kepner, C. H. and Tregor, B. B. (1965) *The Rational Manager*, McGraw-Hill: New York.
3 Nolan, V. (1987) *Problem Solving*, Sphere: London.
4 De Bono, E. (1991) *Handbook for the Positive Revolution*, Penguin: Harmondsworth.
5 De Bono, E. (1977) *Lateral Thinking*, Penguin: Harmondsworth.

MANAGING INFORMATION

17 Recording, storing and retrieving information

| Chapter Objectives | • *What management information do I need?*
• *How should I store and record information so that I can get to it easily?* |

Managers:

- Make plans
- Respond to external factors
- Manage change
- Control resources
- Manage budgets
- Make improvements
- Solve problems
- Make decisions.

There is considerable variety in these responsibilities. Nevertheless, they have at least one thing in common:

None of them can be done effectively without accurate, timely and relevant information.

For example:

- Plans are pointless if you never know whether you are achieving them.
- You cannot respond to external factors if you do not know how they are changing.
- How can you manage change or make improvements if you have no way of knowing when they are necessary?
- Controlling resources and managing budgets depends on knowing how productively they are being used.

INTRODUCING MANAGEMENT

- You cannot <u>solve problems</u> unless you know they exist.

- <u>Decisions</u> can only be effective if you know what they are required to achieve and whether they have succeeded.

* See Chapter 16

Decision making is a central part of management* — and good information is essential to effective decision making. We can categorize the uses of information into that required before, during and after the event. The uses are shown in Figure 17.1.

Used for:	Planning	Monitoring and control	Review and evaluation
Information:	Before the event	During the event	After the event

Figure 17.1

We also need to differentiate between quantitative and qualitative information:

- *Quantitative* information can be measured and expressed as numbers (and normally relates to facts and figures).

- *Qualitative* information is difficult to quantify and normally deals with feelings, attitudes and opinions.

- *Quantitative* information is easy to compare and analyse into patterns and trends.

- *Qualitative* information is messier and more difficult to formalize. Even so, it is a mistake to overlook qualitative information, because it is often the only guide to human factors like staff motivation or customer satisfaction.

Data, information and good information

We said just now that effective decisions depend on good information. But what is good information? To answer that question, we need to explore the difference between data and information and then examine what makes information good.

Data

Data are raw facts, figures, expressions of attitudes or opinion. They (the word data is technically plural) are the raw material from which information is derived.

213

Case Study

> You are told that your team's output last week was 132 units. You are asked if you are satisfied with that performance.

What more would you need to know before you could answer the question?

The fact that your team produced 132 units is only data. It may be accurate. It may be worth remembering. But it tells you nothing.

For it to be useful, you need to be able to compare it with something. So, if you are told that the output of 132 units was 98% of target and 7 units higher than last week, the figures start to tell you something.

Information

Information is data which have been processed and analysed to make them useful. It provides answers to questions and is a basis for decisions.

However, not all information is good. Consider the following situation:

Insight

> You receive information about your team's output on a monthly basis. It comes in the form of actual output compared with targets and previous months' performance. It is now November and you have just received output information for your team's performance in September. It shows a performance of 98% against target. However, your team are paid a bonus for achieving this target. They tell you that their own, informed records show that in September they achieved 103% of target. Also, your performance is assessed on your team's output compared with that of other teams

Why is September's output information not good information?

Good information

To be good, information must meet the following criteria. It must be:

Relevant — in other words, it must tell you what you need to know.

Accurate — it must be true and reliable.

Timely — it must arrive soon enough for you to be able to make decisions based on it.

Complete — it must also tell you all you need to know.

Concise — but without drowning you in unnecessary detail!

In our case study, the information is relevant (it is valuable for monitoring and control) but not complete (no comparisons with other teams). It is neither reliable nor timely. Because your team is telling you something different about output (which should be accurate because it is based on data gathered at the point of production), either they are wrong or the information is. You do not know which, so can rely on neither. The information also arrives too late for you to take any corrective action for two months. That is too long to wait before correcting under-performance.

Formal and informal information

Good information may be either formal or informal. Formal information is recorded and accessible via a recognized system (management accounts, perhaps, or a goods received record, or an analysis of timesheets or MIS). Informal information is like the output claims made by the team in our last case study – comments made in passing, not recorded and irregular.

Both types of information have strengths and weaknesses. A summary of these is given in Figure 17.2

On the face of it, the comparison is weighted in favour of formal information. In reality, the two types are complementary. Both are essential because each tells you things the other cannot.

215

Formal information	Informal information
Should be accurate and reliable	May be subjective and biased
Available easily (regularly or on demand)	Depends on having the right contacts
Processed for you	Requires you to draw your own conclusions
Content dictated by the system	Allows you to ask what you want to know
Deals best with facts and figures	Gives access to opinions, feelings, attitudes
Shows trends and patterns	One-off

Figure 17.2

Collecting information

Good information is relevant — it tells you what you need to know. As a result, the first priorities in collecting information are:

- Deciding what information you need;
- Identifying suitable sources.

Needs and sources of information

At the start of this chapter, we listed a manager's responsibilities. You will spend most of your time dealing with the day-to-day running of your operation. As a result, the information most relevant to you is likely to deal with relatively short-term, internal matters. However, managers at all levels should have an understanding of external factors, how they are affecting customers, community competition and technology. So it would be a mistake to overlook external sources of information like:

- Government statistics;
- Industry statistics;
- Specialist reports;
- Newspaper, radio and TV reports;
- Trade magazines;
- Experts' comments.

Most of the information you need will be required to support tactical decisions. By definition, these will be frequent, implemented straight away and of limited long-term impact. In a well run organization that information should be readily available from formal, internal systems. It may be from different sources.

Local information

In other words, generated in your section by your team. It may be derived from production counts, quality checks, materials stocks or attendance records. You will certainly have easy access to it although how good it is may depend on the quality of the system which produces it. Nevertheless, you should have some influence over its relevance, accuracy, timeliness, completion and con-ciseness.

Remote information

This information will be produced elsewhere in your organization – for example, future demand from internal customers, maintenance schedules, materials deliveries. Whether you get the information you need when you need it and in the form you need, will depend both on your relationship with other teams and the flexibility of the information systems they operate.

Central information

This is normally information based on data coming from different parts of the organization, collected, processed and analysed at a central point, then distributed. It is likely to be more complete than any other information available to you, but may be late, irrelevant and contain too much detail. Of all the internal information systems available to you, this is likely to be the most difficult to change. Doing so will almost certainly involve representation through your manager, because of the inevitable impact of changes both on the rest of the organization and the department which collates and processes the information.

Not all the information you require will be tactical though. With the advent of delegated decision making you may be involved in longer-term planning of your team's operation, or in improvement

217

or change projects. These will be less frequent and sometimes one-off. They may mean you need:

- External information;
- Access to central information you do not usually see;
- Informal, internal information.

In the first two cases, finding the sources of information may involve you in some research into what is available in your organization. In the last case, you will probably need to create your own.

Most organizations have more information than their managers realize. Ask yourself:

- Does my organization have a central resource library?
- Where are the archives kept and how do I gain access to them?
- What happens to trade and professional journals? Are they stored? If so, where?
- Who are the best people to ask for: Personnel information? Financial information? Sales records? Customer and competition information? Production information? Environmental trends?

There is no set way of doing this. It is a matter of nosing around, asking your manager, asking colleagues and contacts.

Informal, internal information will come from none of those sources. You will need to set up:

- Interviews and discussions;
- Questionnaires;
- Telephone conversations;
- Lunchtime chats;
- Checklists.

In fact, all of the techniques we described earlier in the book when we looked at how to collect information from internal customers.

The results of this research will start off as data. To turn it into information, you will need:

First to record it in a consistent way, on paper or on a computer record.

Secondly to look for trends, patterns and comparisons.

In this way, you are creating a system and turning informal into formal information.

Storing and retrieving information

Most organizations appear to be overflowing with information. Actually, that appearance is deceptive. In reality most organizations are full of data which are often difficult to access, dispersed and often held in a form which contains too much irrelevant detail, is too incomplete and has not been processed in any way. It hardly counts as information, let alone good information.

Insight

Tom has been asked to undertake a development project which will involve making recommendations on how to improve customer satisfaction. As part of the project, he has decided to compare the number of customer complaints with numbers of customers, turnover and profit for the last five years.

Customer relations keep details of complaints for two years. Then they are put into off-site storage. Sales keep records of existing customers. But past customer records are only available from invoices, which are held by accounts for three years and then copied on to microfiche and archived in another part of the building.

Turnover and expenditure for the year to date are held by finance. They do not calculate a reliable profit figure until the year-end. Previous years' turnover and profit figures are contained in the published accounts, which are held by the company secretary.

What will Tom need to do to turn all this data into information

He will need to visit five separate departments plus two different storage sites! He will need to extract all the relevant data (but can only estimate this year's profit) before analysing and processing it in order to make comparisons.

This situation is not unusual. In fact it is to be expected. Tom's project is one-off. It would be excessively expensive to make the comparisons he wants to make on a regular basis. Of course information needs to be accessible but there is no point in producing it just in case someone may possibly want it at some unspecified time in the future. And who knows what form they might want it in anyway!

Nevertheless all organizations need to keep a huge volume of both data and information. Some of it is needed on a day-to-day basis. Some of it is needed as a historical record, and some is required by law – in the UK that applies particularly to personnel records, details of contracts and company financial accounts.

Information systems

The development of information and communication technology over the past few decades has had a significant impact on organizations. Organizations can now process and transmit information globally with relative ease. Despite this, information that is used by businesses continues to be processed both by internal computer systems and by manual systems. The important point is not so much which system is used but, does the system meet the wide range of information needs across the organization? Information systems, whether computerized or manual, need to contribute to the whole process of managing information effectively.

To make an effective choice between a manual or a computerized system for a particular purpose will require consideration of the following criteria:

- Number and location of people who will use it;
- Ease and speed of access;
- Complexity and volume of information;
- Processing power required;
- Equipment cost;
- Input and output costs.

Computerized systems allow information to be held centrally, then called up by individuals on their own computers as required.

Manual systems are only accessible in one place, making them awkward for several people to use. So if the information you use is only relevant to you, a manual system will be fine. If several people use it, particularly if they are dispersed over a sizeable area, computerized systems will be more efficient.

Ease of access and complexity are linked. A simple piece of data or information (like a train time you have recorded to save you remembering it) will usually be quicker to check from a piece of paper than if you have to call it up on the computer screen. However, if you need lengthy or complicated information, it should be easier to access from a computer memory, because the computer will help you find it. Which brings us to our next point.

Manual systems are static. They hold the information. You do the job. Computerized systems are usually embedded in equipment which will do processing jobs for you, like analysis, calculations and formatting.

Equipment cost is an obvious consideration. A pocket diary is cheaper than a desk-top computer! Of course the cost should not be seen in isolation but treated as one factor in a more complex set of criteria.

Input and output costs relate to time, equipment and accuracy. Sending an e-mail to a colleague notifying them of the date, time and venue of a meeting may be a better use of time than making a mental note that you must remember to tell them about the meeting next time you pass their desk.

Manual systems include:

- Card indexes;
- Personal notes;
- Directories;
- Catalogues;
- Files.

221

They may contain:

- Telephone numbers;
- Invoices;
- Payment records;
- Personnel records;
- Product specifications.

Computerized information systems have a range of functions that can contribute to the overall operation of an organization. The technological advances continue to impact on industry sectors in different ways. The following list gives some examples:

Retail – EPOS (electronic point-of-sale) systems/terminals ensure speedier customer checkout, monitor sales and many are now linked to suppliers to ensure stocks are replenished.

Manufacturing – CAD (computer aided design) can be linked to manufacturing processes to improve product time to market. EDI (electronic data interchange) enables speedier and more accurate exchange of data between customers and suppliers.

Financial services – online and Internet banking has revolutionized the way customers can access accounts, financial information and services from the High Street banks and financial institutions.

Storage devices

These are all ways of recording and holding data or information. Technological development is constantly increasing the choice but the most commonly used at the moment are:

Hard disks

These are integral to all personal computers. They store both program files and master files. Despite the increase in hard disk capacity, they should be seen primarily as working disks because when hard disks are nearly full, the computer's processing speed declines seriously.

Floppy disks

Used to input program files and transaction files and also to store updated master files.

Magnetic tape

Now mainly in the form of high speed 'tape streamers' which are used as backup storage for large amounts of data held on hard disk. Their advantage is capacity but their drawback is the need to wind or rewind extensively to find the data you are seeking.

Optical media

CD-ROMs and DVD (Digital Versatile Discs) are high capacity; until recently these were read only devices which meant that they could not be changed. However, recordable CD is now becoming much more available and affordable.

Insight

Graham is a freelance consultant, close to retirement, who runs public speaking training courses for a living. His courses have remained largely unchanged for many years and he has a dozen regular and satisfied clients. He has deliberately avoided any interest in or understanding of computers. His friend, Christine, is the computer manager of a major accountancy firm. She has been trying for a long time to persuade Graham to abandon his manual records in favour of a computer-based system, but without success.

Why do you think Christine's experience leads her to favour computers?

Would you recommend that Graham should take her advice or not?

Christine's employers process large amounts of data frequently and regularly. They also need to keep abreast of frequent changes in accounting law and have many clients and many employees. The volume and complexity of data and the need for many staff to access central information are sound justifications for a computerized system.

Graham on the other hand uses information (in the form of hand-outs) which rarely change. He has relatively few clients and his invoicing and accounting are likely to be simple. If he switches to a computer based system it will take him time to learn, he is likely to make many errors so the cost of learning and equipment, and the aggravation involved do not seem justified.

Information security

There is a significant need for security in the case of information systems. Effective security is necessary to ensure:

- Confidentiality (particularly related to personnel records and customers' financial details);
- Accuracy (information is not useful if it is not reliable);
- Avoidance of loss (think of the results if you lost all of next week's work schedules).

In the case of computerized systems, there is a further need to avoid:

- Hacking (unauthorized tampering with records or programs, normally from a distance, over a telephone line from another computer).
- Viruses (instructions fed into files or programs which corrupt the data stored on them. These normally enter the system from disks which are themselves infected).

Four techniques will reduce the risk of security breaches in both types of system:

1 Restriction of access

For both systems this involves the provision of physical security:

- Locks on doors and remembering to use them;
- Limiting access to authorized people with passes;
- Entry detectors and alarms;
- Locks on filing cabinets, desks and computers;
- Insisting that all records are securely stored when workstations are unattended.

For computer access, we can add:

- Use of passwords and entry codes;
- Separate passwords and access codes to enter confidential files or change data.

2 Division of labour

For both types of system, this involves:

- Having work checked by someone else before it is confirmed;
- Having discrete elements of confidential work done by different people;
- Ensuring that the person authorized to commission work is not also allowed to authorize payment (to avoid loss in the form of fraud).

For computer systems, a related technique is to include validation checks into the programs.

3 Staff relationships

Staff loyalty and competence reduces the risk. These can be enhanced by careful selection, relevant training and suitable reward.

4 Back up

Relevant mainly to the avoidance of loss, backing up computer files by downloading data into a separate storage device is common practice. It is less common with manual systems, although it is worth noting that government departments insist that there should be both a working copy and a file copy of every document.

Before leaving the subject of information security, we should look briefly at a relevant piece of legislation, the UK's Data Protection Act, 1998.

The Act was passed to protect individuals who had data or information about them stored on computer. It requires organizations which keep such records to register with the Data Protection

Register. Under the Act, processing personal data must comply with the eight enforceable principles of good practice, data must be:

- Fairly and lawfully processed;
- Processed for limited purposes;
- Adequate, relevant and not excessive;
- Accurate;
- Not kept longer than necessary;
- Processed in accordance with the data subject's rights;
- Secure;
- Not transferred to countries without adequate protection.

Processing information

We made a brief reference earlier to IT applications. There is a huge variety of programs, capable of undertaking various tasks.

Some programs have a less specific use and are packaged together for general business use. They are known as general purpose software.

We will be familiar to some extent, with the following types of general purpose software:

Word-processing

A word-processing package produces a similar output to a conventional typewriter. However, it offers these additional benefits:

- The ability to erase, insert and move text around the document without re-typing the whole thing.
- The chance to experiment with type-sizes and type-faces and to use a wide variety of them in the same document.
- Spelling and grammar checks.
- The opportunity to incorporate diagrams and other graphics.
- A colour printing facility.

Databases

A database is a collection of individual files, each organized in the same way. A file is made up of a number of blocks of data, each known as a 'field'. So far, it is very similar to a manual card index system.

However, a database has several advantages over its manual equivalent:

- Individual fields can be changed or updated without the need to copy the rest.
- A central database can be accessed and worked on by different people in different places.
- It is possible to sort records on the basis of one or more fields (for example, all hospital patients between the ages of 25 and 40 who have attended casualty with a broken arm in the last year).
- Records can be arranged or rearranged in any order the user chooses.
- A single record can be traced even if you only know the content of a couple of fields (for example, if you know the road but not the number, you could ask for all customers in that road; of course knowing the name as well would speed up the process).
- A database can be combined with a word-processing package to produce individualized letters automatically.

Spreadsheets

A spreadsheet is a table, made up of rows and columns. Where a row and a column meet is called a 'cell'. They are used mainly to perform 'what if' calculations which they do after they have been instructed to apply given formulae between cells. Look at the example in the next Case Study.

Case Study

> The street lighting department of Coalville Local Authority has been told to cut its wage costs. It currently has five staff, who change on average 20 light bulbs a week. It is forecast that, next year, 4,000 bulbs will need changing.

Calculate how many light bulbs a week each worker will need to change if the team is reduced to four.

The calculation is relatively easy on a calculator: we make the answer 22 on the basis of 46 working weeks a year.

A spreadsheet though with the relevant data to work on and formulae to apply would be able very quickly to calculate how much overtime would be necessary (and its cost), the annual number of bulbs which a reduced team could handle as a maximum, the effect of shortening the working week, and so on.

Desk-Top Publishing (DTP)

Using mainly a combination of sophisticated word-processing and graphics techniques, a desk-top publishing package will produce high quality masters ready for reproduction. It is worth pointing out though that the final result depends for its quality on the user having some eye for an effective layout and on reasonable copying facilities.

Transmitting information

Later in this section we shall examine in detail techniques for communicating effectively face-to-face and in writing. These are the traditional methods of transmitting information and still used most frequently.

However, the development of information and communication technology has extended the list of communication methods to include (as well as the telephone):

- the facsimile (fax) machine
- e-mail
- teleconferencing
- computer networking
- the Internet.

From this list it is important to differentiate between one-way and two-way communication. Faxes, e-mails, computer networks and the Internet are all one-way. In other words, messages can be transmitted when no-one is at the other end, stored and retrieved when the other person arrives. That is one of their major benefits but it also brings two drawbacks:

- You cannot be sure the message has been received;
- It is difficult to judge the receiver's reaction to the message.

The transmitter can receive confirmation that the message has arrived in the case of fax and e-mail, but that does not mean it has been either read or understood!

It would be wrong though to underestimate the advantages brought by electronic communication:

- The telephone reduces the delay (and to an extent the cost) of long distance communication.
- Faxes increase the speed of written communication.
- E-mail addresses the problems of distance and time difference.
- Teleconferencing eliminates travelling time.
- Computer networking improves information transfer between offices and sites and reduces the cost of shared facilities like printers or a common database.
- The Internet makes common database searching for information faster and more convenient.

Nevertheless it is interesting to note that as electronic communication has led to increasing numbers of people 'tele-commuting' (working from home but linked by electronic media), organizations have recognized the need to bring tele-commuters together regularly to enjoy the benefits of being in a group. In other words, electronic information transfer solves the practical difficulties, but does not address the human aspects of communication.

Review

Now check your understanding of this chapter by completing the following activities:

1 Data are:

Information is:

2 To be good, information must be:
(list five criteria)   T _ _ _ _ _
                                   R _ _ _ _ _ _ _
                                   A _ _ _ _ _ _ _ _
                                   C _ _ _ _ _
                                   C _ _ _ _ _

3 Internal information may be
    L _ _ _ _ , R _ _ _ _ _ , or C _ _ _ _ _ _

4 Why is effective information security necessary?

Workplace Activity

If you are currently in a management job, relate this chapter to your own experience by answering the following questions:

1 How good is the management control information you receive? How could it be improved?

2 Where would you find external information in your job?

3 What information systems do you use?

4 Are they the most suitable for the information you need? If not, how could you change them?

5 How secure is the information you use? How could information security be improved?

6 How have the advances in information technology impacted on your organization?

18 Principles of effective communication

<table>
<tr>
<td>Chapter
Objectives</td>
<td>
• What makes communication effective?
• What are the best ways of informing, persuading and influencing?
</td>
</tr>
</table>

The purpose of communication – whether in writing, face-to-face or via electronic media – is not simply to transmit information. Rather, it is to achieve a result. The desired result may take any one of a number of forms:

- An instruction to one of your team is intended to bring about action – they carry out the instruction.

- Pointing out unacceptable behaviour, perhaps as part of a disciplinary process, is intended to stop that behaviour in future.

- Congratulating your team on a job well done is intended to motivate them to continue working well.

- Management control information is intended to facilitate decisions about corrective action.

- An announcement to patients in a doctor's waiting room that the doctor is running 30 minutes late is intended to forewarn them and prevent complaints.

Of course transmitting information may not have the desired effect. To understand why not – and what to do about it – it helps to get to grips with the communications model which follows.

A communications model

The communication process involves a sender and receiver (Figure 18.1):

231

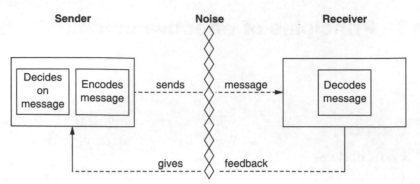

Figure 18.1

- The 'sender' is the person transmitting the information.
- The 'receiver' is the person for whom it is intended.
- The 'message' is the information itself.
- 'Encoding' is the process of translating the information in the sender's head into the message.
- 'Decoding' is the process by which the receiver interprets the message.
- 'Noise' is anything which gets in the way of the message being received and properly understood.
- 'Feedback' is confirmation that the receiver has understood the message.

The model itself is simple. However, each of the elements in it is rather more complex. Because effective communication is not a straightforward mechanical process, the most helpful way of exploring the complexities is to examine what can go wrong at each stage.

Deciding on the message

If you are not clear in your own mind what you want to communicate, you stand no chance of getting your receiver to understand it. In that situation we often fall into the trap of either leaving out important information or giving the receiver so much information that the overall message becomes confusing or incomprehensible.

Encoding the message

Receivers will have different levels of:

- Knowledge and experience;
- Language skills;
- Confidence.

If you are sending a message to a maintenance engineer to get a piece of equipment repaired, you do not need to explain how it works — the engineer will know. However, if you want an inexperienced operator to use the machine for the first time, it would be sensible to provide a basic understanding of the machine.

The basic rule about language is to keep it as simple as you can, avoiding ambiguous and emotive statements.

Direct messages will suit confident receivers. Those with less confidence may need a gentler and more reassuring tone.

You may come across the ABC of communication, indicating that a message should be:

- Accurate;
- Brief;
- Clear.

Of course, all messages should be accurate — but difficult messages may need some careful phrasing. How brief you can be will depend on how much your receiver needs to know, and what constitutes clarity will depend on things like knowledge, experience, education and language ability.

Sending the message

* See Chapter 17

In the last chapter*, we explored different ways of transmitting information. The list was not totally complete. We could have added other communication media like:

- Sign language;
- Pictures;
- Braille;
- Body language.

And the list would still be incomplete!

233

At this stage there are two important factors to consider. The first is the need to select the most suitable communication medium. Suitability will depend on:

- The purpose you want to achieve;
- Whether you need immediate feedback;
- The length and complexity of the message;
- The urgency of transmitting the information;
- The urgency of achieving your purpose;
- Who your intended receivers are;
- Where your receivers are located;
- How close your working relationships are with your receivers.

The second factor to remember is to keep your message consistent. For example:

- With face-to-face communication your words must be consistent with your body language.
- With sales literature, a message designed to impress must be presented impressively.
- An urgent message must be transmitted in a way which conveys urgency.

Insight

> Walking down the corridor, Alison notices smoke and some flames coming from under a locked cupboard door. She is the fire marshal for her floor.
>
> Alison will need to send some messages.

What will be the purpose of these messages?

Who will the receivers be?

How should she send them?

As a member of the workforce, Alison has a general duty of care to raise the alarm if she sees signs of a fire. So one purpose of her messages will be to alert all other members of staff in the building.

As fire marshal, she is responsible for ensuring that other staff on the floor follow laid-down evacuation procedures. So this will be another purpose of her messages.

They are different messages and she will send them differently. To raise the alarm, she will press the nearest alarm button to ring fire bells throughout the building.

To ensure that staff on her floor evacuate the building, she will have to make some choices and take some decisions. If she is confident that people know the procedures and will obey them, shouting 'Fire!' may be enough. If she has any doubt, she may need to visit individual offices, inform people separately and tell them what to do.

In any case, the messages are both urgent and it is equally urgent that Alison achieves her purpose. There is no way she can get feedback that everyone in the building knows about the fire, but she can get immediate feedback from people on her floor by seeing them start to move.

Noise

Messages can be distorted in many ways. For example:

- Physical distortions like conveying a verbal message in a noisy location;
- Using jargon which is not understood;
- Transmitting a message to a receiver who dislikes or resents you;
- Transmitting a difficult message to someone who rejects it entirely or receives it selectively.

Decoding the message

So far, we have concentrated on the responsibilities of the sender to get the message right and clear, and send it in a suitable and consistent way. But there is a burden of responsibility on the receiver, too. Decoding the message involves:

- Working out what the sender intended.
- Highlighting any uncertainty or confusion.
- Seeking clarification.

This brings us to the final stage of the process.

Giving feedback

All messages result in feedback. That may be surprising in view of what we said in the last chapter — about one-way and two-way communication. But then we were discussing effective communication which achieves its purpose. And from that point of view, some forms of feedback are more useful and valuable than others.

Formal or informal feedback

Formal feedback is a deliberate response to the message. It may be 'I understand and will do it now', or 'I do not know how to do that. Will you explain?'. Informal feedback involves the interpretation of unintended signals from the receiver. For example, if you ask a team member 'Are you happy about doing that?' and your receiver says 'Yes' but with gritted teeth and clenched fists, the feedback is that your message has been badly received and the task may not be done, or done badly.

Immediate or delayed feedback

As the descriptions suggest, immediate feedback may take the form of a response straight away in the case of telephone or face-to-face communication, or by return in the case of written communication. Delayed feedback may contradict a formal response, initially made after a week or two. The response may not be what was desired. If you send a message requesting action and still nothing happens even after a long period, the informal delayed feedback is 'No, I will not', 'I cannot be bothered', 'I am too busy'.

The most useful feedback is formal and immediate. It allows you to take corrective action which may take the form of further clarification or persuasion.

Delayed feedback is difficult to deal with. Your response to silence will depend on how well you know the receiver and your working relationship. You may respond by:

- Chasing for a reply;
- Stressing the urgency of your message;

- Going to someone else;
- Changing the message.

Informing, persuading and influencing

It is the human aspects of communication which make it succeed – or fail. Technically, there are some fairly simple guidelines to follow in encoding and sending a message.

- Consider who is receiving your message, e.g.
- Their knowledge and experience;
- Their level of confidence;
- Their willingness to co-operate – or not;
- Your relationship with them.

Informing people is not an end in itself. You inform to achieve a result. To achieve that result you need to understand the people involved. Nowhere is that more important than when your purpose is to change people's attitudes, opinions or actions, or to encourage them to do something which they had not thought of doing. In other words, when your purpose is to persuade or influence.

Managers are in the business of selling. Not products or services in most cases but ideas. You are selling an idea when you:

- Make a recommendation to your manager;
- Suggest improvements to your team;
- Apply for a promotion;
- Ask for overtime.

If you want people to accept – or buy – an idea, they will only do so if they can see how they will benefit from it. Benefits result from satisfying people's needs.

We examined the sorts of needs or expectations people have from work when we looked at motivation in an earlier chapter*. As far as persuading and influencing are concerned, the most relevant approach to motivation is that of Abraham Maslow, who said that people needed:

* See Chapter 6

- The basic requirements for life (food, drink and so on);

237

- Security;
- Acceptance and belonging, social contact;
- Respect and recognition;
- The opportunity for personal growth.

So when you set out to sell your ideas, whether to your team, colleagues or your manager, you should be sure you know the answers to these questions:

- What is of greatest importance to those people? What is their greatest need?
- How could my idea, suggestion or request help them to satisfy that need?
- How can my message make the link between their need and my idea?

Insight

> A rumour about large scale redundancies has been going round the organization, which has worried your team. They are specialists and concerned that finding alternative work will be difficult and take time. You want them to work unpaid overtime.

What do you see as their priority needs at the moment?

How might you persuade them to accept unpaid overtime working?

Your team are likely to be most preoccupied with their basic needs (continuing to feed themselves and their families) and with the security of their jobs. If you can present unpaid overtime as a way of making their jobs more secure and maintaining their ability to buy their basic needs, you will go a long way to gaining their acceptance.

Insight

> You know your line manager is intensely ambitious. He believes himself to be highly competent but for some reason other managers do not seem to like him very much.
>
> You want him to help you implement some new working practices for which you will need money from his budget.

238

What do you think his priority need might be?

How would you persuade him to support your recommendation?

Other managers may not like your line manager much but it does not sound as though his priority is acceptance and belonging. It is more likely that he wants respect and recognition as a first step towards personal growth in the form of a promotion.

If your recommendation makes him look good, he will probably support it.

Review

Now check your understanding of this chapter by completing the following activities:

1 Insert the relevant words into Figure 18.2 – the communications model:

2 What is the ABC of communication?

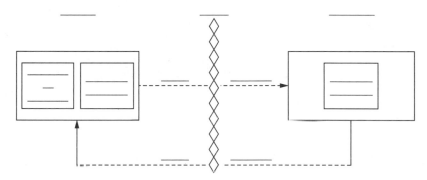

Figure 18.2

3 List five factors to consider when deciding on the suitability of a communication medium.

4 Explain the difference between formal and informal feedback.

5 What makes people buy ideas?

Workplace Activity

If you are currently in a management position, apply this chapter to your own experience by answering the following questions:

1 What are the levels of knowledge and experience, language skills and confidence of the different members of your team?

2 How will this affect the way you communicate with them?

3 How satisfied are you that you use the most suitable communications media?

4 What improvements could you make?

5 How do you obtain feedback from your team?

6 How persuasive and influential do you think your messages are? What could you do to make them more so?

19 Communicating effectively – in writing

Chapter Objectives	• *What information do others need from me?*
	• *How do I make my written communication effective?*

Most of us avoid written communication as much as we can. There are some good reasons for this:

- Talking to people is quicker;
- It requires less effort;
- We get immediate feedback about people's reactions and attitudes;
- It allows us to adapt our message according to the feedback we receive;
- We are not confident about our ability to get grammar, spelling and layout right.

Nevertheless, there are also situations where written communication is at least preferable, if not essential:

- If you want to send the same message to a large number of people.
- If, for legal reasons or to protect yourself, you need a record of your message.
- If your message is too long or complicated to send over the telephone or face-to-face.
- If it is difficult for you to make direct contact with your intended receiver.
- If you want your receiver to be able to refer several times to your message, without relying on memory.

In any of these situations your communication will be much more effective if you put it in writing.

It is also worth noting that most of the electronic media we listed in Chapter 17 involve communication in writing. The message may be transmitted electronically but its content is still the equivalent of words on paper. As a result, written communication is growing in use and importance.

Essentials of written communication

Any message should be clear, concise, complete, correct and courteous. But these are especially important in the case of written communication, particularly as messages in writing are permanent and therefore will remain, either to your credit or to haunt you. Here is what the '5Cs' mean for a written message:

Clear

Keep your language simple and suited to your audience. Avoid pompous, complicated language, just because you are writing. Use abbreviations only if appropriate.

Concise

Decide what your reader needs to know and limit your message to that. Keep sentences short. But remember that difficult or unpopular messages may need more justification.

Complete

Unnecessary information is a source of confusion and a waste of time. But without all the necessary information, a written message cannot achieve its purpose. So make sure you include all the facts, evidence and conclusions your reader needs. If this message is one of a series or part of an ongoing correspondence, remember to put it into context.

Correct

Make sure your facts are accurate, your conclusions and recommendations justified. Check your grammar and spelling, either through the relevant validation checks if you are using a word-processing package, or with a dictionary or, if you have doubts, by asking a colleague to read your draft. If your organization has a standard format for letters, memos and reports be sure you know and follow its requirements. We will suggest some formats for these three forms of written communication later in this chapter.

Courteous

This is not just a matter of good manners. People react badly to rudeness which annoys them, may damage your relationship with them and cause them to delay any response in order to pay you back.

What to put in writing

You may need or choose to put information on to paper for the following reasons:

To meet organizational requirements

In most organizations there is a formal requirement to put into writing some or all of the following:

- The minutes of meetings.
- Regular reports of achievement against objectives.
- The outcomes of performance reviews.
- Personnel attendance records.
- Purchase orders.
- Goods received.

In addition, certain written information is required by law and will therefore appear as a requirement somewhere in your organization's procedures manual. Examples are:

- Employment contracts.
- Supplier contracts.
- VAT returns.
- Tax returns.
- Accident records.
- Details of disciplinary action.

Finally, organizations which have adopted formal quality assurance systems, either their own or the relevant version of ISO 9000, will require procedures to be documented; records to be filed and accessible so that an **audit trail** can be carried out.

As a personal record

You may attend a meeting with colleagues, your team or your manager. You will hold face-to-face and telephone conversations. During them, you may give an undertaking to do something or be told something of interest. It is more reliable and easier in the long run to jot down the details on paper rather than trusting to memory.

To confirm agreement

We often discuss possibilities and reach tentative agreement with people face-to-face or over the telephone. This may concern something simple, like a hotel booking or a proposed visit. Or it may be more complex, like asking a colleague to give a presentation on a particular topic to your team. You could of course simply hope that the other party has taken their own personal records and will take the action agreed. It would be safer though to confirm details of the agreement in writing.

To promote discussion

We have already mentioned that written communication is better for long, complex messages and can be circulated more cost-effectively to several people. But it also brings the drawback of delay. All of these factors combine to make written communication, in the form of discussion papers or recommendations for change, the best way of encouraging people to think carefully about alternative solutions to difficult problems or major longterm issues.

To keep people up-to-date

We have stressed the importance of communicating only what people need to know or the information necessary to achieve your purpose. But that often goes beyond communicating just the 'bare bones' of a situation.

Insight

Louise has been authorized by her manager to take on two temporary staff because her permanent staff have fallen behind with invoice preparation. Her temporary staff are inexperienced but Louise decides she can cope with this by carefully monitoring their work. But she falls ill and is off work for a week.

A little later, the complaints start to arrive in the Customer Relations team. Some customers have been invoiced for goods not received, some discounts have been wrongly calculated.

Her manager is called in to a crisis meeting to discuss the situation. He is asked 'why has this happened?' but cannot answer the question.

What should Louise have done differently?

In an ideal world, Louise would have found experienced staff. Less ideally, she would have asked a member of her team to supervise the temporary staff while she was off sick. Neither of these may have been possible. But even in the worst situation she should have made sure that her manager knew what was happening — in writing — in view of the seriousness of the implications. Managers do not welcome surprises, particularly unpleasant ones!

The same principle applies to colleagues and team members. It is not suggested that you should pass on irrelevant information 'just in case it comes in useful'. Remember though that knowledge is power! If you have information which is likely to have implications for other people, remember to pass it on to give them greater control over their own futures and decisions.

Writing memos

You can think of a memo as an internal letter to someone else in your organization. The person you are writing to is therefore likely to have a reasonable understanding of the workings of your organization, so, of the 5Cs of communication the most important for a memo are that it should be:

Clear

So that the receiver understands what it is about; the key information you want to communicate; the response (action or decision) you are looking for. In the case of a memo, jargon is acceptable, provided you are confident that the reader is familiar with it.

Complete

Containing all the necessary, but no more than the necessary, information. Most organizations have a standard format for memos, which will help to prompt you.

Concise

Some organizations demand that memos should be no longer than a single side. Your reader should know the background, so this will help. In any case, long and wordy memos tend to be ignored. Complicated messages may be better as a report.

Standard memo formats usually require:

- Who it is to and from;
- A reference or subject heading;
- The date.

In addition, memos normally only deal with a single subject and, as with any written message, should use simple language. Short paragraphs are also better and can be broken-up with subheadings or numbered points if these make the memo easier to follow.

Writing e-mails

We discussed in Chapter 17 how the developments in information and communication technology have increased the speed and ease of communication both internally and externally for organizations. Electronic mail (e-mail) has increased our ability to communicate to a wider audience. However, the use of e-mail has created a number of problems for some organizations and will certainly haunt some individuals. The fundamental problem appears to be that people do not apply the 5Cs of communication when writing their message, particularly that of being courteous!

E-mail has been developed for ease of communication, and as it is always written the message still needs to be clear, concise, complete, correct as well as courteous.

Writing letters

Letters may be to suppliers, customers, job applicants, official bodies (government departments or trade associations) or other organizations. Most organizations also write letters to staff members on personal or confidential matters.

Writing letters may be a regular part of your job, or a rare event. In the first case, you will find it helpful to compare your standard approach with what follows. In the latter case, you may want to convert our suggestions into a checklist for future reference.

An effective letter depends on knowing the answers to three questions.

Who am I writing to?

If you know their name, use it. Write to 'Dear Mr Allen', rather than 'Dear Sir'. It is perfectly acceptable to write 'Dear Phil' if you know the person well and use their first name in conversation. The more personal you can make the letter, the better it will read.

Considering the person will also help you to use a suitable style and vocabulary. The general rule is to avoid jargon. But if the person is a long-standing contact, jargon is an acceptable way of shortening your message, provided your reader will understand it.

Why am I writing?

Is it to inform, persuade or influence? Remember the issues of needs and benefits from the last chapter.

Is this letter a response to someone else's, or the start of a correspondence intended to achieve my own purpose? If the former, include a reference to the earlier letter. If the latter, think about the content necessary to achieve your purpose.

Regardless of the situation, make some careful decisions about the information your reader will need and make sure you have all of it.

How should the message be presented?

When you have the necessary information, arrange it in a logical order. The first paragraph should explain the purpose, background or context. The middle paragraphs should contain the relevant facts, justifications or arguments, again arranged logically. The final paragraph should set out the desired action or response.

As with memos, ensure your letter conforms to your organization's standard layout (position of receiver's name and address; date and reference; spacing and margins; headings, subheadings and paragraph numbers; and so on).

Finally, remember your purpose. If you are writing to persuade or influence, you may be able to include sales literature; put the letter into a folder with supporting documents; arrange special binding. If you are writing to inform (perhaps about delivery schedules or changes to procedures), you may need to include charts, instructions or other enclosures.

Armed with the answers to these questions, you can then draft your letter. Remember to:

- Include a reference or subject heading;
- Keep the letter as concise and courteous as you can;
- Use subheadings or paragraph numbering if these are consistent with your organization's standard layout and will improve clarity;
- Check that the content is correct.

Writing reports

Reports are written:

- To provide a comprehensive survey of external events;
- To provide a comprehensive survey of internal developments or performance;
- As a basis for consultation;
- As a basis for discussion.

By definition therefore reports are long, contain a lot of information and present major challenges related to structure and organization.

That introduction is not meant to put you off. Instead, it is intended as a warning that writing reports demands time, effort and discipline. But it can be made a lot easier if you follow a standard routine. Again, the creation of an effective report starts with answering some fundamental questions. You should not be surprised that these are similar to those which relate to writing an effective letter.

What is the purpose of the report?

As with a letter, a report may be intended to inform, persuade or influence. A report to inform will emphasize facts and evidence. A report to persuade or influence will emphasize justifications and benefits. In the latter case, the more revolutionary the report's proposals are the better the justifications will need to be.

Who will read the report?

This question takes us back to the issue of individual needs, again linked to the purpose of the report. A regular report, like one on team achievement or a management update, can be relatively short and is likely to consist of facts and figures with a brief commentary. Its readers will have seen previous reports of the same kind and, bluntly, will not pay it a great deal of attention. A one-off report on the other hand is likely to address a significant issue. It may well be controversial and the subject may be unfamiliar to its readers. A report of this kind will require far more background, explanation and, probably, evidence from external sources.

Guidelines for report presentation

In case your organization has no standard format for reports, the following structure provides a useful starting point, based on an analysis of what is logical from the reader's viewpoint.

Title page

Obvious but necessary! If your readers receive lots of reports, they want to be able to find the relevant one without difficulty.

Contents page

Helps readers find their way around the report quickly and without a struggle. Long reports may need individual sections to be subdivided. Remember to include page numbers.

Summary

It is preferable to put the summary right at the front. But write it last otherwise you will not know what you are summarizing. This will allow very busy readers to get an idea of what your report says, without having to read all the justification.

Introduction

Explains the purpose of the report and how the information contained in it was collected.

Main body

The evidence of the report, limited to facts and figures. Avoid interpretation or conclusions. These come later and will be suspect and unjustified before all the evidence is available.

Break the main body up by using headings and numbering to make the report easier to follow and more user-friendly.

Conclusions

Must be based on the evidence. Avoid the temptation to slip in conclusions which are unsupported. And readers who notice will doubt the rest of the conclusions. May be combined with recommendations in a shorter report.

Recommendations

Must be justified by your conclusions. Should specify a logical series of actions arising from the situation described in the report. Use the SMART (see page 148) principle when formulating your recommendations.

Appendices or annexes

Mainly source materials (internal or external) which provide the basis for the main body of the report. Add these at the end to avoid making the main body too dense or muddled for the reader to grasp easily.

Assembling your report

Here is a step-by-step approach to writing a report which will meet your readers' needs and achieve your purpose:

1 Be sure about the purpose

This will usually be based on a brief from a more senior manager. Be certain you know what your manager wants and, if you have doubts, ask for clarification. Your manager may expect the report to result in particular conclusions and recommendations. If your research indicates these are unfounded, seek guidance from your manager before finalizing the report.

2 Identify relevant evidence

This may be from internal or external sources. It may be current or historical. It may include facts, attitudes or opinions. You may need to ask around to find it. Make sure you can quote the sources and include them in your appendices.

3 Organize the evidence

Analyse your evidence to establish a shortlist of main themes. Arrange it logically, bringing together evidence which belongs under each of these themes.

4 Draw your conclusions

You or your manager may be hoping the evidence leads to certain conclusions. You will need to ensure your conclusions are justified.

5 Decide on recommendations

These need to be practical. When making your recommendations, ensure that the organization has the budget, resources and flexibility to deliver them.

6 Write your summary

By definition, a summary is short. Never more than one page, preferably less. Highlight the main points of your report but leave the rest of the report to fill in the detail.

7 Check the content

Ensure that the report meets its intended purpose; the evidence supports the conclusions; the recommendations are practical; the content is presented in a logical order; the structure meets your organization's requirements; the grammar and spelling are accurate.

Review

Now check your understanding of this chapter by completing the following activities:

1 List five situations where written communication is the preferable form.

2 What do the '5Cs of communication' stand for?

3 What are the main points to consider when constructing a letter?

Workplace Activity

If you are currently in a management position, relate this chapter to your own experiences by answering the following questions:

1 Which of the following do you write:

Memos?

Letters?

Reports?

2 Which give you most difficulty and why?

3 Does your organization have standard formats for memos, letters and reports?

If so, where would you find them?

4 How could you improve the letters you write?

5 How could you improve the reports you write?

INTRODUCING MANAGEMENT

20 Communicating effectively – face-to-face

<table>
<tr><td>**Chapter Objectives**</td><td>● *How do I communicate effectively – face-to-face?*</td></tr>
</table>

In the previous chapter we discussed the essentials of written communication. As managers you probably spend a large percentage of your time communicating with people on a face-to-face basis; this may involve your team, colleagues, other managers, customers and suppliers. In all of these circumstances you need to be able to communicate effectively. So often in the workplace a simple message can be misunderstood with disastrous consequences. Communication is a two-way process and you need to ensure that you do communicate effectively, you listen actively and give constructive feedback. This chapter covers:

● Listening skills.

● Interpreting body language.

● Formal interviews with team members.

● Informal conversations with team members.

● Briefing your manager.

● Making presentations.

● Contributing to meetings.

Many of the techniques involved are common to several of these processes. However, there are differences too. We shall therefore avoid repeating common techniques, but instead concentrate on highlighting the difference.

Listening skills

'We have two ears and one mouth as a sign that we should listen twice as much as we talk'.

That may be an exaggeration but there is still a lot of truth in it! Communication is about achieving results and feedback is an important part of communication.

Consequently you should be ready to listen to:

- Suggestions from members of your team.
- Objections to your own suggestions.

Effective listening demands some self-discipline. It depends on:

- A willingness to stop talking;
- Showing interest in the other person by facial expression and body language;
- Asking questions to encourage and clarify;
- Patience, particularly in face of hesitant or inarticulate speakers;
- Avoidance of prejudice; your least capable staff member may still have points worth listening to.

Questions to encourage and clarify are a topic in themselves as shown in the case study.

Case Study

> Sandra has suggested that Khalid tackle a task differently. Khalid objects.
>
> Sandra could respond with:
>
> (a) 'So you're rejecting my idea, are you?'
>
> (b) 'Why don't you think it will work?'
>
> (c) 'How else could we speed up the job?'

Which of these three responses would you recommend.

The first is not encouraging. It is aggressive and likely to lead to a yes-or-no answer.

The second may lead to further discussion of possible improvements. But as it stands, it sounds defensive and challenging.

254

The third is the most likely to lead to a productive exchange of ideas, because it is neutral and actively seeking suggestions.

Interpreting body language

Research reported by Michael Argyle indicated that the messages we send to other people can be demonstrated as in Figure 20.1.

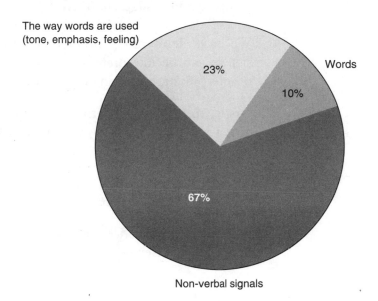

Figure 20.1

In the West, people are trained and expected to pay most attention to words and their meaning. As Figure 20.1 shows, that means missing two-thirds of the messages others send to us.

There are three aspects to body language.

Space

People standing very close may be seeking to dominate — try not to invade the personal space of others, it can be very intimidating.

Posture and gesture

Folded arms may indicate anger or defensiveness. But they may also reflect that the individual is cold.

A shrug of the shoulders may indicate ignorance or lack of interest.

Looking at the ground may indicate shyness, discomfort or lack of attention.

Nods generally indicate agreement.

Smiles offer encouragement. Frowns may indicate disagreement or careful attention.

Eye contact suggests interest.

We have deliberately pointed out that individual non-verbal signals can be interpreted in a variety of ways. The two secrets of interpreting body language successfully are:

Firstly, to look for patterns of non-verbal signals. Several signals giving the same message are trustworthy. Individual signals are not.

Secondly, to recognize that different cultures use non-verbal signals to convey different messages.

In America and the UK, putting your thumb up is a positive sign of approval. Elsewhere, its meaning is very different!

Formal interviews with team members

Formal interviews with your team members will be for the purpose of:

- Task briefing;
- Performance reviews;
- Discipline.

There are, of course, significant differences between those three purposes but the basic interview structure remains the same.

The interview process has three stages:

- Before the interview;
- During the interview;
- After the interview.

Before the interview

As preparation, you should:

- Decide what you want from the interview and how relaxed it should be;
- Work out how long it needs to last in order to achieve your objective;
- Assemble the necessary information and any relevant paper-work;
- Plan the interview itself; the sequence in which you will cover points; when you will talk and when you will ask questions; what you will say and the questions you will ask;
- Book and arrange the room.

The standard points about the need for privacy, avoiding distractions and interruptions apply. How you arrange the room will depend on whether it is to be a relaxed exchange of views (when comfortable chairs and no barriers between you and your team member will be most effective) or whether, as in the case of a disciplinary interview, you want to create a more formal environment.

During the interview

There are three stages to the interview itself. Opening the interview will involve setting the scene and explaining its objective and structure. To create a relaxed atmosphere the opening stage should be friendly and start with a general chat. In a more authoritarian interview, it is better to get straight down to the matter in hand.

The main part of the interview should follow a logical sequence and combine statements, questions and, obviously, listening. The balance between you and your team members' inputs to the conversation will depend on your team members' personality (confidence, experience and so on), and on the purpose of the interview. As we suggested earlier, asking questions and encouraging your team members to talk is essential to effective communication. But, typically, task briefings will make you the main speaker; performance reviews should involve most input from your team members; and disciplinary interviews fit somewhere in the middle. Remember to:

257

- Maintain control by asking relevant questions to bring your team members back to your agenda.

- Use body language which is consistent with your message and the purpose of the interview.

- Manage the time.

Closing the interview will involve summarizing what has been discussed and confirming the actions you and your team members will take, usually with objectives and deadlines. Remember to take notes and to inform your own manager of any aspect of the interview he or she needs to know about.

After the interview

Complete any relevant paperwork. Take any action you have agreed during the interview. Monitor your team members' action and performance.

Informal conversations with team members

By definition, the content of informal conversations is difficult to predict, particularly if they are initiated by your team members. If a team member says to you:

'Can I have a word?', or

'Have you heard about . . .?', or

'Do you know what's happening with . . .?' you cannot be sure what will come next. When that happens, try to establish what your team member wants to discuss. Then make a judgement as to whether you have the necessary information to deal with the subject. If you do not, give yourself some research or thinking time. Arrange a later time to meet, or simply reply along the lines of:

'I'm a bit tied up at the moment, can I come back to you in an hour or so?' But remember to honour the arrangement or the promise and use the time to get your information or ideas together.

Informal conversations you initiate yourself are rather easier to prepare for. They are essential parts of:

- management by walking about;

- checking on morale;
- monitoring progress;
- identifying individual needs and motivation;
- knowing and gaining the respect of your team.

Since any communication has a purpose, it helps to work out a series of provisional questions to which you want answers or the information you want to send. The conversation may not go quite as you planned, but the preparation you have done will give you some structure to follow and help to ensure that you achieve your objective

Case Study

> Ahmed has arrived early at the school where he works as Head of Physics, in order to prepare a lesson for later in the day. He is in the laboratory checking that the necessary equipment is available when Shirley, the part-time laboratory assistant, comes in. She asks:
>
> 'Can you spare a moment? I wanted a chat.'
>
> Ahmed replies: 'I really want to finish this first. But could you come back to see me here at break-time? What did you want to discuss?'
>
> Shirley explains that she wants to talk about her future.

What preparation should Ahmed do before their conversation?

A discussion about Shirley's future could deal with any one of a wide range of topics. She may want to discuss:

The possibility of working full-time.

Any promotions going.

Taking up another job elsewhere.

Leaving work to start a family.

Ahmed can prepare for the conversation firstly by thinking back to see if Shirley has said anything recently to indicate what she might want to talk about; secondly, by looking through her personnel record – appraisal history, family situation, qualifications, any reference to career plans and so on. Depending on the outcome of the first two stages, he may want to:

MANAGING INFORMATION

- Check any forthcoming vacancies in his department or in any other school.
- Prepare some thoughts on Shirley's promotion prospects, based on her performance, qualifications and experience.
- Check the school's maternity provision.

Of course, Shirley may want to discuss a totally different aspect of her future. So Ahmed will need to ask questions to find out at the beginning of the conversation. But he has now researched a lot of the possible topics and is less likely to be caught out by the unexpected.

Briefing your manager

You may need to brief your manager:

- as part of a formal review of your own performance;
- to provide an update on your team's performance;
- to get ideas and suggestions for future improvements or to solve a problem.

To give an effective briefing, you will need to bring together techniques we have covered in various places elsewhere in this book. We can summarize these techniques in the form of four questions:

1 What do I want from this briefing?

Start by establishing your own purpose. To inform, persuade or influence? To gain promotion, development or a pay increase? To give a positive impression of your team? To make changes or improvements? To solve a problem? To provide an update?

2 What does my manager want from this briefing?

In some situations, your manager will want a quick, brief, factual summary. In others, your manager will expect a longer explanation of ideas, opinions and attitudes. It is likely to be ineffective if you go into a briefing with objectives which are widely different from those of your manager. As far as possible, try to ensure that:

- You raise the issues you want to discuss at a time when your manager is prepared to deal with them.

- The briefing is long enough to do them justice.
- Your manager knows the issues and can prepare for them.
- You know your manager's expectations from a particular briefing.
- You match your objectives to those expectations.

3 What information does my manager need?

In the case of regular progress updates or reviews of performance against targets, your manager is likely to be content with a concise statement of facts and figures, with a brief explanation of problem areas and your plans to resolve them. But remember that managers do not welcome surprises, so make sure your information is also complete and correct.

If your objectives for the briefing are more far-reaching (gaining permission or seeking development opportunities, for example), you will need to give thought to the benefits these will bring for your manager.

If you are presenting ideas or opinions, remember that they should be justified by evidence as well as the anticipated benefits.

4 How should I present the information?

Face-to-face communication is often better if supported by written backup. Indeed, your organization may require regular performance updates in writing. Even if it does not, facts and figures are easier to understand and remember if they are presented in the form of tables, charts, graphs or diagrams. Your briefing will then be limited to explanation and discussion of the documents in front of you both.

Proposals for change need time to consider. So prepare a discussion paper and let your manager have it in advance, so that the briefing can then focus on the implications of your suggestions and possible alternatives to them.

Making presentations

Increasingly organizations are requiring staff to make formal presentations. These may, for example, take the form of briefings or be part of the selection process. Many managers find this a daunting process. Nevertheless, both the fear and the risk of failure can be reduced by careful planning and following some simple steps. These are:

- Decide the purpose.
- Decide the content.
- Plan the structure.
- Make notes.
- Prepare support materials.
- Practise your presentation.
- Observe the audience.

Decide the purpose

The first step is to decide what you want to achieve from your presentation. Decide on your objectives. For example, is your presentation simply giving information or are you trying to sell an idea?

Decide the content

Work out what you will need to say in order to achieve your purpose. A factual briefing will be limited to 'must knows'. A persuasive briefing may include 'should knows' and 'could knows'.

Plan the structure

Arrange your content into a logical sequence. Guidelines for a structure are:

Tell them:

what you are going to tell them. This is the introduction which should be a bullet-point summary of your content, with a statement of the objective of the presentation.

Tell them:

the main body of the briefing, presenting your content in a logical order. You may decide to encourage discussion from your audience as you go along, but do not allow them to digress too far.

Tell them:

what you have told them. A reminder of your content (we tend to remember most clearly the last thing we heard). Make your conclusion positive and definite. Stress benefits and give your presentation a clearly recognizable finish.

Make notes

Limit your notes to headings and bullet-points. Write them in capitals so you can read them easily, or cards which will be less obvious and distracting. Avoid writing your briefing out in full and then reading it word for word! However, you will be most nervous at the start, so write out your introductory sentence in full – and also write in full any points, facts or figures you need to quote exactly. You may find it useful to use colours to highlight points and to record cross-references to support materials.

Prepare support materials

These may be handouts or fact-sheets you want to distribute after the presentation. Or visual aids in the form of overhead projector acetates, prepared flipcharts or a Powerpoint presentation. Make sure that visual aids are big and clear. And remember when using handouts that people will expect to read them when you give them out so give them at the end of your presentation otherwise they will read the handout and not listen to your presentation.

Practice your presentation

Some speakers will rehearse in front of a mirror, others will use a tape recorder. Make sure you know how to use any equipment like an overhead projector. Listen to your own words – do any sound clumsy or unclear? Check your timing – but bear in mind that questions and discussions will always make your actual briefing longer than your rehearsal.

Observe the audience

When giving your briefing, maintain eye contact. Watch body language to judge reaction and understanding. Remember, too, to match your facial expression and gestures to the objectives you want to achieve. Show enthusiasm and smile. Use hand gestures to clarify and emphasize points. Avoid the temptation to

263

fiddle with papers, a pen, jewellery or change in your pocket. Any of these will distract and your message will be lost.

> You are preparing to make a formal presentation to your team on next month's output targets. They are higher than last month's, which your team struggled to meet, although they succeeded.

What objectives will you want your presentation to achieve?

What content will you include to achieve them?

You need to communicate the targets, but will also need to encourage your team and convince them that the targets are achievable. The briefing will need to include a factual statement of the targets but you would be well-advised to present an analysis of your team's performance against past targets (assuming that they have had a past history of success in meeting them) and convincing evidence that the new targets are not excessively higher than those they have already met (if this is the case). If you have any encouraging news about, for example, extra staff or other resources, you should of course include that as well.

Effective meetings

You may have seen a sign something like this one pinned up on an office wall:

Fed up with being on your own?

Want to avoid making decisions?

Need a break from work?

Attend a meeting!

You may have found it amusing — or too true to be funny.

Potentially, meetings have the capacity to improve:

- Team loyalty;
- Team knowledge;

- Planning;
- Problem-solving;
- Decision-making;
- Team commitment;

but only if all those who participate understand and fulfil their roles, and the meeting is effective and productive.

Meetings can be an extremely effective way of exchanging information but they also have the potential to be time-consuming, unnecessary and unproductive. So when planning a meeting ask yourself the following questions:

Is this meeting really necessary?

What would be the outcome if the meeting were not held?

Once you are satisfied that the meeting is necessary then plan for it by deciding who should attend, when and where it should take place, give notification and prepare an agenda.

Of course you are likely to be involved in both formal and informal meetings. Formal meetings tend to be called in advance, follow formal procedures, are structured with an agenda, require decisions to be taken and actions agreed. Minutes of the meeting record the discussions and the agreed actions.

Informal meetings are as the word suggests less formal; they may take place in the canteen, a corridor, an office. As they are often spontaneous it is unlikely that there would be an agenda or minutes but you may decide to compile action notes following the discussion.

Contributing to meetings

It is likely that you undertake a variety of roles in different meetings. In your team meetings you will have the role of chair; you may be a participant in senior management meetings; you may have the role of secretary/note-taker in committee meetings. Whatever the role, it is about taking responsibility for how the meeting performs and the results achieved. This means sharing responsibility for any actions taken, being co-operative with other members of the meeting and having common goals.

We can now look at the role of participant, secretary and chair in turn.

The role of participant

Participants should be called to meetings because they have relevant knowledge, skills or experience to contribute. These may not be directly related to the topics on the agenda, but the chair has decided that they could be relevant and valuable.

In consequence, participants should prepare for a meeting by:

- Studying the agenda and identifying the topics to which they could contribute.

- Carrying out any necessary preparatory reading (including background papers enclosed with the agenda) and research to assemble the information related to those topics.

- Of course arriving on time contributes to the effectiveness of the meeting. In fact, some minutes now list members' arrival times, so that late-comers can be identified.

During the meeting, participants should:

- Ensure that they contribute relevant knowledge and experience;

- Express support for a disagreement with others' points, but objectively and with justification;

- Avoid irrelevant points and going off on a tangent;

- Take note of actions they have agreed to carry out.

After the meeting, participants should:

- Take the actions they have agreed at the meeting, without waiting for the minutes which might be late.

The role of the secretary

In some places, the role of the secretary is limited to the task of taking minutes. However, the role can be made more satisfying and more productive by extending it to include:

- Consulting with the chair to agree the content of the agenda, then preparing it and sending it out;

266

- Booking the location;
- Notifying members of the date, time and location of the meeting;
- Taking apologies for absence;
- Arranging the room – seating plans, notepads, refreshments and so on;
- Supporting the chair by monitoring time and checking all agenda items have been fully covered;
- Clarifying actions agreed;
- Drafting minutes and checking them with the chair for accuracy and completeness;
- Circulating minutes;
- Following up actions, if asked to do so by the chair.

Chairing meetings

In the main, the meetings you chair are likely to be informal meetings of your team. Nevertheless, like most other forms of communication, they will need a clear purpose and a structure. They should result in actions and involve feedback from the participants.

To meet all these criteria, the chair should:

Decide on the objectives the meeting is to achieve

This could be a single objective, or different ones for each item on the agenda. Some items may be for information only, others will need discussion and agreement of actions to be taken.

Design the structure

Basically, this means organizing the agenda. If the meeting is intended to make decisions on related issues, make sure the items are in a logical sequence so that a decision is taken before issues which depend on its outcome are taken.

Decide who should attend

To be cost-effective, meetings should only involve people who have a relevant contribution to make. Equally, make sure you include everyone who can affect the decisions to be taken and the resulting actions.

Manage the time

Start on time. Discourage unproductive discussions. Spend less time on unimportant topics than on the key issues (some agendas specify how long will be spent on individual items).

Open the meeting by explaining its purpose, rules and anticipated finishing time.

Involve everyone

Look out for any members who are not participating and bring them into the discussion.

Discourage domination

In other words, do not let those with the loudest voices or the biggest egos take over.

Control the meeting

Keep to time. Stick to the agenda. Assert your authority without overpowering the members.

Clarify, summarize and confirm

Make sure everyone understands the arguments being put forward and the actions which have been proposed. Confirm the actions finally agreed.

| **Review** | Now check your understanding of this chapter by completing the following activities: |

1 List three aspects of body language.
2 What should you do before a formal interview with a member of your staff?
3 What are the four questions you should answer when planning a briefing for your manager?

If you are currently in a management position, relate this chapter to your own experience by answering the following questions:

1 How good a listener are you?

How could you improve?

2 In what situations do you hold formal interviews with your staff?

How effective are they and what could you change to make them better?

3 How easy is it to brief your manager?

What could you do to make briefings more effective?

4 What steps do you need to take to improve your presentation skills?

5 What meetings do you attend?

How could you improve your contribution?

6 To what extent do you follow this chapter's guidelines for chairing team briefings?

What will you do differently now that you have read them?

Reference

1 Argyle, M. (1969) *Social Interactions*, Methuen: London.

Website addresses

www.iuke.co.uk
Business to business best practice exchange programme. Opportunities for benchmarking on topics including information management and technology, processes and supply chain development.

MANAGING INFORMATION

Section 5 Managing Resources

- *What financial information do I need?*
- *Why are financial accounts useful?*
- *How should I use a budget?*
- *What are the best ways of controlling costs?*
- *How do I get the best from my resources?*

MANAGING RESOURCES

271

21 Financial information and management control

Chapter Objectives	• *What financial information do I need?*

Earlier in this book we have stressed the need for managers to monitor and control the use of resources. We have also pointed out that monitoring and control are dependent on your ability to measure both inputs and outputs. Consider the situation given in the insight.

Insight

Julia is in charge of a local government department responsible for refuse collection. It is the time of year when budgets are prepared. Julia is told that, in order to improve her team's performance, she can have either a new dustcart or three additional staff.

What information will Julia need to enable her to make a decision?

Faced with a straight choice between these two alternatives, Julia will need to know how much extra output she will gain from each, so that she can choose the best.

In most situations, managers are expected to maximize output from minimal inputs. Julia therefore needs to know:

- the cost of the additional inputs such as the extra staff and the dustcart;
- the increased volume that will result from each option.

MANAGING RESOURCES

273

Then she can make a value-for-money decision. But that is only possible if Julia can measure the value of the inputs and the value of the outputs.

However, there are problems associated with giving everything a financial value. Some outputs cannot be given a financial value. How could you put a value on your firm's:

- Customer loyalty?
- Customer satisfaction?
- Staff loyalty?
- Staff morale?
- Management competence?
- Effective leadership?

We accept that these outputs are all important so how can we quantify them?

Taking customer loyalty as an example: customers cost money to attract. A business that does not retain customers must replenish its customer base in order to maintain sales. Such poor customer loyalty could be costed by calculating the money that would need to be spent to attract new business.

Looking at morale: when morale is high, staff stick around. There is no reason to leave. However when morale is low employees leave. Such staff turnover can be costed on the basis of the additional cost of advertising, filling vacancies, and training new staff.

Financial information provides us with a common measure of outputs which allows us to make decisions. As well as helping us make decisions, financial information can measure the health of an organization.

Annual financial accounts, which are dealt with in our next chapter, give a picture of what the organization owns and what it owes, whether it is trading profitably or at a loss, and its ability to continue to finance its operation.

Management accounts provide more detailed and frequent information so that managers can assess past performance early enough to take remedial action. The starting point for this process

* See Chapter 22

is the construction of budgets, which we will examine in Chapter 22*, followed by a discussion of control methods in our final chapter.

Financial information and decision-making

We explored the general principles of decision-making earlier. Here we will concentrate on the financial implications of the process, remembering of course that most results of decisions can be translated into financial values.

Financial information helps managers decide upon:

- What to do?
- How to do it?
- Whether we can afford it?

Financial information is important in decision-making, but taking decisions purely on the basis of financial data does not take into account a large range of non-financial factors.

What shall we do?

We can use financial information to help answer this question at a strategic level as it affects the organization as a whole. This will result in long-term decisions concerning products, services and markets. Or we can answer it at an operational level, resulting in short-term, day-to-day decisions.

At a strategic level, organizations need to decide:

- What markets should we operate in?
- What products or services shall we offer?

The answers to these questions will depend upon the

- Attractiveness of different markets;
- Productivity of existing and new products;
- Investment return on new products.

All of these can be quantified in financial terms.

Strategic decisions such as

- What markets should we attack?
- Which products should we produce?
- What services should we offer?

will benefit from information on:

- Size of the markets in which we currently operate. How much do all customers in our markets spend?
- The sales trend. Are our sales growing, declining or are they remaining at a constant level?
- The market share in the markets in which we operate. Are we the major provider in any of our markets or are we a small operator compared to our major rivals?
- The size of any new markets we might enter;
- Their anticipated growth;
- Whether they are dominated by a single supplier which will make entry difficult. Or whether they are served by a lot of small suppliers;
- The performance of our existing products (sales volumes, turnover, profitability);
- Their current trends and forecasted growth;
- Predicted performance of proposed new products;
- Development, launch and promotion costs;
- Investment in new equipment.

You are unlikely at this stage to be involved in decisions at a strategic level. However, it is worth recognizing the extent to which financial information lies at the heart of them.

At an operational or tactical level, you will still be involved in decisions. As we pointed out earlier, the financial information you will need to help make them will include:

- The cost of inputs;
- The value of outputs you are seeking;
- The cost of doing nothing.

The cost of inputs

Costs can be categorized according to how they change with output or time.

Fixed costs

Remain relatively unchanged regardless of whether output is going up or down. These include costs such as: rent, rates, heating, lighting.

Figure 21.1

Variable costs

Vary directly according to the level of output. These include costs such as: materials used in processes, products, commission paid to salespeople. When the business is busy, it will incur more variable costs than when it is quiet.

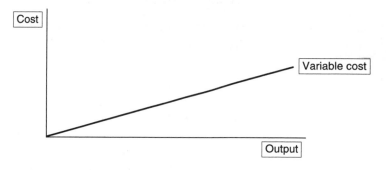

Figure 21.2

Of course no costs are truly fixed, on what basis would the following costs vary:

● Heat and light

- Electricity usage of machinery
- Production line staff?

Heat and light will vary according to the time of year. More heat will be required in the winter. This is a fixed cost as it does not vary relative to output.

Electricity usage on machinery may change as a result of more efficient use. This is classed as a fixed cost, again, because it does not vary in relation to increases or decrease in output.

Production line staff costs may not vary at all in the short run, if they are salaried. When extra staff are employed the costs will rise in a stepped fashion. This cost is a stepped cost, and has features in common with both fixed and variable costs.

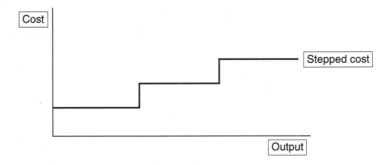

Figure 21.3

Revenue helps to pay costs

For a firm to make profit its revenue must exceed its costs. Any revenue should at least cover the variable costs of production. Any revenue received on top of this contributes to the payment of the firm's fixed costs. This 'contribution towards paying fixed costs' is a bit of a mouthful so it is shortened to 'CONTRIBUTION'. The calculation of contribution is very useful for managers.

CONTRIBUTION = sales value − variable cost

It is very useful because it can be used in break even analysis. Break even analysis identifies the output level at which the value of the outputs exactly equals the cost of the inputs, i.e. where our total costs (TC) equal our total revenue (TR).

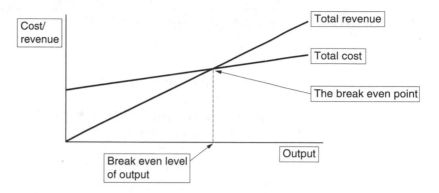

Figure 21.4   Break even chart

Insight

> Product selling price: £25
>
> Variable costs: £15
>
> Monthly fixed costs: £500

How many units of this product will need to be made and sold to break even?

Selling price of £25 − variable cost of £15 gives contribution for each unit of £10.

£500 fixed costs divided by unit contribution of £10 gives a break even point of 50.

We can therefore deduce that if we sell less than 50 units we shall make a loss; and that if we sell more than 50 units we shall make a profit. Break even is very helpful when deciding a price for a product or order. Indeed it can help to decide whether to accept an order at all.

If output volumes have not yet reached break even point, any orders will be welcome, at any price provided it makes some 'contribution' to the payment of fixed costs.

Operating above break even point but below full capacity allows you more flexibility. As a result of your fixed costs being covered, you can choose to price an order with nil contribution if necessary. Alternatively you can choose to maximize contribution on orders. This decision may well rest upon how other customers might react if you offered a new customer a special deal.

MANAGING RESOURCES

Selling price: £25

Variable costs: £15

Monthly fixed costs: £500

You are currently producing 150 units a month and have the capacity to increase this to 180 units.

A new customer wants to order this product at £23 and take 20 units a month.

- Your current profit is

  Total revenue − Total Costs = Profit

  Total revenue − (Variable Costs + Fixed Costs) =

  (£25 × 150) − [(£15 × 150) + £500] = £1,000.

This can be calculated in a much quicker way if we use contribution

Total contribution − Fixed Costs = Profit
(Contribution per unit × output) − Fixed Costs = Profit

(£10 × 150) − £500 = £1,000.

The new customer's order would increase your total output to 170 units which is still within your capacity. But each extra unit's contribution towards fixed costs would fall to £8 (Selling price of £23 minus − £15 variable costs). That is not a big problem. The original 150 units are still contributing £10 each to fixed costs and as long as your original customers don't find out about this new order you won't have to adjust your original price.

Total contribution would then be

For the first 150 units: £10 × 150 plus

For the special order of an extra 20 units: £8 × 20

= £1,500 + £160

= £1,660

Taking away your £500 fixed costs would then result in an increased profit of £1,160.

However, what would happen to your profit if ALL your customers demanded the product at £23?

(Contribution per unit × output) Fixed Costs = Profit
(£8 × 170) − £500 = £860.

The critical factor which affects your ability to vary prices, is whether your current customers are in a postion to find out what prices you charge to your other customers. If they are likely to find out, it is unwise to offer discounts on new or special orders.

This all has most relevance in that you can price yourself more competitively if you have exceeded your break even point, because you need only cover your variable costs in order to increase profit!

Of course, if you are already producing at full capacity, the only way of increasing output would be by adding extra resources, which would result in a stepped-increase in fixed costs.

Break even is also useful when making decisions about whether the best way to tackle a situation is to do nothing.

How shall we do it?

Different actions will require different inputs and create different outputs. The inputs can be costed and outputs forecasted to determine the most cost-effective or profitable solution.

This question again has relevance at both strategic and operational levels. At a strategic level, the decision will depend upon what resources are required and how much will they cost?

How much investment will be needed and where the money will come from? How long it will take to recover the investment. How risky is this course of action?

All of these factors can be quantified, although the third and fourth will be subject to varying levels of uncertainty.

Investment appraisal helps when we are comparing alternative methods of delivering strategic objectives. There are three main forms of investment appraisal.

281

The payback period

This method measures how long it will take to pay back the initial investment cost with revenue i.e. for revenue to equal investment.

You have the option of investing in two possible ventures. Selling beer and selling cigarettes at your social club. You have conducted research and forecast the following revenues and necessary investment.

	Cigarettes	Beer
Initial investment	(10,000)	(20,000)
Yr 1 cash	4,000	9,000
Yr 2 cash	5,000	9,000
Yr 3 cash	5,000	12,000
Yr 4 cash	4,000	10,000

How long does it take to repay your investment on each?

Cigarettes pay back the £10,000 investment after 3 years as does beer.

What are the problems with this form of calculation?

The problems here are that we cannot see which gives us the best return on our investment. All payback does, is give us a time-scale of how quickly the investment gives us a return.

The average rate of return

This takes the predicted life of the investment and calculates the average annual percentage return on the investment over its whole life. Let us take our earlier example again to see which is best:

	Cigarettes	Beer
Initial investment	(10,000)	(20,000)
Yr 1 revenue	4,000	9,000
Yr 2 revenue	5,000	9,000
Yr 3 revenue	5,000	12,000

	Cigarettes	Beer
Yr 4 revenue	4,000	10,000
Total revenue	18,000	40,000
4 yr profit	8,000	20,000
Average yearly profit	2,000	5,000
As a percentage of our investment		
ARR	20%	25%

Therefore **beer** is better, because it gives a better average return.

Net present value

This method of investment appraisal is calculated in the same way as average rate of return but recognizes that money received in the future will have reduced value at today's prices as a result of inflation. Therefore future revenues are discounted.

These methods are strategic in nature and, at an operational level, your role in deciding on investment decisions is more likely to be based upon knowing:

How much spare capacity you have?

What the cost of increasing capacity would be?

What additional resources would alternative decisions require?

Are they available and how much would they cost?

Which of these various alternative actions would address the situation most cost-effectively?

In an ideal world, extra capacity and additional resources would be freely available – though at a price. In the real world however some resources are fixed, and therefore limited. They cannot be increased, either because no more are available or because your organization has, for example, put a block on capital spending.

In these situations you have three choices. You can:

Buy in from elsewhere.

Choose your action on the basis of resource limitations.

Make a deliberate choice to do nothing because the necessary resources are not available.

The following are brief comments on these three alternatives.

Buying in from elsewhere (often known as the 'make or buy' decision) gives you access to:

Resources you need on a short-term basis, like temporary staff, consultancy support or extra transport.

Top-up inputs at busy times. These are acceptable, provided that their cost does not change a profitable product or service into a loss-maker.

An alternative to in-house delivery. Many organizations are following the advice of Peters and Waterman that they should 'stick to the knitting'. In other words, do only those things they are good at doing. However, the risk of that approach is that it may make redundant in-house facilities which cannot be eliminated.

Case Study

> Leander Construction is a small housing developer. For many years, it made its own window and door frames, before recognizing that its main expertise lay in building houses rather than woodwork. As a result, it closed down the woodworking facility, made staff redundant and sold the machines. However, it still has the workshop on a long lease, which it cannot terminate before it expires. The workshop rental costs £100,000 per year.
>
> It buys in windows and doors from a specialist firm at £100 per unit and purchases 2,000 each year.

What is the time cost of each unit? i.e. what is the real cost of buying in each window when we still have to pay for the lease of the workshop?

To calculate the time cost of each unit, we need to take account of the cost of the redundant in-house workshop. The annual workshop rental of £100,000 should be spread over the 2,000 units bought each year. As a result, the time cost of each unit is:

$$£100 + \left(\frac{£100,000}{2,000} \right) = £150$$

Choosing your action according to resource limitations involves identifying the 'limiting factor'. This may be:

Equipment;

Raw materials;

Staff availability;

Expertise.

Insight

> Tom is production supervisor for a firm making printed packaging. He has received an urgent order for a simple two-colour job and has two machines which are capable of producing it.
>
> It is 10 o'clock in the morning. The job has to be completed by 4 o'clock this afternoon. The job requires 6,000 printing impressions. Machine A is capable of a maximum of 1,000 impressions per hour. Machine B can deliver 1,200 impressions per hour. Machine A costs 5p per impression. Machine B, which is more up to date and offers higher quality, costs 6p per impression.

Which machine should Tom use?

The answer to this question is both quantitative and qualitative. Both machines have the capacity to complete the job in the time. However, in the case of Machine A, this will only be possible if nothing goes wrong – no snags, no need for adjustments during the print run. Machine A is only likely to be the better choice if the cost of the job makes its higher contribution necessary and if the quality specification can be achieved despite its poorer quality.

You will choose to do nothing if either:

Revenue is exceeded by your costs

or

your alternatives require resources which are not available to you.

Both can be quantified.

Can we afford it?

285

This question can be answered based on

A comparison of input costs with available budget.

An investment appraisal.

A comparison of the output value of this project with those of alternatives.

But, of course, if this is the favourite project of a senior manager or an important customer, you may need to take account of qualitative considerations as well!

Review

Now check your understanding of this chapter by completing the following activities:

1 List three uses of financial information.

2 Why is financial information not a complete basis for management decisions?

3 In accounting terms, break even is the point at which
T _ _ _ _ R _ _ _ _ _ _ exactly covers T _ _ _ _
C _ _ _ _

4 The three main forms of investment appraisal are:
The P _ _ _ _ _ _ P _ _ _ _ _ _
The A _ _ _ _ _ _ R _ _ _ _ of R _ _ _ _ _
N _ _ P _ _ _ _ _ _ V _ _ _ _

5 When is the best operational choice a decision to do nothing?

Workplace Activity

If you are currently in a management position, relate this chapter to your own experience by answering the following questions:

1 What financial information is available to you?

2 Is it sufficient to enable you to make effective management decisions? If not, how could you gain access to more?

3 How well does your organization measure more subjective factors like customer satisfaction or supplier loyalty? What more could it do?

4 How does your organization make strategic decisions? If you do not know, who could you ask?

5 What do you see as the main limiting factor in your operation?

6 To what extent do you use quantitative analysis when making decisions? What more should you do?

Reference

1 Peters, T. and Waterman, R. (1982) *In Search of Excellence*, Harper & Row: New York.

22 Understanding financial accounts

Chapter Objectives	• *Why are financial accounts useful?*

For many managers, financial accounts are irrelevant. At best, they are given a complimentary copy and scan it for items of interest.

- Did we make a profit last year?
- Is there anything about me or my team?

At worst, financial accounts are produced once or twice a year, never circulated and never seen by the workforce.

This is a shame because financial accounts contain a wealth of data which, when analysed, can provide valuable information about the current financial health of an organization; and a useful guide to its likely future performance.

Uses of financial accounts

The production of financial accounts on an annual basis and in a set format is a legal requirement for:

- Limited companies and
- charities.

Sole traders and partnerships have more flexibility in the way they present their financial statements; but they are still required to submit a statement of annual profit to the Inland Revenue so that tax liabilities can be assessed.

INTRODUCING MANAGEMENT

Public sector organizations like central government departments, local authorities or health trusts, which are funded by public money, are required to account to government, the public, or both for the way they have used that money.

In each case, as you will have noticed, financial accounts are required so that others can make judgements and draw conclusions about the performance of the organization.

People to whom organizations are accountable are normally called 'stakeholders'. They are made up of groups, or people who have an interest in or are affected by the organization. Traditionally the view was that management was only accountable to the one group of stakeholders – the shareholders of the company. This is no longer the case. For example, customers of the organization's products or services are important stakeholders as neglecting them may result in them going elsewhere. Equally as important are the employees who need to be considered as important stakeholders when decisions are made, for example, those which affect work practices.

Colin Coulson-Thomas provides a useful broad view:

'Stakeholders to whom the board is accountable include the shareholders, customers, suppliers, employees, the government and the general public.'

Stakeholders are both within and external to the organization (see Figure 22.1).

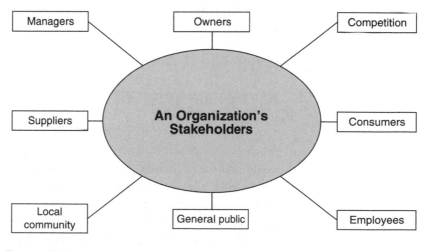

Figure 22.1

So how can these various groups use an organization's financial accounts?

Shareholders (who are the owners of limited companies) will want to know how profitable and stable the business is, so they can assess how well managers are using their assets. Potential shareholders may also want to compare the financial performance of different businesses, in order to decide where to invest their money.

Customers will want to know whether the organization is likely to provide satisfactory products and services. Financial accounts will not provide this information in detail but do provide an indication of past reliability and whether the organization is likely to stay in business to meet their needs.

Suppliers will also want to assess whether the organization is likely to survive long enough to be a worthwhile customer. They will also be interested in whether it will have enough money to pay their bills in future and how long they will have to wait in future. Banks will want to know how much other debt the organization is carrying, how secure loans are and whether the organization will be able to pay the interest and repay the debt. All this information can be extracted from the financial accounts.

Employees will rightly be interested in the organization's ability to continue paying wages and salaries. They will also want to know how secure their pensions are. To a certain extent this can be derived from past profits; the value of assets and cash owned by the organization: labour costs compared with total costs and costs incurred in past years.

Potential employees can use financial accounts to decide who to join, by assessing poor financial performance and profitability, future security and growth prospects.

Government, as we mentioned earlier, is legally entitled to know trading and profit figures as a basis for calculating tax liability. It will also use accounting data as a source of statistical information so it can trace wider business trends.

The general public fits into several of the categories listed above. They may be shareholders in limited companies, customers of both private and public sector organizations, suppliers of money to, for example, local government or the local school. They may also be either actual or potential employees. As the wider community, they may be interested in the financial performance of local organizations and its implications for unemployment rates and the money available for local investment (in both the community and other businesses).

Financial accounts: the profit and loss account

This is the standard name for the financial statement which sets out where an organization's revenue has come from and how it has been spent. Since some organizations are either not expected to make a profit or forbidden by law from doing so (public sector organizations and charities are the most obvious examples), their equivalents are known as income (or revenue) and expenditure accounts.

The simplest form of profit and loss account is that which relates to a sole trader. An example is shown in Figure 22.2.

Profit and Loss Account for F. J. Reynolds, Consultant
For the period 1 January to 31 December 2 _ _ _

	£	£
Invoices		52,000
LESS EXPENSES:		
Typing and bookkeeping	1,800	
Postage and stationery	1,200	
Use of home	560	
Telephone and fax	880	
Bank charges	730	
Motor and travel expenses	2,300	
Hotel accommodation	1,600	
Depreciation of motor vehicles	630	
Professional development	1,400	
		11,100
Net Profit		40,900

Figure 22.2

A sole trader's profit and loss account is a historical record of the revenue earned during a period and the expenses incurred to earn that revenue. It is important to note that the money involved may not have reached or left the trader's bank account during the period. For example, invoices raised at the end of the period may still be outstanding. But the work has been done and the money earned. Equally, bills received at the end of the period may not have been paid. In our example, the last telephone bill may not have arrived yet but the calls have still been made and will have to be paid for eventually.

Some of the entries in our example Profit and Loss Account are worth exploring further.

Revenue

In our example, all the money due to the trader is the result of work done. Consequently, all the revenue appears in the form of invoices. In other situations (for example, a retail shop or market trader) revenue may arrive in cash. In other businesses, revenue may come from:

- investment interest;
- property rental;
- bank interest;
- commission on sales;
- fees for work done.

All these items make up what is often known as 'turnover'.

Some bills will not have been paid by customers before the end of the period. But the work has still been done. Invoices raised but not paid constitute debts and the customers are debtors.

Expenses

Different businesses have different expenses. Depending on the nature of the business, they may take the form of:

- wages and salaries;
- heating and lighting;
- telephone calls and fax transmissions;
- interest on loans;
- equipment or property rental;

- printing and stationery;
- recruitment costs;
- hire of temporary staff.

In our example, the consultant obviously works from home because the Profit and Loss Account says so. In this case 'use of home' is equivalent to the more general heat and light heading. Fred Reynolds has no permanent staff – the business is too small to need them. Instead, he uses a local service for typing and book-keeping – the closest item in his account to wages and salaries.

Depreciation

Fred Reynolds runs a car, which he uses to visit clients. It is therefore a legitimate business expense. Over time, the car will wear out. In the same way, the fixed assets like machinery, office furniture or computers of other businesses will wear out – but not normally in a single year. In a Profit and Loss Account, depreciation reflects the cost of that wear during the period.

There is no accurate way of calculating depreciation. Staying with our car example for a moment, a mid-range car which covers high mileage or is neglected could be worn out after five years! A quality car which is not used much on the other hand could still be going strong after ten or fifteen years – or even longer.

Depreciation of computers is another revealing example. Computer development is currently taking pace at such a rate that new models are announced almost as soon as the old ones have been sold. The new models are faster and software for the old ones ceases to be available.

So what is a reasonable working life for computers? Despite these difficulties, the depreciation of equipment follows a simple formula:

- Take the purchase price of the equipment
- Decide on its working life in years
- Work out its likely residual value, i.e. how much it will be worth at the end of the period
- Calculate the value it will lose during each year of its working life.

There are two main ways of carrying out the last calculation. The 'straight line' method assumes that the equipment will lose the same amount of value during each year of its working life. So a piece of equipment which costs £1,000 will last for 10 years and be worth nothing at the end of its life, will depreciate by £100 each year.

The 'reducing balance' method applies the same percentage of depreciation to each year of the equipment's life. For example:

A piece of equipment is bought for £1,000 and is expected to last for 10 years. So the annual rate of depreciation is 10%.

- At the end of the first year it will be worth £900 (£1,000 less 10%)
- At the end of the second year it will be worth £900 less 10%, which equals £810
- At the end of the third year it will be worth £729, which is £810 less 10%.

The reducing balance method recognizes that equipment loses its value more slowly over time.

Case Study

Rajit Patel sets up as a sole trader offering a bookkeeping service. He buys a computer for £1,300 which he believes will last him for three years. He also buys a software package for £150 (which counts as an operating rather than a capital expense and therefore can be included in the costs of the first year). In his first year, Rajit does business to the value of £24,000. He works from a spare bedroom at home, which takes up 15% of the total floor-space. Household expenses (heating, lighting, water) amount to £1,800. He has installed a separate telephone line and a combined telephone and fax machine. The cost of the telephone and fax calls is £700 during the year. The telephone/fax machine cost £300 and Rajit estimates it will last for 5 years. He has had some stationery printed for which he has paid £800. Rajit's wife does his typing at a notional cost of £300, although no money actually changes hands. His stamps cost £150.

Prepare Rajit's profit and loss account for his first year of trading.

There is no set order for the items in a profit and loss account. So the sequence in which you included Rajit's expenses does not matter. But it is normal for revenue to come first. Figure 22.3 is our version (with explanations in parentheses where we think these are helpful).

Rajit Patel: Profit and Loss Account

For the 12 month period ended 31 March 2 _ _ _

(Profit and loss accounts can be for any length of time. It is normal to specify either the start and finish date, or the end date and the length of the period.)

	£	£
Revenue		24,000
(or 'fees earned' or 'invoices' or 'sales'. The description is immaterial provided it is accurate. In the case of a shop, it could be 'cash received' or 'income')		
LESS EXPENSES:		
Stationery	800	
Postage	150	
Use of home (could be 'heat, light, etc.' In Rajit's case this is 15% of total household expenditure)	270	
Secretarial expenses	300	
(The fact that no money has changed hands is irrelevant provided that this is a genuine cost to the business.)		
Software	150	
Telephone and fax	700	
Depreciation	493	
(We have used the simpler straight line method and applied it to both Rajit's computer and combined telephone/fax, assuming that they will have no value at the end of their estimated working life.)		
		2,863
Net Profit		21,137

Figure 22.3

We have assumed several things:

- That Rajit never uses his own car for business purposes;
- That any outstanding debts at the end of the period will be paid;
- That his computer and telephone/fax machine will have no value at the end of their lives.

Profit and loss accounts for limited companies are a little more complicated. Because they normally have shareholders who will expect a return on their investments, the profit and loss accounts of limited companies will include a 'dividends' heading.

In addition, larger businesses will probably bring in independent accountants to prepare their accounts. Their fees will be a further expense in the profit and loss accounts.

In the UK, limited companies are also subject to 'corporation tax' which is calculated on net profit and shown after it as a further item on the profit and loss account.

Financial accounts: the balance sheet

An organization's balance sheet shows what it owns – and what it owes. Whereas the profit and loss account is a historical record showing how much an organization has received and spent over a period, the balance sheet is a snapshot of what the organization owns and owes at one moment in time.

There is no legal requirement for a sole trader to prepare or submit a balance sheet. The reasons for this are obvious. Many sole traders own little and, if they are in a business which trades in cash, do not owe much either. For example, if we go back to Fred Reynolds whom we met earlier, his business appears to own little if anything other than his car, and he will have been required to pay most of his debts before the end of the year, with the exception of his bank loan.

However, some sole traders run businesses which genuinely benefit from the details contained in a balance sheet. The owner—manager of a retail corner shop is a good example. Figure 22.4 is a balance sheet, which would be typical of that kind of business.

John Norman, trading as Open All Hours

Balance Sheet at 31 December 2 _ _ _

	£	£	£
Fixed assets:			
Display and storage racking			
– cost		14,000	
– depreciation		2,800	11,200
Current assets:			
Stock	7,000		
Debtors	400		
Prepaid expenses	300		
Cash and bank	2,000	9,700	
Less current liabilities:			
Creditors	3,200		
Accrued expenses	300	3,500	
Working capital			6,200
			17,400
Less long-term liabilities:			
Loan			10,000
			7,400
Financed by:			
Capital at 1 January 2 _ _ _			7,000
Profit for year 2 _ _ _			11,000
			18,000
Less drawings			10,600
Capital at 31 December 2 _ _ _			7,400

Figure 22.4

We will now look in more detail at some of these headings.

Assets

These are what the business owns. Fixed assets are the productive assets the business intends to use for a long period of time. In our example, the only fixed assets shown are the display and storage racks for the shop. You can deduce from the figures that these are being depreciated by the straight line method. They were either bought last year and were expected to last for five years, or the year before with an expected life of ten years. In the case of storage equipment, the latter is more likely. Depreciation of fixed assets is a usual entry in a balance sheet and the figure of cost less depreciation is called the 'net book value'. This can only ever be approximate. In the case of a building for example its value will be shown as at the last valuation. An organization may only re-value its buildings every ten years, which means that the value shown can be significantly out of date.

Current assets are those which go on to create cash for the business. These only exist for a short time, i.e. less than one year and then become cash. Examples include stock, raw materials, bank and cash balances, debtors and prepaid expenses.

In our example, most of John Norman's sales are paid for immediately in cash. However, he does allow a few of his regular customers to run a monthly credit account. They are the debtors shown in the balance sheet. His prepaid expenses relate to things like advance payment of a telephone line rental.

Liabilities

These are what the business owes. Long-term liabilities are those which are due for repayment after more than a year, like bank loans or a mortgage. Current liabilities are due for repayment in less than a year, like debts to suppliers (which appear as creditors) and accrued expenses. In our example, accrued expenses are a bill for electricity consumed during the last quarter, which John has not paid yet. If he had a bank overdraft, this would also be shown as a current liability because the bank is entitled to demand immediate repayment.

Working capital

The example balance sheet we have been using is fairly detailed. Some contain much less data. The working capital calculation is often omitted, although it is, in fact, a very important one. This is because it shows how much money the business could put together quickly, if it found itself in a tight corner. Under those circumstances, it would not want to sell off its fixed assets, because the business depends on them to keep going. But it would also not need to pay its long-term liabilities. So the working capital figure is calculated by deducting current liabilities from current assets, leaving what is otherwise known as 'net current assets'. The figure that results is the amount of money the firm has left over after paying all of its current short-term bills.

Financed by

A balance sheet shows what a business owns, but also where the money has come from to pay for it. The two items should balance (hence the name). For a sole trader, the business is financed by the owner's capital (money put in at the start of the business or during its life). It is also financed by profits – those made in previous years and left in the business (called 'retained profits' or reserves) and those made in the year just ended.

The balance sheet of a limited company is a little different at this point. Capital will have come from the sale of shares. When a company decides to issue shares, its directors will decide how much money they want to raise. They will then decide how many shares to issue and at what price. All shares have, in effect, a value printed on them. They may be 50p shares or £1 shares, for example. This is called the 'nominal', 'par' or 'face value'. The company may sell its shares at their face value, or decide that people will pay more for them. In that case the shares' issue price will be higher than their face value and the difference is called the 'share premium'.

The 'Financed by:' section of a limited company's balance sheet will therefore contain figures for:

- Share capital;
- Share premium;
- Retained profits or reserves.

Interpreting financial accounts

We have already seen that the data contained in a profit and loss account and balance sheet tell us a great deal about the financial performance of an organization. It is perfectly possible to look at a profit and loss account and make judgements like:

- That business isn't making much;
- They seem to have borrowed a lot;
- The cost of goods isn't leaving much profit;
- They're paying a lot in salaries.

Based on the balance sheet, we might say things like:

- That machinery must be pretty old;
- There's not much there for a rainy day;
- As a supplier, I'd be worried about getting my bills paid;
- They're holding a lot of stock.

All of those judgements would be based on informal comparisons between what we see and what we would expect. The judgement may well be accurate but the comparisons are subjective and can only be tentative.

As we have suggested elsewhere, monitoring performance depends on comparing one set of data with another. The comparisons may be with targets, with historical performance, with other teams or other organizations. The major advantages of using financial data for comparison are that they are numerical, reasonably accurate and usually based on common criteria. There are also accepted standards to indicate whether the results of the comparisons are presenting an acceptable or unacceptable performance.

Financial comparisons are mainly expressed in the form of ratios. The most common types of ratios are:

- profitability ratios;
- liquidity ratios;
- capital ratios;
- dividend ratios.

We shall look at examples of each of these now.

Profitability ratios

These measure the performance or efficiency of a business. They are helpful to managers looking to decide whether efficiency needs to be improved, to set product prices or to make decisions about where to source components or raw materials. They can also help potential investors decide whether shares in a particular business are a wise investment.

There are two main types of profitability ratio. The first is a set of percentages calculated by comparing profit with sales. All can be calculated from the profit and loss account.

The formula for gross margin or gross profit percentage is:

$$\text{Gross profit} = \frac{\text{Gross profit}}{\text{Sales}} \times 100$$

The resulting percentage can be compared with other businesses in the industry or with historical performance. A declining gross margin may suggest that the business is losing control of its costs, or that increased competition is forcing it to reduce prices.

The net profit percentage is calculated as follows:

$$\text{Net profit percentage} = \frac{\text{Net profit before tax}}{\text{Sales}} \times 100$$

It provides a useful source of performance comparison between companies because it is an overall measure of efficiency. It is less use as a management tool because it is too broad to identify any particular aspect of costs.

Return on capital employed (ROCE) shows how productively a business is using its assets and is therefore a useful guide for investors. It compares profit before tax from the profit and loss account with capital employed from the balance sheet. The formula is:

$$\text{ROCE} = \frac{\text{Net profit before tax}}{\text{Capital employed}} \times 100$$

There are no standard guidelines for what these various percentages should be. However in general terms, the higher the better. Comparisons with other firms in the same industry will indicate what is acceptable.

Liquidity ratios

Two ratios measure an organization's ability to pay its debts (useful information for both managers and suppliers!).

The current ratio compares current assets with current liabilities from the balance sheet. The formula is:

Current ratio = Current assets : Current liabilities

Consider the case study in Figure 22.5.

301

Modern Knitwear has been invited to supply sweaters to Fiona's Fashions, an independent clothing shop. Looking at the shop's published balance sheet, they find the following:

	£	£
Current assets:		
Stocks	13,000	
Debtors	2,000	
Prepaid expenses	500	
Cash and bank	1,000	
		16,500
Less current liabilities:		
Creditors	9,000	
Accrued expenses	300	
		9,300

Figure 22.5

The shop's current ratio is 16,500 : 9,300 or 1.77:1.

This means that the shop will be able to pay its debts.

We have said that the shop will be able to pay its debts, but it will need time to sell its stocks. It is in a fashion business, so some of its stock may be out-of-date and difficult to sell.

Another way of calculating liquidity is by using the 'quick' or 'acid test' ratio. This takes the same data as before, but excludes stock from the assets.

In our example, the acid test ratio for Fiona's Fashions is:

3,500 : 9,300 = 0.38 : 1

This is very low. The normal standard is 1 : 1 and the shop now looks a very poor business risk from a supplier's viewpoint. On the other hand, if the ratios are very high, it means that too much money is tied up unproductively in stock or cash.

Capital ratios

A limited company can bring in capital by issuing shares or borrowing money. There are two main types of shares: ordinary shares and preference shares. Ordinary shareholders may only get a dividend when the company makes a profit – they share the risk with the business. Preference shareholders are entitled to a fixed dividend each year whether the firm makes a profit or not. In the same way, those who lend money to the company are entitled to a fixed rate of interest each year.

The normal capital ratio is the gearing ratio. This compares equity capital in the form of Ordinary Shares on one hand with fixed rate capital (loans and preference shares) on the other. The ratio is:

$$\text{Gearing ratio} = \frac{\text{Fixed rate capital}}{\text{Capital employed}} \times 100$$

Analysts say that a business with a gearing ratio of over 50% is highly geared.

A highly geared business is more at risk than one with a low gearing because it will still need to pay loan interest and dividends to preference shareholders, even when its trading performance has been poor.

Dividend ratios

Potential investors will want to know how much return will come from the shares they have bought. That return will come in the form of a dividend. Dividend per share can be calculated from the balance sheet and profit and loss account.

A balance sheet lists details of issued share capital. The profit and loss account gives details of dividends paid. It is therefore possible to calculate dividend per share. Try the following example:

Case Study

	£
Issued share capital in 50p shares	100,000
Dividends paid	2,000

What was the dividend per share?

It is important to note that the shares were 50p shares, so 200,000 have been issued. Consequently the dividend was 1p per share.

That may seem generous. But potential investors will not usually pay the face value of shares. There is no reason why a 50p share should not have a market value of £1, £5 or even £10. So our investors will also need to check the stock market selling price of any shares they are interested in.

| **Review** | Now check your understanding of this chapter by completing the following activities: |

1 Name six of an organization's stakeholders.

2 What does a profit and loss account tell you?

3 What does a balance sheet tell you?

4 A business had a gross margin last year of 10%. What else would you need to know before deciding if that was good or bad.

5 A company has a business loan of £15,000, preference shares of £5,000 and equity shares of £20,000. What is its gearing ratio?

| **Workplace Activity** | If you are currently in a management position, relate this chapter to your own experience by answering the following questions: |

1 Have you ever seen your organization's financial accounts?
   How could you get hold of them?

2 How would you define your organization's stakeholders?
   Is that consistent with your organization's view?

3 What is the biggest expense item on your organization's profit and loss account?

4 What is the biggest asset (fixed or current) on your organization's balance sheet?

5 Calculate your organization's current and acid test ratios.
   What do they tell you?

6 Which other organizations would provide relevant comparisons with your own?

References

1 Coulson-Thomas, C. (1993) *Developing Directors*, McGraw-Hill: New York.

23 Preparing and using budgets

| Chapter Objectives | ● *How should I use a budget?* |

* See Chapter 8
A key responsibility for managers is monitoring and controlling performance, as we saw in Section 3*. We also described the clumsy but effective system of 'top-down, bottom-up' strategic planning which is commonly used to set performance objectives.

The principles which underpin setting objectives, monitoring and controlling performance apply equally to budgets.

The process of preparing budgets

All organizations need answers to the following questions:

- What do we want to achieve?
- What are we capable of achieving?
- What resources will we need?
- What resources can we afford?
- How productive will they be?

The answers to all these questions come from the linked processes of developing objectives and preparing budgets. They apply to organizations as a whole, separate functions (marketing, finance, personnel, production, administration), departments, sections and teams.

What do we want to achieve?

There is no objective way of answering this question. The simplest approach would be to take last year's performance and add a percentage to it. A more rounded approach would be to consider what the organization's main stakeholders — in this case shareholders and customers, but possibly also government and the general public — expect or require from it. Yet another approach would be to take the organization's long-term aims (perhaps for growth, expansion or an increase in market share, or for productivity improvement or cost reduction) and to work out next year's contribution to them. Regardless of how the answer is reached, it will ultimately result in performance objectives and financial targets.

What are we capable of achieving?

There are both internal and external factors to consider here. The internal factors relate to capacity, resources and productivity. The external factors are to do with what the market wants from us and how much customers are willing to pay.

Organizations typically prepare three high-level budgets:

- Cash budget;
- Sales budget;
- Production budget.

These are the headings normally used in a commercial manufacturing environment. In other contexts, the budget titles may be different but the main purpose of each remains the same:

The cash budget sets out how much money will be available to pay for inputs or resources like staff, materials, equipment, training, transport, heat, light and so on.

The sales budget appears to be the most commercial of the three. But think of it as setting out the anticipated demand for the organization's products or services. Then you will see that it applies equally to the likely demand for consultancy meetings; the number of children likely to apply to a local school; or the number of VAT enquiries which are likely to be received by the local Customs and Excise office.

The production budget sounds as if it relates mainly to manufacturing. However, it is equally relevant to a road haulage business (how many trucks? how many drivers?), to a training business (how many courses? how many participants?) or to an accounts department (how many invoices? how many queries?).

For any organization, one of these three budgets provides the *limiting budget factor*. This is the factor which determines the maximum size of the other budgets. That factor may be:

- the availability of skilled staff;
- machine time;
- market demand;
- cash flow.

Regardless of what it is, the limiting budget factor will be the starting point for the preparation of all other budgets.

Case Study

> Last year, the first-year intake into Wallcorn School was fifty-six pupils. It has two reception teachers, each of whom has a classroom with thirty desks. Neither has space for more. The education authority is prepared to fund a further teacher but all classrooms are being used. Sixty-eight children have applied to join the school next year.

What is the limiting budget factor in this situation?

The school has more demand that it can cope with, so its equivalent of a sales budget will not limit its activities. It has access to extra money to pay another teacher so the cash budget will be adequate. Its limiting factor is space — the two reception classrooms can accommodate no more than sixty pupils together and nowhere else is available.

What resources will we need?

We identified resources in an earlier chapter as consisting of:

- People;
- Plant;

- Equipment;
- Materials.

Historical data will identify the quality and quantity of production these resources can achieve. A comparison with planned output will reveal whether they will be sufficient. This in turn will show whether:

- New people need to be recruited or existing staff trained to produce more;
- Plant needs to be extended or reorganized;
- Equipment needs to be upgraded or replaced;
- More or better materials need to be sought.

If any of these are not possible, they will become the limiting budget factor and output plans will need to be revised. Alternatively, the comparison may show excess resources and a need to reduce the scale of the operation.

What resources can we afford?

This is another potential limiting budget factor, related to the cash budget. Increasingly, public sector organizations are subject to tight cash limits and are being required to deliver more for less. Even in commercial organizations, the drive for increased competitiveness and cost reductions is making cash saving a priority. Which leads us to our final question.

How productive will they be?

Once upon a time, productivity was not a key issue. If existing resources did not produce enough, you added more. Nowadays, the emphasis is on gaining more output from the same, or fewer, resources. An increasing adoption of the internal customer—supplier relationship also means that help from other teams or departments comes at a price.

- If you want someone trained, it will cost you;
- If you want a wall moved, it will cost you;
- If you want a machine adjusted to run faster, it will cost you.

Any action necessary to improve productivity will need to be included in your budgets, unless it is something you can do for yourself.

Budgets and people

Like any other performance objectives, budgets need to be achievable. Otherwise they are seen as irrelevant and will be ignored. Equally, budgets which are too easy to achieve will also be ignored, because those responsible will soon recognize that they can exceed the budget without making a conscious effort.

* See Chapter 13

The 'top-down, bottom-up'* approach to planning involves the people responsible for achieving budgets in preparing them. That has the following advantages:

- The budgets are realistic;
- The people involved understand them;
- They are motivated to achieve them;
- And, surprisingly, the budgets are likely to be more demanding because people set higher standards for themselves than is generally recognized.

However, if budgets are to be realistic, motivating and achievable they must be kept up to date if circumstances change. There are countless examples of production budgets remaining the same while cash budgets are cut, making the output targets neither realistic nor achievable.

The master budgets

Sales, production and cash budgets, together with subsidiary budgets like the labour budget, materials budget, administration budget, transport budget and capital budget will be brought together to produce a set of master budgets. These will consist of a budgeted profit and loss account, balance sheet and a cash flow forecast.

The first two are similar to the historical financial accounts we examined in the last chapter. The last is a deceptively simple statement with huge implications for an organization's survival. Its purpose is to set out when money will come into the business

MANAGING RESOURCES

and whether it will be sufficient to meet expenditure in the same period.

Case Study

Roland has just started business as a sub-contract builder. He has taken on Alan as an assistant and decided to pay himself £800 and Alan £600 per month. He has also bought a van, for which he has borrowed £10,000 from the bank. The bank manager has insisted on Roland preparing a cash flow statement, which is shown later. Roland has also landed a brick-laying contract with a bigger builder, which he estimates will bring in £2,000 a month, paid in at the end of the following month. He has saved £3,000 which he will pay into the business in May, when he also expects to make the first payment on his van and start work on his new contract. His cash flow forecast is shown in Figure 23.1

Unfortunately, the weather in August is terrible and the building site is shut down for the month.

	May (£)	June (£)	July (£)	August (£)	September (£)	October (£)
Income	3,000	2,000	2,000	2,000	2,000	2,000
Expenditure						
Bank loan	500	500	500	500	500	500
Wages	1,400	1,400	1,400	1,400	1,400	1,400
Van running costs	50	50	50	50	50	50
Total Expenditure	1,950	1,950	1,950	1,950	1,950	1,950
Balance	1,050	50	50	50	50	50
Balance Brought Forward	Nil	1,050	1,100	1,150	1,200	1,250
Balance Carried Forward	1,050	1,100	1,150	1,200	1,250	1,300

Figure 23.1

When will Roland run out of money?

According to Roland's forecast, the work he did in July will be paid for in August and he will carry forward £1,200 into September. However he will not have worked in August. If he does not use the van, he can save £50 of expenditure. He may also be able to lay Alan off for the month saving another £600.

The bank loan interest is fixed however and will have to be paid. We must also assume that he needs his own £800 wages to meet household expenses. His expenditure for August will therefore be:

Bank loan	£500
Wages	£800
Total	£1,300

This will allow him to carry forward £1,850 into September. However, assuming work on the site starts again, his expenditure in September will return to £1,950 and he will get no cash into the business. He will therefore run out of money in September.

Monitoring and controlling budgets

Budgets are statements in financial terms of:

- The quality of outputs required to meet the organization's objectives.
- The inputs which the organization has decided it can afford to meet those objectives.

As we explained in an earlier chapter, different teams, sections and departments in an organization depend on each other and supply each other. Consequently, the plans and budgets of individual parts of an organization should reflect the needs of its internal customers and what they can afford or are prepared to pay. They should provide a way of co-ordinating diverse activities in an organization to ensure they contribute what is required to achieve its overall objectives.

That means budgets are not just the results of some tedious number-crunching, prepared and issued at the start of the plan period, which can then be filed and forgotten while you get on with managing the real work of your team. Instead, they make a valuable contribution to monitoring and controlling that work which, as we have seen, is a central part of management.

Budgets are normally prepared to last for a year then broken down into monthly targets. Properly prepared budgets take account of monthly variations in demand and the difference in level and type of activity during that month. So budgets are only estimates based on the best available information at the time.

Analysing budget statements

At the end of each monthly budget period, you are likely to get a statement showing you and your team's performance against the budget. Any differences between planned and actual performance will be shown as a variance.

Variances can be favourable or adverse. Favourable variances indicate that more output has been achieved, or less money spent, than planned. Adverse variances result from producing less output or spending more money than planned. It is tempting to assume that adverse variances are negative and need action, but favourable variances are positive and can be ignored. But that is not always true, as the case study shows.

Case Study

Performance against budget in June for the staff canteen of Healthwise Pharmaceuticals

	June			Year-to-date (January–June)		
	Budget (£)	Actual (£)	Variance (£)	Budget (£)	Actual (£)	Variance (£)
Income						
Meals sold	1,500	1,000	500A	9,000	7,000	2,000A
Snacks and drinks sold	1,000	1,200	200F	6,000	6,400	400F
	2,500	2,200	300A	15,000	13,400	1,600A
Expenditure						
Snacks and canned drinks	800	960	160A	4,800	5, 120	320A
Ingredients	750	500	250F	4,500	3,500	1,000F
Wages	800	800	–	4,800	4,800	–
Staff training	100	–	100F	200	–	200F
Maintenance	50	50	–	3,000	3,000	–
	2,500	2,310	190F	17,300	16,420	880F

Which of these variances concern you?

Do they show any pattern?

The canteen output (measured by its income) is below budget both in June and in the year to date. However, the variance in June (expressed as a percentage of budget) is higher than in the year to date. In other words, the situation is worsening. There is another pattern here, too. Staff are buying fewer meals but more snacks. This trend is also more pronounced in June than in the year to date.

Looking at expenditure, the overall variance is favourable but this masks the presence of an adverse variance in the value of snacks and canned drinks bought. However, this is what you would expect as sales of these are above budget. You might have noticed though that the profit margin on snacks is lower than that on meals. So if present trends continue, the canteen will find it harder in future to break even, which is the apparent intention. It is also worth noting that the apparently favourable variance on staff training results from the fact that no training has been done this year at all.

The budget is just a set of figures. It does not include explanations so you cannot draw any definite conclusions without doing some investigation. The variances may result from a badly constructed budget. But the other possible explanation is that the meals are poor and staff are moving to more palatable snacks instead. And could the lack of training be contributing to poor quality meals?

Investigating variances

If you were involved in preparing your budget, you should know the assumptions on which it was based. You should know the anticipated output demand and where it was expected to come from. You should also know the basis on which costs and expenditure were calculated.

So the first step in investigating variances is to compare reality with the assumption on which the budget was based. For example:

- Was output down because your team was less productive than expected, or because your customers required less? In either case, why?
- Were material costs higher because more were wasted, or because central purchasing changed supplier?
- Were wage costs up because of extra overtime, or because of a general wage increase which was higher than expected?

313

Controllable and non-controllable variances

The next step in investigating variances is to decide whether the causes of them were inside or outside your control. Of the examples we just gave, team productivity, waste and overtime costs are usually within a manager's control. Customer demand, central purchasing and organization-wide wage increases are not. Unless, of course, customer demand has fallen because they are not satisfied with your output.

There is clearly nothing you can do directly about non-controllable variances. But if their causes are likely to continue, they will have an impact on your future performance against budget. And, bluntly, that will make your budgets both unreliable and irrelevant. This is a matter to refer to your manager. Ask yourself in advance:

- Can my manager influence changes to my budget?
- Can my manager control causes which I cannot?
- If so, what do I want my manager to do?

* See Chapter 16

Controllable variances are different, of course. For them, you should follow the process set out in Chapter 16*:

- What is the real cause of the variance?
- Who else will be involved in putting it right?
- What will an ideal solution look like?
- What choices do I have?
- Which is the best?
- And how will I implement it?

Add to these the overriding questions:

- Is the variance important enough to deal with?
- Or is it a one-off and likely to disappear of its own accord?

Flexible budgets

The standard way for organizations to prepare budgets is as we have described:

- Overall objectives are agreed and set

- The cost of achieving them is agreed and set
- Local budgets are determined according with them.

This process assumes that the future can be predicted accurately. Of course, this is not the case:

- Demand will vary
- Efficiency and productivity will vary
- Costs will vary.

Changes in any of these factors will have a significant impact on budgets. Some are in the control of the organization and its managers. But others are not. This is the issue which flexible budgets are designed to address.

Typically they are based on a series of predictions. They assume a:

- Most likely case;
- Best case;
- Worst case;

for each budget. Separate budgets are then worked out for each case.

Of course, this is a nightmare for managers. It involves constantly updating budgets, either in line with organizational guidelines or with managers' individual analyses of the current situation. Nevertheless, computer spreadsheets which allow extensive 'what if?' analysis, make flexible budgets possible to introduce, if not easy to monitor and control.

Review

Now check your understanding of this chapter by completing the following activities:

1 What is the purpose of a budget?

2 Organizations typically prepare:

   C _ _ _ budgets

   S _ _ _ _ budgets

   P _ _ _ _ _ _ _ _ _ budgets

315

3 Master budgets consist of three statements. What are they?

4 A difference between planned and actual performance is called a
V _ _ _ _ _ _ _

5 How does a flexible budget operate?

**If you are currently in a management position, relate this chapter
to your own experience by answering the following questions:**

1 What is the limiting budget factor for your operation?

2 How much do you contribute to the preparation of your own
budget? If your answer is 'not enough', how could you influence
it more?

3 Which of the factors in your budget are under your control?
And outside your control?

4 How much freedom do you have to change factors which
should be under your control? What more would you like?

5 What, if anything, can you do to change non-controllable
factors?

6 Does your organization operate fixed or flexible budgets? What
are their positive and negative aspects for you?

INTRODUCING MANAGEMENT

24 Managing and controlling costs and resources

Chapter Objectives	• *What are the best ways of controlling costs?*
	• *How do I get the best from my resources?*

Monitoring and controlling costs and getting the best from your resources are a key task for you as a manager.

Managing costs and resources is a six-stage process:

- Knowing what you want to achieve;
- Identifying the quality and quantity of inputs needed to achieve it;
- Setting standards for measurement;
- Monitoring performance against them;
- Taking corrective action if necessary;
- Comparing results with plans.

This chapter will:

- Provide a brief explanation of each of those six stages;
- Describe in more detail some techniques specific to controlling costs and resources which we have not yet examined;
- Consider inventory *or stock* as a resource and some quality issues associated with it.

The control process

Knowing what you want to achieve

We have already stressed that effective control depends on being able to compare actual performance with plans expressed in quantified terms. But we have also pointed out that quantified plans are reflections of qualitative judgements. In other words, they start with general aims like:

- To satisfy customer demand;
- To improve productivity;
- To reduce costs.

Then they are quantified by being refined into numerical or financial values like:

- To achieve sales of £3.2 million;
- To increase output from 1,200 units to 1,400 units per machine per week;
- To make savings of £150,000 in energy costs this year compared with last year.

These quantified targets will, ideally, be agreed with you then issued to you formally as:

- Individual objectives;
- Team objectives;
- Departmental budgets;
- Team budgets.

Identifying input quality and quantity

The objectives and budgets set through the annual planning process are not usually detailed enough for the day-to-day control of costs and resources which will be your primary responsibility. In order to carry out that responsibility, you will need quantified statements of:

- Machine hours;
- Labour hours;
- Raw material volumes;
- Output targets.

These are relatively straightforward to calculate.

The question of input quality is more complicated. For example:

- You know the number of labour hours required for a particular job. But what skills and experience will your staff need?

- You know how much raw materials you need. But of what quality must it be to meet your output and waste targets?

As mentioned earlier, you can only exercise control if you can compare numbers. To do that, you will need a specification for each of the inputs required to achieve your outputs. The exact form of each specification will vary according to the nature of the input.

The specification for people may include the successful completion of a craft training programme, specific professional qualifications or so many hours', months' or years' experience.

Materials specifications will probably involve statements of, for example, purity, size, tolerances, durability, breaking strain and so on.

Even production equipment – machines – may have quality specifications related to maximum outputs available, reliability and maintenance requirements.

Case Study

> James is a cabin attendant for an airline running services between London Heathrow and Paris Charles de Gaulle airports. James serves passengers a light meal during the flight. The meal is prepared and packed on trays by an outside catering firm. The aircraft has 150 seats for passengers and storage space for 160 meals. The airline has recently changed to a cheaper catering firm. Of the meals they supply, 8% are found to be missing some of the food – normally either the bread roll or the fruit.

What impact will this have on James's ability to feed his passengers?

An 8% failure rate means that if 160 meals are loaded on to the aircraft, thirteen of them will be rejected by the passengers. If the aircraft is not full, the airline can adjust by loading more meals than passengers flying. But if the plane is full, three passengers will not be fed.

Setting standards

These relate to both inputs, as we have described, and outputs. The standards need to:

- Measure both quality and quantity;
- Reflect the complexity of the process which creates the output.

For example, producing ball-bearings is a quick, one-stage process which will need simple standards frequently applied. Building a battleship on the other hand is a long process with multiple stages. Useful standards will break the process down into individual stages and probably sub-stages as well. But the standards are likely to be applied less often than for ball-bearings.

One approach which is often used for repetitive processes is based on standard performance rates. Often called 'standard costing' it involves:

- An analysis of an individual task, job or product, normally by work study measurements;
- The quantity of inputs required (materials, time, energy);
- The costs of those inputs.

These result in standards of measurement which can be used as a basis for job or product costing and pricing.

Monitoring performance

We have described the principles of performance monitoring elsewhere. Here, it is worth noting the variety of monitoring systems and documents available to you:

- Timesheets;
- Overtime statements;
- Reject rates;
- Customer complaints and letters of praise;
- Purchase invoices;
- Sales invoices;
- Budget statements;
- Goods received notes;

- Standard performance rates;
- Standard costings.

Taking corrective action

* See Chapter 23

The last chapter* introduced the idea of controllable and non-controllable variances. We suggested the importance of differentiating between them:

- Variances you can control;
- Variances your manager can control – or at least influence;
- Variances totally outside your organization's control.

Similar considerations apply to the process of controlling costs and resources.

* See Chapter 22

Costs can be separated into*:

- Variable and fixed costs;
- Direct and indirect costs;
- Overheads.

Variable costs vary directly with the volume of output produced. With a transport fleet, for example, fuel costs will increase directly in line with the number of miles covered. Fixed costs still vary, but less directly. Thus, in our example, the depreciation costs of trucks in the fleet will stay the same, even if they cover no mileage. However, if the distance to be covered continues to increase, it will ultimately be necessary to buy an extra truck and depreciation will go up.

Direct costs are those which can be attributed directly to the output process. In a manufacturing environment, the workers who operate the machines are sources of direct costs. The sales force, on the other hand, is not involved in production. Their salaries are indirect costs. Similarly, the components used in manufacture are direct material costs, whereas the costs of stationery and clearing materials are indirect costs.

Overheads are a form of indirect costs, but even further removed from the production process. For example, an office will typically have reception staff and telephonists. However, they service all the

MANAGING RESOURCES

operations carried out in the office and are therefore overheads. Overheads may relate to:

- Sales and distribution;
- Administration;
- Heating and lighting;
- Office and factory rental.

Typically, you will have more control of variable and direct costs than of the remainder. Therefore, although your budget may charge you a notional rent for the space your team occupies, you are unlikely to be able to control either the rate per square metre or the space for which you are charged.

Comparing results

This is the final stage of the control process. It involves checking whether the corrective action you have taken has eliminated the variances between plans and performance. On a regular basis, the feedback information you get will come through monthly budgeting control techniques or the more frequent control documents we listed earlier. Improvement or change projects are also, of course, methods of narrowing the gap between actual performance and what you would like to achieve. Their success will need to be compared with the targets and objectives you set for the project at the beginning.

Case Study

> Swinbourne Local Authority has a Training Officer who runs induction and sales programmes from an office and training room at the back of the building. When courses are running, delegates receive free coffee and meals and are given training notes to take away and written exercises to complete during the programme.

What are the Training Officer's: Variable costs? Fixed costs? What overheads are likely to apply? How would you recommend the Training Officer to control inputs and outputs?

The most obvious variable costs are the delegates' drinks, meals and the handouts given to them. If no delegates attend, these costs will not be incurred.

The primary fixed costs will be the Training Officer's salary, pension and depreciation on the equipment used.

Overheads will take the form of heating, lighting and, possibly, a central administrative or clerical service used by several functions in the building.

Managing resources

So far, we have lumped together costs and resources. Strictly though managers do not control costs. Costs are no more than a set of financial values applied to the use of resources. So the manager's job is to manage resources in the most cost-effective way.

A complete list of resources used by an organization would include:

- Land;
- Buildings;
- Finance;
- Equipment;
- Materials;
- Information;
- Energy;
- Time;
- People.

Managers have little control over location. The decision to buy or lease a particular site will have been taken a long time ago and relocation decisions are taken at the most senior level.

It is much the same with buildings, although, as we have already explained, you may be able to re-arrange your team's work area to make it more comfortable or efficient. You may also be able to influence how clean it is or the way it is decorated. You will recognize these as a couple of the hygiene factors which Herzberg* suggested can dissatisfy people, although getting them better than right will not make people work any harder.

*See Chapter 6

Finance is a different matter. You probably have no control over actual cash, unless you have access to a small amount of petty cash for incidental expenses. However, you may well be able to:

- Influence investment decisions
- Influence or instruct your team concerning the standard of hotels they use, whether they travel first or second class and so on.

The remaining items on our list are even more under your control and management.

Managing equipment

Equipment is used wastefully when it is:

- Inadequately maintained;
- Used by people who lack the proper training;
- Unsuitable for the purpose;
- Insufficient for the purpose.

The results of these kinds of ill-usage are:

- Breakdowns;
- Poor quality;
- Damage;
- Reduced output.

Depending on your situation, you may be able to:

- Alter or improve the standard, frequency or nature of main-tenance schedules;
- Train staff to use equipment properly;
- Influence recruitment decisions;
- Recommend the acquisition of the right equipment.

*See Chapter 18

In most cases you will do this most successfully by using the persuading and influencing* skills we described earlier.

Managing materials

In a manufacturing environment, materials will consist of:

- Components;
- Raw materials;
- Disposable items like lubricants or cleaning stuffs;
- Finished goods.

In a retail environment, materials will be:

- Stock lines;
- Service items;
- Till rolls, order forms, customer information leaflets and so on.

An office-based organization will use:

- Stationery;
- Binders;
- Computer paper;
- Pens, pencils, markers.

All of these will need to be purchased, held in stock and accounted for.

In an earlier chapter, we described:

<table>
<tr><td>* See Chapter 13</td><td>

*ABC analysis**
An analysis of stock by volume and item value. So that different stock control systems can be applied to different stock categories to ensure they are effective but not unnecessarily costly.

</td></tr>
<tr><td>* See Chapter 13</td><td>

*Just-in-time techniques**
These keep an organization's materials stocks to the necessary minimum by using an on-demand system, which makes stock-holding largely the supplier's responsibility.

</td></tr>
</table>

We will now say a little more about purchasing and security.

Purchasing involves:

(a) *Finding the right supplier*
In other words, suppliers who can deliver the right products, at the right time, to the right quality, in the right quantities and at the

right price. Tight and accurate product specifications are important here.

(b) *Negotiating terms*

It is often said that 'there is always a cheaper supplier'. But alternatives may be cheaper because the quality is poorer. Negotiating terms is a matter of ensuring what you are getting gives you the best price for the quality you need.

(c) *Ordering goods*

Ordering 'little but often' keeps down the cost of holding stock. But it also increases the administrative costs. ABC analysis can help here, by identifying those high value, low volume items which are costly to hold in stock and therefore justify frequent re-orders.

Effective security addresses the issues of external theft, employee theft and employee fraud. It is interesting to note that, in most retail operations, employee theft is a far bigger source of loss than shoplifting. (Retail managers tend to find this fact uncomfortable and therefore put most of their effort into preventing shoplifters, who present the minority of problems.)

Theft requires:

- Something worth stealing;
- A thief;
- An opportunity;
- A means of removal.

The likelihood of theft can be reduced by:

- Limiting knowledge of valuable items (goods or information) to those who need to know;
- Careful selection of staff;
- Controlling visitor access;
- Adequate physical security (locks, bolts, alarms, fences and so on);
- Strict guidelines on what can be removed from premises and when.

Managing information

As a manager, you depend on information. Your effectiveness will be tied up with, for example:

- Materials specifications;
- Production schedules;
- Customer orders;
- Control information.

*See Chapter 17

We suggested earlier* that good information needed to be:

- Relevant;
- Accurate;
- Timely;
- Complete;
- Concise.

The essence of managing information is to:

- Decide the information you and your team need, based on these criteria;
- Compare the information you get with that specification of your ideal requirements.

Identify the shortcomings

Take personal action to address them *or* find someone else in the organization who can bring what you get in line with what you need.

Managing energy

We can draw a distinction between physical energy (heat, light, power) and human energy in the shape of effort. Managing physical energy will involve you reminding staff to switch off unused equipment and unnecessary lighting; checking for examples of waste; looking for and recommending ways of improving energy waste.

*See Chapter 6

Improving the use of human activity* can be undertaken through performance review; training; motivation — encouragement and finding more effective ways of doing things.

MANAGING RESOURCES

Managing time

The time taken to complete a job is a measure of efficiency. You can manage time by:

- Monitoring staff attendance records;
- Assessing and addressing machine and staff productivity;
- Revising operating methods;
- Reviewing production and maintaining schedules.

Time is a precious resource that vast numbers of managers complain that they do not have enough of! We have probably all, at some time or another attended a time management course often resulting in disappointing results. Improving the management of one's time cannot be achieved on a quick fix basis. It requires a systematic and planned approach with small step changes and realistic goals. But managing your time does not start with planning, it actually starts with information. You need to understand, for example, how your time is used and misused, how much of your time is actually spent on unplanned, unproductive activities, how many times you are interrupted and why.

How much of your time is lost through the following?

Failure to define priorities – resulting in important tasks being neglected or hurried.

Procrastinating – so that you have to work late to complete those monthly reports.

Inefficient delegation – remember Jim in our case study in Chapter 7?

Attending meetings – meetings are a potentially costly activity particularly if they are not really necessary.

Spending time analysing (this is productive) how your time is wasted and lost can be extremely beneficial in enabling you to plan to make better use of this precious resource in the future.

Laurie Mullins suggests that the essentials of good time management include:

'Clear objectives, careful forward planning, the definition of priorities and action; and the ability to delegate successfully.'

328

Managing people

In the same way as you manage and control equipment, materials and information you need to manage people. However, people are a unique and special resource and managing them is not simply a control process! As we have shown you in previous chapters getting the best from your team means knowing your people, treating and valuing them as individuals as well as understanding what motivates them. Nonetheless they still need to be productive in the most efficient and effective way as possible.

Your role involves getting the best possible results from people by:

- Making sure you know what you require from them (output standards, quality, quantity and so on);
- Communicating those requirements to them;
- Agreeing and providing them with methods of measuring actual against required performance;
- Encouraging them to seek reasons for any shortfalls;
- Involving them in finding solutions;
- Providing or arranging help in implementing them (which may be in the form of training, additional or more suitable resources).

In other words, it involves applying a minor but important variation of the control process with which we started this chapter.

Review

Now check your understanding of this chapter by completing the following activities:

1 Give three examples of quantified statements needed for day-to-day control.
2 What might a person specification include?
3 Standard performance rates are:
    - Hourly payment rates for a particular job.
    - Measures of the inputs used on a job under normal circumstances.
    - Output quantities expected from a member of staff under normal circumstances.

329

- Output volumes which must be achieved before a bonus is earned.

(Tick one)

4 Explain the difference between variable and fixed costs.

5 List three examples of poor time management.

Workplace Activity

If you are currently in a management position, relate this chapter to your own experience by answering the following questions:

1 How much attention do you pay to the quality specifications needed for your inputs?

What more could you do?

2 What performance monitoring documents do you see regularly?

Which performance standards do they relate to?

3 List the costs charged to you in your budget.

Which can you control?

4 How does your organization carry out purchasing?

If you do not know, how could you find out?

5 How can you and your team reduce costs?

6 What changes could you introduce which would make your team/department more cost-efficient?

Reference

1 Mullins, L. (2002) *Management and Organizational Behaviour*, Sixth edition, Prentice Hall: Harlow.

Website addresses

www.carol.co.uk
Provides company annual reports on-line.

www.severn-trent.co.uk
A good example of a corporate company website; provides financial performance information as well as involvement in community affairs.

INTRODUCING MANAGEMENT

Answers to review questions

Section 1 Managing in Context

Chapter 1 Achieving results

1 **a** Plan; **b** Organize; **c** Command; **d** Control; **e** Co-ordinate.

2 Information; People; Activities; Resources.

3 Passing down authority and therefore control down an organization's hierarchy.

Chapter 2 Managing resources

1 Adding value.

2 Inputs.

3 Consumable; Renewable.

4 Customer choice; Political decisions; Weather; Social change; Competition; Technology.

5 Managers do not work in isolation; Management is an ever changing dynamic process.

Chapter 3 Focusing on customers

1 Knowing customer needs enables us to satisfy them.

2 Internal and external.

3 Purpose; Use.

4 Political; Economics; Social; Technological; Legal; Environmental.

5

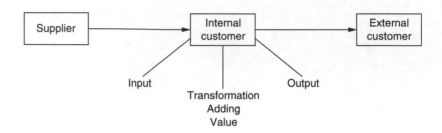

Chapter 4   Understanding the culture

1 Do things round here.

2 History; Size; Ownership; Purpose.

3 Does well: Consistent decisions; Manages large organizations; Everyone knows what to do because there will be rules and policies that tell you.

Does badly: Slow to react to change; Change will only happen once; Procedures have been rewritten.

4 Does well: Handles change well; Quick response; Handling crises.

Does badly: Organization falls apart if the 'leader' retires or falls ill; Can't handle large numbers of staff.

5 Implement; Management attitude; Training.

Chapter 5   Understanding the environment

1 Policital; Economic; Social; Technological; Legal; Environmental.

2 False.

3 Creches; More part-time working.

4 False.

Section 2   Managing People

Chapter 6   Motivating people

1   Getting people to WANT to do what you WANT them to do.

2

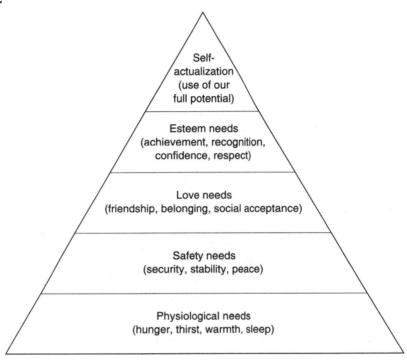

3   Salary = hygiene; Opportunity for promotion = motivator; Responsibility = motivator; Status = hygiene; Working conditions = hygiene; Supervision = hygiene; Sense of achievement = motivator.

4   Effort; Effort; Reward; Reward.

5   Expectancy theory suggests that if you do not honour your promises, your staff will come to expect you NOT to honour your promises in future. Therefore, this is likely to have a negative effect upon staff motivation.

Chapter 7   Leading and delegating

1   N/A.

2   Good.

3 Action-centred leadership

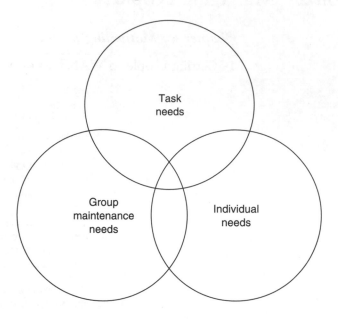

4 Makes productive use of time; Avoids managerial overload; Improves the job satisfaction of the team; Develops their skills; Improves their promotion prospects.

5 Joints or consults.

Chapter 8   Managing teams

1 Common purpose; Interdependency; Respect; Selection; Commitment.

2 See completed Figure 8.3 on page 335.

3 *Co-ordinator:* mature, confident, trusting, chairman, clarifies; *Innovator:* creative, unorthodox, solves difficult problems; *Monitor—evaluator:* sober, strategic, discerning, makes judgements, lacks ability to inspire.

4 Because the group's objectives supersede those of the organization and its work suffers.

5 Information, understanding; Impossible, incomparable; Norms, principles, procedures; Hostility.

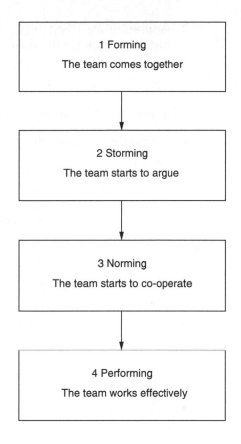

Figure 8.3

Chapter 9 Improving performance

1 Managing By Walking About
It means, spending more time with team members informally, to get to know them and their problems.

2 Distrust, managers or reviewers don't understand the system, lack of preparation, complicated paperwork, process is rushed, different managers apply different standards, managers are biased.

3 Immediate, limited, shows respect, puts the improvement into context, is two way.

4 Training is for short term (for now and near future) Development is for long term (for career ambitions and future promotions).

5 A disciplinary procedure addresses under-performance by look-ing at the achievement of targets/standards

Chapter 10   Managing change

1 Ownership (people do not like change if it is imposed so they have to be informed and involved in the process).

2

3 Unfreezing; Changing; Refreezing.

4 Information; Consultation; Enthusiasm.

5 Review the outcome (isolate inefficiencies and opportunities for refinement); Ensure people change through changing targets/objectives and monitor this through appraisal; What have we learned from the process of change? How can we apply this lesson to the next time we have to change?

Section 3   Managing Activities

Chapter 11   Changing inputs into outputs

1 Transformation; Outputs.

2 Activities carried out that provide a source to customers which is its basic reason for existing.

3 1c; 2a; 3b.

4 Your staff.

Chapter 12   Meeting customer needs

1   Failure.

2   Time; Significant management effort; Training/re-education; New or adjusted processes/systems.

3   Co-operation between suppliers and customers which allows for greater information flow and therefore bringing the two closer together.

4   Product; Place; Time; Price; Way.

5   Everyone.

6   Primary research: focus groups, interviews, Delphi groups, postal phone questionnaires
Secondary research: sales records, government statistics.

Chapter 13   Planning, organizing and controlling work

1   Where senior management set broad organizational aims, lower levels then say how they could contribute towards attaining these aims.

2   Specific; Measurable; Achievable; Realistic; Time-based.

3   Outputs; Standards; Corrective; Action.

4   A firm which has demand which varies greatly works ineffi-ciently because when it is busy, it is too busy, unable to keep up with demand for its products. It therefore has to contract out work which is expensive or turn work away. When it is not busy however, it will have staff and equipment lying around idle. Smoothing demand allows the firm to constantly work at manageable level whilst maximizing the efficiency of its resources.

5   (*a*) 10–15% volume, 70–80% value; (*b*) 20% volume, 15% value; (*c*) 60% volume, 5–10% value.

Chapter 14   Managing the workplace

1   Duration; Frequency; Sequence.

2   Sequence; Minimum.

3   Easy access; Flexibility; Productive use of space; Comfort/safety; Efficient work flow; Minimum distances of travel for people/resources/products.

4 Employees; Employers; Managers.

5 Legal costs from civil actions from injured parties; Recruitment costs to replace dissatisfied employees; Production costs increase as down time increases due to stoppages for injuries or incidents.

Chapter 15   Making improvements

1 Results identify new possibilities; Spreads risks; Prepares the organization for the next change; Gets people used to change and 'newness'.

2 Continuously improving productive efficiency in small incremental steps through empowered employees, i.e. continuous improvement.

3 Improvement teams; Project teams; Cross-functional/Inter-departmental teams.

4 Gives the team focus; Ensures a common direction; Defines spheres of responsibility and the extent to which they are expected to improve processes/outputs.

5 Changes processes/information flows/documentation systems. May cause disruption.

Section 4   Managing Information

Chapter 16   Solving problems and making decisions

1 Analytical; Creative.

2 In order to decide if any action should be taken and if so how urgently.

3 People; Environment; Methods; Plant; Equipment; Materials.

4 To ensure they are clear, unambiguous, agreed and understood.

5 Your objectives; Constraints.

Chapter 17 Recording, storing and retrieving information

1 Raw facts, figures – on their own, they mean nothing. Information is: data which have been processed and analysed and therefore can be used to justify decisions.

2 Timely; Relevant; Accurate; Concise; Complete.

3 Local; Remote; Central.

4 It ensures confidentiality, accuracy and less risk of loss (in the case of IT protection from backing and computer viruses).

Chapter 18 Principles of effective communication

1

2 Be: Accurate; Brief; Clear.

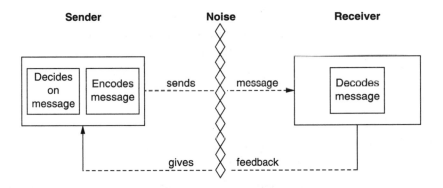

3 What's the purpose of your communication? Do you need immediate feedback? How long is the message? How urgent is the message? Who is going to receive the message? Where are your receivers? What is your relationship with the receivers?

4 Formal feedback is a conscious response from the receiver; Informal feedback is an unconscious response from the receiver.

5 By knowing how your idea will benefit them; By you making them understand and appreciate your idea.

ANSWERS

Chapter 19   *Communicating effectively – in writing*

1 If you need to communicate to large numbers; If you need to record for legal or other reasons; If the message is complicated; If you find it difficult to contact the receiver; If the receiver will need to refer to your message.

2 Clear, Concise, Complete, Correct, Courteous.

3 To whom, why and how should the message be presented.

Chapter 20   *Communicating effectively – face-to-face*

1 Space; Posture; Facial Expression.

2 Decide upon your objectives; Decide how long the interview needs to last; Assemble the necessary documentation; Plan the interview; Arrange an interview.

3 1 What do I want? 2 What does my manager want? 3 What information does my manager need? 4 How should I present the information?

Section 5   Managing Resources

Chapter 21   *Financial information and management control*

1 What markets we should attack; What products we should make; What services we should provide; Measure customer loyalty; Measure staff morale; Calculate break even point; Make investment decisions.

2 Because there will be qualitative arguments to take account of.

3 Total Revenue; Total Costs.

4 Payable Period; Average Rate Return; Net Present Value.

5 When the costs of doing something exceed the costs of doing nothing. When the problem will be solved by a larger initiative in the future.

Chapter 22 Understanding financial accounts

1 Employees, general public, managers, customers, suppliers, government, local community.

2 How much profit you have made over the accounting period.

3 What the organization owns and owes at any one point in time.

4 What it was the year before and what everybody else in the industry makes as a gross margin.

5 $\dfrac{15{,}000 + 5{,}000}{20{,}000 + 15{,}000 + 5{,}000} = 50\%$

Chapter 23 Preparing and using budgets

1 To monitor and control revenue and expenditure in order to achieve corporate objectives.

2 Cash; Sales; Production.

3 Budgeted Profit and Loss; Cash Flow; Balance sheet.

4 Variance.

5 Flexible budgets are renegotiated upon; External changes that might affect revenues or expenditures.

Chapter 24 Managing and controlling costs and resources

1 Machine hours; Raw material volumes; Output targets; Labour hours.

2 The ideal set of qualifications; Abilities/experience of the desired candidate.

3 Output quantities expected from a member of staff under normal circumstances.

4 Variable costs vary in line with output; Fixed costs remain fixed regardless of the levels of output.

5 Failing to define priorities; Inefficient delegation; Procrastinating; Holding unnecessary meetings.

Glossary

Section 1

19   **Change**   What will happen when the pain of the present ways is greater than the expected pains of the future.

19   **Total Quality Management**   A management philosophy based on the idea that quality is the best way of competing in the market.

19   **Supply Chain**   The chain of internal and external customers along which inputs/outputs flow.

20   **Internal Customers**   Your fellow employees to whom you supply services. Total Quality Management suggests that you should treat these internal customers as if they were external customers.

27   **Added Value**   An imperative concept in TQM is that every output should add value and therefore contribute to customer satisfaction.

31   **Entrepreneurial**   A person, organization or culture with a flair for grasping business opportunities and taking risks.

32   **Authority**   What you need more of, if you are going to do a job properly. You need to have been given the 'right or power' to make decisions and use resources.

32   **Delegation**   The passing of authority to make decisions (and therefore control) down the hierarchy.

33   **Flat Structure**   A management structure which has relatively few layers of hierarchy. As a result, managers have more members in their team, which means they must delegate a high proportion of tasks and decisions.

34   **Hierarchy**   Inescapable component of organizations, that will never be abolished, despite the best efforts of many Chief Executives. Whether it is tall or flat it is there to make the organization manageable.

342

41 **Investment** The sacrifice of consumption now in order to benefit to a greater extent in the future.

41 **Corporation Tax** The tax companies pay as a percentage of their profits. Smaller firms pay around 20% whilst larger firms pay around 30%. These percentages alter in the budget each year.

43 **Economic Cycle** A regular pattern of up and downturns in demand in the economy. Each cycle lasts for around 7–10 years. Recessions, the lean periods for most businesses, need to be weathered. The early 1980s and 1990s saw many businesses fail as a result of recessions in the economic cycle.

Section 2

56 **Delegation** The passing of authority to make decisions (and therefore control) down the hierarchy.

56 **Responsibility** Responsibility for decisions and results is theoretically transferred down the hierarchy in delegation. However, accountability for the organization's deeds or misdeeds always lies with the directors.

67 **Leadership** Leaders inspire loyalty, respect, trust and affection.

74 **Authority** The right or power to use resources or make decisions.

74 **Accountability** The extent to which employees are responsible for their actions. If you were given responsibility to carry out a task, you will be held accountable, if it is not done. Overall accountability for the organization lies with the directors.

Section 3

128 **Supply Chain** The chain of internal and external customers along which inputs/outputs flow.

128 **Internal Customers** Your fellow employees to whom you supply services. Total Quality Management suggest that you should treat these internal customers as if they were external customers.

136 **Total Quality** The business philosophy that tries to get individual teams to think of those they work for as customers, even if they are fellow employees.

Index

INTRODUCING MANAGEMENT